BUS-PASS BRITAIN

50 OF THE NATION'S FAVOURITE BUS JOURNEYS

edited by
Nicky Gardner and
Susanne Kries

D1392748

Edition 1
Bradt Travel Guides Ltd, UK

(photo © Chris Steer / IS)

 The circled number by each photo refers to the relevant bus journey.

Marking time in **Guildford**.

(photo © Jan Mika / DT)

A classic London sight: a **Routemaster bus** on the first journey in this book.

London and the Home Counties

(photo © hidden europe)

Surrey villages are fine spots to linger. An extravagant confection of chimneys at Albury on our **Pilgrim's Way** bus route. Other appealing villages on the same route are Shere and Abinger Hammer.

(photo © Brian Grigg)

⑦

An Aylesbury-bound number 61 **trundles through Ivinghoe** in Buckinghamshire.

③

Picture-perfect Rye is an excellent place to stop when **riding The Wave**, the name given to the bus route that links Dover with Hastings.

(photo © clubfoto / IS)

The chalk cliffs at **Seven Sisters** on the Sussex coast are a highlight of the bus journey from Brighton to Eastbourne.

④

(photo © Jenny Jones)

(photo © Pam Johnston)

14

One of a number of seasonal summer services in this book, the 300 from **Minehead to Lynmouth** is the perfect way to explore Exmoor National Park. At one point in its journey, this open-top double-decker negotiates a 1 in 4 hill.

Stop to relax at several points along the **Jurassic Coast bus route** that links Exeter with Poole.

13

(photo © GAPS / IS)

17

Cruise the Cornish coast to Penzance, but better still hop off the bus and walk over the tidal causeway to St Michael's Mount.

(photo © Paula Connelly / IS)

⑨

Silbury Hill is a landmark on the Trans-Wilts Express bus route from Trowbridge to Swindon.

South and Southwest England

The **Purbeck Breezer** from Bournemouth to Swanage is the only route in this book where a bus journey includes a ride on a ferry.

⑪

⑫

Both Dorset and Devon are blessed with superb networks of rural bus services, many of which give **good access to the coast.** Sidmouth on Journey 12 is pictured here.

The **Pontcysyllte Aqueduct** (below) is a tribute to the ingenuity that surrounded an earlier age of slow travel. The aqueduct carries the Llangollen Canal over the Dee Valley.

The bus ride beside the **Mawddach Estuary**, part of Journey 19, is one of the finest in Wales. This view of the estuary, with its distinctive bridge (used by trains, cyclists and pedestrians) is from the destination of the route in Barmouth.

Wales

Journey 18 through mid-Wales to Llandrindod Wells is blessed with some fine vistas, among them good views on a clear day of the **distant Brecon Beacons**.

(photo © fotoVoyager / IS)

Rural bus routes in mid-Wales afford access to some of the remotest terrain in the Principality. The sparsely populated hills of Elenydd are part of the **broader Cambrian Mountains chain**.

(photo © Caril Privezentzev / DT)

20

An improbable piece of Flemish-influenced design in the 'seven eyes of Ruthin' – just a detail from **Ruthin's intriguing roofscape**. The town is the destination of Journey 20 in *Bus-Pass Britain*.

The seaside and university town of Aberystwyth makes a very fine overnight stop on bus journeys through Wales. In a prime position on the seafront, **Old College** is an eclectic architectural feast. The building is still used by the **University of Wales**.

(photo © Jan Keirle / DT)

Lincoln Cathedral, the high point on our route from Lincoln to the coast at Skegness.

Timber-framed perfection in the old Grammar School at **Market Harborough**, a good place to stop and explore on our route from Northampton to Leicester.

Central England

The busy **South Quay in King's Lynn** is one of over forty harbour communities featured in *Bus-Pass Britain*. King's Lynn marks the end of our route from Cromer.

Take time to savour the **quieter side of England**. Diss is at the start of our bus journey exploring the Waveney Valley on the borders of Norfolk and Suffolk.

The **bridge and castle in Ludlow**, a town that cherishes its affiliation with the Cittaslow (slow city) movement. Ludlow is the jumping-off point on our journey to Hereford.

Explore **urban Britain** in several of the journeys in *Bus-Pass Britain*. Birmingham (pictured here) features in Journey 24, where we follow the longest urban bus route in Europe.

Towns and cities in the region boast some **famously choppy roofscapes**. York is a fine example.

Pennines and Yorkshire

Chatsworth House makes a perfect stop on the bus journey from Matlock through the Peak District to Sheffield.

Bus have largely eclipsed canals as a form of slow travel. The **Huddersfield Narrow Canal** in the Saddleworth area.

(photo © Ian Wilson / DT)

Aysgarth Falls is a great spot to pause when travelling by bus through Wensleydale in North Yorkshire.

(photo © Khrizmo / IS)

The **perfect thatch** at Rievaulx in the North York Moors National Park. Even very remote villages in the area are well served by seasonal **Moorsbus** services.

Sun, sea and sand in **Scarborough**, the southern end of our bus journey from Whitby.

(photo © hidden europe)

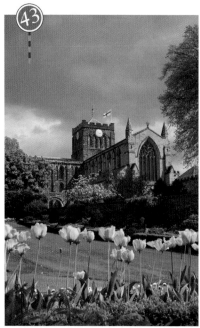

43

Ride our route **along Hadrian's Wall** and you may still encounter the occasional Roman soldier.

44

Hexham is a hub for local bus routes in rural Northumberland. Masonry salvaged from nearby Roman forts and Hadrian's Wall gave the builders a head start in constructing **Hexham Abbey**.

Cumbria
and Northumberland

 39

Red squirrels are in decline in many parts of England, but they still thrive in woodland refuges in Cumbria, as here at Whinlatter in the Lake District.

Lake District bus journeys combine easily with boat trips. Journey 41 over Kirkstone Pass ends at Glenridding Pier (pictured above) on **Ullswater**. Victorian vintage boats offer year-round service on the lake.

A perfect stopover on the ride from Keswick to Windermere, the **village of Ambleside** offers a feast of fine pubs and cafés. Cruises on Windermere leave from the pier at Waterhead just south of the village.

A Newcastle-bound 501 bus in the village of Craster on the **coast of Northumberland**. The bus route features in Journey 45 in this book.

End of the road for Journey 49 at **Rannoch railway station**. But you can continue your explorations by train. Rannoch even has a direct night train to London.

Glasgow's new **Riverside Museum**, opened in summer 2011, is devoted to the history of transport and travel.

Scotland

 Storm clouds over the **Kyles of Bute** on our bus journey across the Cowal peninsula.

Inverness Castle, overlooking the River Ness, is close to the start point of the last of our fifty journeys – a run north from Inverness to Thurso.

(photo © Eric Newton)

The ride from Glasgow to Kintyre skirts the shores of Loch Lomond.

(photo © Mcwarrior / DT)

The magnificent Gothic ruins of Melrose Abbey on our Tweed Valley bus route.

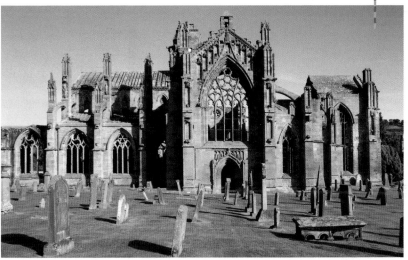

(photo © Creativehearts / DT)

Bus-Pass Britain
50 Favourite Journeys

KEY
— London and the Home Counties
— South and Southwest England
— Wales
— Central England
— Pennines and Yorkshire
— Cumbria and Northumberland
— Scotland

Bradt

N

Orkney Islands

Thurso   John o'Groats
50

Outer Hebrides

Stornoway

Skye

Fraserburgh

Moray Firth
Inverness
Loch Ness   Spey   Don   Dee Aberdeen
Mallaig   *GRAMPIAN MTS.*
Ben Nevis   **49** Pitlochry   Montrose
Tay
Mull Oban   Perth Dundee
48 **SCOTLAND**
Forth
47 Glasgow   Edinburgh   Firth of Forth
Clyde
Campbeltown *Arran* Ayr   Tweed **46** Berwick-upon-Tweed
Nith   *CHEVIOT HILLS* *The Cheviot* **45**
Stranraer   **43**   Newcastle upon Tyne
Carlisle   **44** Tyne Durham
39 **42**   Middlesbrough
Keswick   **36** Scarborough
40 **41**   Northallerton **38**
Isle of Man   **35** Swale **37**
P E N N I N E S   **34** York
I R I S H   S E A   **34** Leeds Kingston upon Hull
N O R T H   S E A

33 **32**
Manchester   **29** Sheffield   **28** Skegness
Liverpool   Buxton   **31**   Lincoln   **26** Cromer
Snowdon **20**   **30** Derby Trent   King's Lynn Norwich
19   Wrexham   **ENGLAND**
Wolverhampton   Leicester **25** Peterborough   **27**
WALES   Birmingham **24**   Coventry Northampton Cambridge Ipswich
Aberystwyth   **21** **22**   Severn Northampton
Cardigan   **18** Hereford   **23** Oxford **7** Luton   **1**
Swansea   Gloucester   *COTSWOLD HILLS* Swindon **9** Reading London **2**
Cardiff   Bristol   **8** **5** **6** Thames Chatham
14   **10** **9** Andover Guildford   **3** Dover
Minehead   Taunton Salisbury Southampton *SOUTH DOWNS* **4** Folkestone
16 **12** **13** Poole Brighton Hastings
DARTMOOR Exeter   **11** Eastbourne
Plymouth **15** *Portland Bill* *Isle of Wight*
17   *E N G L I S H   C H A N N E L*
Isles of Scilly Penzance

0 ___ 100km
0 ___ 60 miles

Foreword

Until 2008 it never occurred to me to take a bus for pleasure; it was simply a way of travelling from A to B. Then it was announced that the existing regional bus passes in England would be extended to embrace the whole country. Suddenly we pensioners had free travel throughout England, and my horizons broadened. I am now hooked.

Buses divert to what was described by a fellow passenger on one journey as 'all those silly places.' They meander through villages, potter down country lanes, and squeeze between cottages nearly removing the thatched roofs, while we are free to gaze into gardens and over the countryside. Bus travel gives you glimpses of places you want to return to, snatches of conversation which make you smile, and serendipitous stays in towns that you never knew you wanted to see. I spotted a neighbour on a local bus and asked her where she was going. 'Exeter. When I get to the bus station I'll just get on the next bus that takes my fancy and see somewhere new.' How lucky we are to have this freedom!

We at Bradt Travel Guides wanted to produce a book to encourage others – and not just pensioners – to explore Britain by bus, but how were we to find an author to research it? Then I met some of the committee of the University of the Third Age (U3A) and we realised that their members held the answer. A competition was organised to find the nation's fifty favourite routes (see the map opposite) attracting many entries from U3A members and from a wider public. This book is the result. You're in for a treat!

Hilary Bradt

Bus–Pass Britain: 50 of the Nation's Favourite Bus Journeys
First published October 2011
Bradt Travel Guides Ltd
IDC House, The Vale, Chalfont St Peter, Bucks SL9 9RZ, England
www.bradtguides.com

Bus-Pass Britain project managers: Nicky Gardner and Susanne Kries
Book editors: Nicky Gardner and Susanne Kries
Book design: Shane O'Dwyer
Cover illustration: James Nunn
Colour map: David McCutcheon (www.dvdmaps.co.uk)
Route sketch maps: hidden europe
Typesetting and layout: hidden europe (www.hiddeneurope.co.uk)
Print management: Jellyfish Print Solutions

ISBN-13: 978 1 84162 376 4
British Library Cataloguing in Publication Data
A catalogue record for this book is available from the British Library

Some **photographs** have been sourced from photo agencies. Where this is the case, the following abbreviations have been added next to the name of the photographer: DT (Dreamstime.com), IS (iStockphoto.com).

Printed and bound in India by Replika Press

Welcome Aboard

The humble omnibus has no pretensions to grandeur. And most of the journeys we all make by bus are mundane. There is no romance in the short hop to the local shops, no hint of adventure in waiting for the last bus home on a winter evening.

But there is another side to **bus travel in Britain**. The prosaic familiarity of the routes we know well contrasts with the **delicious exoticism** of the routes that lead beyond our home territory. Yes, there is life beyond the edge of the conurbation.

The destination blinds of the buses we see every day frame our mental maps. Local buses often take us to the nerve ends of our own communities. But no-one decrees that we must turn round there and return home. With time and a little planning, we can **hop from bus to bus** on journeys that extend across several counties. We can stop off here and there to explore market towns, national parks and unsung places.

Bus-Pass Britain is a **celebration of British bus journeys**. We do not claim that the fifty essays in this volume describe the very best of British bus routes, nor indeed that our anthology amounts to a comprehensive compendium of the range of bus journeys that are on offer in England, Wales and Scotland. No, our aim is rather different – we present fifty routes that have special meaning for the writers who describe them in this volume. Some authors recount bus journeys they make every day, while others have opted to highlight routes far from home which cast a particular spell. This book is one **written by the public and for the public**. And, for most of our authors in *Bus-Pass Britain*, it is the first time that they have seen their prose appear in print.

A Community of Writers and Travellers

British buses are often civil and **sociable spaces**. Buses are places for chance encounters and spaces for performance. Start and end points on each of the fifty journeys in this book are linked by changing landscapes and a rotating cast of characters. At its best, the local bus is a real **community on wheels**. And there has been something essentially communitarian about the project which nursed *Bus-Pass Britain* from a mere idea to this book.

Bradt Travel Guides is a company with conviction, one long noted for favouring the road less travelled. When Bradt invited members of the public to suggest their **favourite British bus routes**, no-one quite expected the fine mix of proposals that would flow in – from double-deck delights in the Lake District to the bus that meanders over marshlands to an isolated community on the Isle of Grain in the Thames Estuary. The U3A (University of the Third Age) was a good partner in encouraging submissions.

Some of the texts received by Bradt sparkled immediately, with perfect, fluent prose which nicely captured the peculiar appeal of exploring Britain by bus. In other cases, there has been some modest editorial intervention. Not so much, we hope, as to mask the many different voices that lie at the heart of this book. A handful of the essays, very much the minority, are by professional travel writers with a connection to Bradt Travel Guides. Among the latter is Hilary Bradt, co-founder of the company that bears her name.

Bus networks: a national asset

We hope this book will encourage and inspire readers to explore Britain by bus. UK residents of a certain age can do this for free, by virtue of the **bus passes** that allow pensioners to travel without charge on most bus services within the country in which they live – an odd restriction that hardly encourages pass holders in Wales to venture over the frontier into England or vice versa.

But you don't need a bus pass to explore Britain by bus, and we know many younger travellers, some of them contributors to this book, who appreciate that in its **local bus networks** Britain has a tremendous national asset. Yet, in a tight fiscal environment, lightly-used bus services which rely on public subsidy are an easy target for local authorities looking to cut budgets. Britain's bus networks will grow and thrive only if those not yet eligible for a bus pass make good use of buses now. Bus operators rely on full-fare passengers to maintain a viable service. The solution to the problem of funding local bus services is not to scrap **concessionary travel schemes**, but to ensure that a wider travelling public in Britain forsake their cars and take a bus instead.

From Zennor to Unst and back again

We have trundled on **red double-deckers** through Metroland – tea and buttered toast country – and ridden with the local postie on the post bus along remote valleys in the Scottish Highlands. There is **a fabulous variety** in British bus routes. Western Greyhound's route 508 battles out to Zennor on Cornwall's north coast in even the worst Atlantic gales, while at the other end of the British Isles P&T route 28 criss-crosses the island of Unst in the Shetlands, along the way serving what is surely the most well-appointed bus shelter in all of Europe. And between those two extremes is a dense mesh of thousands of local bus routes.

The day will probably come when technology will usher in the driverless bus. But for now, especially on rural routes, the bus driver's welcoming smile and helping hand are key ingredients of the bus journey. Happily, there is in Britain the long-standing custom of passengers **thanking their bus driver** as they alight from the bus. It's a courtesy that, if ever it existed at all, has long since disappeared on the continent. So we must close our introductory comments with a word of thanks. And that must be to the authors of *Bus-Pass Britain* for the energy and enthusiasm with which they accepted the Bradt challenge. And to the bus drivers who safely escorted them along the fifty journeys in *Bus-Pass Britain*.

Nicky Gardner and Susanne Kries
Editors, *Bus-Pass Britain*

HOW TO USE THIS BOOK

This book is as easy to use as hopping on your local bus. We have divided Great Britain into **seven regions**. Well do we know that the coverage is not absolutely even, but we preferred to give priority to routes that many readers can easily follow. That lends a bias to routes in more populated parts of Britain, rather than having a book showcasing journeys in truly remote areas. You will find an **index map** showing the location of each of our **50 routes** in the colour pages at the start of this book. Journeys vary from 30 minutes to more than three hours. And we have a mix of operators with some journeys run by large national companies and others relying on small locally-based bus operators.

Each route is accompanied by a **simple sketch map** – nothing fancy, but just enough detail for you to identify the main *en-route* points mentioned in the text. We give a **typical travel time** in minutes between each point on that map. Bear in mind that on some routes these average travel times can vary considerably from one trip to another. In urban areas, timetables often allow for longer journey times at peak hours. In rural areas, occasional buses may make deviations off the main route to serve villages that might otherwise have no bus service.

In the **introductory notes** at the **start of each route**, we give an indication of service frequency, an important consideration if you are planning to stop off along the length of a journey. Some of our routes run several times each hour, others as little as thrice daily. Careful planning always pays off. We also always cite the Ordnance Survey 1:50,000 **Landranger maps** relevant to each route in the order in which they occur if you follow the route as we describe it. And we mention the likely travel time if you follow the entire journey. Where a journey intersects with another route in this book, we mention that too.

Within each regional section you will find a **'bus stop' feature**. These are moments to pause between journeys and reflect on some aspect of British bus travel. At the end of the book, in our **reference section** (starting on page 235), you will find lots of good tips on journey planning and a briefing on **bus-pass basics**. And, to round things off, there is a detailed index of place names mentioned in the book.

Finally, we should add a note of caution. Bus timetables are famously volatile. They often vary from season to season. Bus numbers and routings also change. Cuts in public subsidies mean that frequencies on some routes are being trimmed for 2012, and some services cut altogether. Not, as far as we know, any of those featured in *Bus-Pass Britain*. But it always pays to check the current situation before setting out.

FIFTY BUS JOURNEYS

London Regent Street to Blackwall Chatham to Grain Dover to Hastings Brighton to Eastbourne Aldershot to Guildford Guildford to Redhill Luton to Aylesbury Newbury to Andover Trowbridge to Swindon Wells to Taunton Bournemouth to Swanage Exeter to Lyme Regis Lyme Regis to Poole Minehead to Lynmouth Plymouth to Dartmouth Dartmoor circular route Helston to Penzance Hereford to Llandrindod Wells Wrexham to Barmouth Mold to Ruthin Aberystwyth to Tregaron Ludlow to Hereford Banbury to Chipping Norton Birmingham circular route Northampton to Leicester Cromer to King's Lynn Diss to Beccles Lincoln to Skegness Buxton to Macclesfield Hanley to Buxton Matlock to Sheffield Hyde to Oldham Oldham to Ashton-under-Lyne Leeds to Ripon Bedale to Hawes Whitby to Scarborough Scarborough to York Northallerton to Helmsley Lake District circular route Keswick to Windermere Bowness to Glenridding Penrith to Patterdale Carlisle to Hexham Carlisle to Newcastle upon Tyne Newcastle upon Tyne to Berwick-upon-Tweed Berwick-upon-Tweed to Galashiels Dunoon to Portavadie Glasgow to Campbeltown Pitlochry to Rannoch Moor Inverness to Thurso

London & the Home Counties

Londonand buses have long been natural partners, so much so that for many visitors to Britain the **red double-decker bus** is still the most enduring image of the capital. Red buses symbolise the urban heartbeat. And in the days prior to bus privatisation, which splashed a kaleidoscope of brash colour over Britain's buses, green vehicles – not always double-deckers – reflected the more measured pulse of life in London's leafy hinterland.

Excursions beyond the capital

These distinctions were important for an earlier generation of Londoners. Red meant workaday routine, but green meant relaxation. The **Green Line services** beckoned urbanites to venture outside the capital. In the 1950s and 1960s destinations like Westerham, Windsor and Whipsnade were popular Sunday excursions for car-less families who lived in crowded London. The distinctive Green Line single-deck buses, with their handsome roof boards detailing the route, were synonymous with adventure. These were routes that boldly spanned the capital, improbably linking Reigate with High Wycombe (Green Line 711) or Luton with Dorking (Green Line 712) in the days when buses could navigate through central London unhampered by traffic congestion. The Green Line network of 'country' routes succumbed to changing travel trends, as families took to cars to explore Surrey lanes and Chiltern villages.

Nowadays you might smile that anyone ever thought there was anything green about **Luton**. But look carefully and even prosaic Luton has its charms as this book reveals. The bus from

Luton to Aylesbury (Journey 7) is as much fun today as ever it was in the sepia-tinged memories of yesteryear. And the Bedfordshire clanger tastes just as good. The very term 'Home Counties' imposes an amorphous uniformity on places that are very different, and local bus services remain a superb way of tapping into all that is distinctive in **London's hinterland**. In our selection of routes from the region, we take in places that are rightly famous but throw in a few improbable diversions – like the bus that trundles out to the **Isle of Grain** in the Thames Estuary (Journey 2). Elsewhere in this section of *Bus-Pass Britain*, we cruise the **Channel coast** (Journey 3), follow the **Pilgrim's Way** (Journey 6) and hop on a double-decker to explore Britain's newest **national park** (Journey 4).

The London challenge

Let us start with **London**. But how might one capture the flavour of one of Europe's largest cities in just a single bus route? No easy choice as we juggled the competing merits of very different routes. Should we opt for a journey through sedate suburbs, gritty urban wastelands or grand boulevards? In the end we went for a route which reveals quintessential London and includes some of the city's most celebrated sights.

Many other London bus routes begged for inclusion, and you may like to try our three near-misses. All date back to before World War II. Number 88 from **Camden to Clapham** is a very fine run, though nowadays not as interesting as it was in the 1930s when the route continued south beyond Clapham to a then still rural Belmont. Another classic is the 313 to Botany Bay, a further route that has survived for more than 75 years. Botany Bay is an improbably remote spot on the northern fringes of Greater London. Back in 1939 the only London bus route to cross *under* the Thames in Blackwall Tunnel was the 108. And that's still the case today. The 108 from **Lewisham to Stratford** via Blackwall Tunnel affords wonderful insights into parts of east London that have been thoroughly rejuvenated in recent years. ∎

Simply Red: A Capital Route

Alastair Willis

Regent Street

Service no. 15 | Journey time 45–65mins

OS Landranger 176, 177. Daily, every 7–10mins.
Operator: Stagecoach.

Blackwall

London's number 15 bus route really is capital. It is an artery linking the West End with the contrasting East End and Docklands, along the way passing some of London's finest buildings and vistas. Other services may have the edge when it comes to grand sights, but the 15 has a trump card that will appeal to bus travellers with a sense of transport history.

The busy section of the route from Trafalgar Square to Tower Hill benefits from extra daytime buses that ply just this part of the entire journey. And the vehicles that operate those supplementary services are 50-year-old **Routemasters**.

This is a chance for bus-pass holders to cast back to the days of their youth. Yes, we rode to school on open-platform double-deckers where we paid our fares to a conductor who sternly patrolled her or his vehicle and was quick to reprimand noisy and wayward passengers. I first rode a Routemaster in 1959. That was six long decades ago, a year when Max Bygraves was a hit at the London Palladium, and the Morris Mini-Minor made its debut at the London Motor Show.

This is definitely a journey where the best seats are upstairs at the front, rather than downstairs with the ebb and flow of visitors and Londoners who crowd the lower section of the bus. There's about a fortnight holiday's worth of things to see and do along route 15. I use it most frequently as a **'gallery hopper' service** that conveniently links the Royal Academy of Arts, the National Gallery (and its near neighbour the National Portrait Gallery), the Courtauld Gallery, Tate Modern, and Whitechapel Gallery.

REGENT STREET TO ST PAUL'S CATHEDRAL

For many years route 15 started back at Paddington. But London's civic authorities were keen to remove some of the buses that jostled for space on busy Oxford Street, so now the service leaves from just south of **Oxford Circus**, on Regent Street near Hamley's toy shop. Few bus stops enjoy such gracious surroundings, for **Regent Street** is very grand. Once aboard, the bus dives down into Theatreland. Amid the frenzied neon advertisements, there's angelic Eros still poised nude on his plinth at Piccadilly Circus, and nowhere near as controversial today as when he first appeared in 1893. Modern man (and woman) is not so easily shocked.

Trafalgar Square is altogether grander than Piccadilly Circus, with Nelson commanding proceedings from 167ft aloft. I'm always intrigued to see the latest commissioned artwork on the formerly empty northwest plinth in Trafalgar Square.

There's a glimpse of the Savoy, the grand old dame of London hotels, as we drive along the Strand. Gilbert and Sullivan's operettas were first produced in the theatre next door, and indeed it was profits from opera that allowed theatre impresario Richard D'Oyly Carte to fund the building of the Savoy hotel.

A little further east, our bus pauses by the late 18th-century **Somerset House**, which was England's first purpose-built

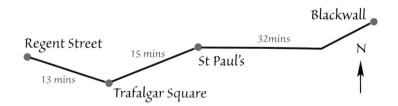

government office block. Nowadays it is a place not just for bureaucrats but for art, for it houses the Courtauld Gallery with its outstanding collection of Impressionist and post-Impressionist art.

Grand buildings follow in quick succession as our driver navigates the busy London traffic. The cathedral-like **Royal Courts of Justice** are Victorian Gothic in style. When high-profile court cases are heard it's interesting to watch the television crews, busily filming the comings and goings at the courts. This area, and nearby **Fleet Street**, are great places to wander. The Inner and Middle Temples, full of little courtyards and alleys, are a respite from the noise of busy streets. These lanes and squares seem unchanged for decades, though the same cannot be said of Fleet Street. Once busy with journalists, editors and printers, but no more! The great newspapers have forsaken Fleet Street, moving east along route 15 to the Docklands.

DOCKLAND BOUND

Then it's all stops east as our bus glides past **St Paul's Cathedral** and along Cannon Street to the Monument. The 202ft tall **Monument to the Great Fire of London** is a fluted Doric column, as much a London

A Routemaster bus in the wild. This specimen has escaped its natural London habitat and now works in Devon (photo © Peter Elvidge / DT)

ROUTEMASTER BUSES

Routemaster buses were introduced in 1956. Nearly 3,000 were built. **Retired Routemasters** are a popular export product. Over 1,000 survive in all corners of the world, many now deployed on sightseeing tours. An old London Routemaster even plies the streets of Ushuaia in remote Tierra del Fuego (southern Argentina). And you'll still find the bright red, iconic Routemasters on two heritage routes in London. They run from **Trafalgar Square to Tower Hill** (part of the number 15 service, as described in this article) and from **Trafalgar Square to Kensington** (a section of the number 9 bus route). This means that, with one change of bus at Trafalgar Square, you can travel from Kensington to Tower Hill on heritage buses – and all for regular fares or by just showing a valid bus pass. These two Routemaster services operate between 09.30 and 18.30.

icon as the Routemaster bus, but very much older. It was built in 1671 to commemorate the fire that, five years earlier, had so devastated the City of London. There is a marvellous view from the top of the column.

The next major landmark is the Tower of London, where I always break my journey for the picture-postcard views of **Tower Bridge** from St Katherine's Docks. The docks are Thomas Telford's most notable work in London, and they once specialised in handling high-value imports like brandy, spices and perfumes. These were the first of the London docks to be rehabilitated, back in 1973.

The Routemasters never venture east of Tower Hill, but the regular modern buses on route 15 certainly do. And it is well worth heading on to the end of the route, which continues past Aldgate into **Whitechapel**. This is a very different London, an area once afflicted by great poverty, and even today conspicuously less affluent than many other parts of the city. Limehouse, Poplar and Blackwall are quite another world from where our journey started in smart Regent Street just an hour earlier. Yet urban regeneration

TWO CATHEDRALS WALK

St Paul's Cathedral (open 08.30–16.30 Mon–Sat, Sun for worship only; entrance £14.50) is worth a visit in its own right, but for me there is another good reason for hopping off the 15 bus at St Paul's. It is the start of a short walk that nicely captures many flavours of London life. From the south entrance of St Paul's head down the wide walkway over the London **Millennium Footbridge**. Stop now and then to look back over the Thames at the Cathedral dome, the *Swiss Re* 'gherkin' and other architectural landmarks that dot the London skyline. **Tate Modern** (☎ 020 7887 8888; www.tate.org.uk/modern; open 10.00–18.00 Sun–Thu, 10.00–22.00 Fri–Sat; Cafe2 has won a best-family-restaurant award) is the former Bankside Power Station, full of compelling contemporary art. Then walk east to **Shakespeare's Globe**, the beautiful 1980s reconstruction of a 20-sided oak-framed galleried courtyard (☎ 020 7902 1500; www.shakespeares-globe.org; open 09.00–17.00 daily, depending on theatre performances; exhibition entrance £11.50).

Go along past **Clink Prison Museum**, Vinopolis, and The Golden Hinde, through the narrow warehoused streets. The lively Borough Market foodstalls are worth sampling. **Southwark Cathedral** (☎ 020 7367 6700; open 10.00–18.00 daily; excellent, friendly refectory) is a hidden, tranquil gem, Gothic and of medieval origin. Either return by the same route or catch bus RV1 to Tower Gateway (to join route 15 eastbound) or back to Aldwych (to rejoin route 15 westbound).

in the Docklands is changing this area fast, a reminder that our capital city is continually evolving.

Don't miss the **Museum of London Docklands** which tells the story of 2,000 years of history of the Thames and its dockland districts from the time when this was a small Roman port to the present day. For an easy way back to the City, opt for the **Docklands Light Railway** (DLR). The DLR trains are driverless, so grab a front seat for superb views from the elevated railway tracks across an urban area that has utterly reinvented itself. ∎

ABOUT THE AUTHOR | **ALASTAIR WILLIS** lives in Leicestershire and visits London frequently. He often joins the 15 at St Paul's, after travelling by train via St Pancras International to City Thameslink.

CENTENARIAN BUS ROUTES

Several authors in this book describe journeys they have made repeatedly over 50 years or more. Many British bus routes, particularly in **London**, retain the **same numbering** for decade after decade. When we were soliciting suggestions for bus routes to be included in this book, several members of the public nominated the number 11 bus route from Fulham through the West End to the City. One gentleman even mentioned that he had first taken the route 80 years ago. In fact the route dates back to 1908, and although one-way street systems have necessitated a few modern deviations, the number 11 bus still follows essentially the same route from **Fulham Broadway to Liverpool Street** as it did in Edwardian times. The buses have changed of course. No longer must passengers brave the weather on an open top deck. No longer is there any conductor to collect your fare. Nowadays the buses even talk to you, with automated announcements proclaiming the route number, destination and the name of the next stop.

Several other London bus routes can claim **centenarian status**. Number 3 runs from Oxford Circus to Brixton, still following much the same route as when first introduced in November 1908. Another of the new routes launched in 1908 was the number 16 from Victoria to Cricklewood. It is still going strong.

The London bus route we eventually decided to include in this book, the number 15 (page 8), dates back to before World War II, although the extremities of the route have been altered. What has also changed are the fares. To ride the 15 from **Regent Street to Tower Hill** would have cost just a shilling fifty years ago. That is five pence in 'new money'. Today the same short hop costs £2.20 (cash) or £1.30 (with an Oyster card).

One hundred years ago, the idea of a London bus number running into the hundreds was unthinkable. Two digits sufficed to accommodate every possible route. Times have changed, and **bus number inflation** is rife. London's highest numbered route today is bus 969 which makes a twice-weekly meander through west London suburbs to the local Asda supermarket.

Yet in the bus numbers of today, those in the know can still find hints of yesteryear. In the 1930s, residents of Kingston-upon-Thames used to crowd on to the number 65 bus for **summer excursions** to Leatherhead and the North Downs. The buses that ply the same route today are numbered 465. NG

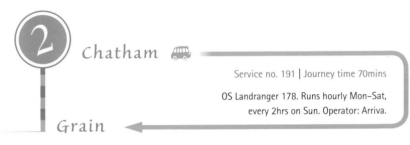

ISLAND ODYSSEY: THE ISLE OF GRAIN

Paul Wren

2 Chatham

Service no. 191 | Journey time 70mins

OS Landranger 178. Runs hourly Mon–Sat, every 2hrs on Sun. Operator: Arriva.

Grain

T he mysterious Isle of Grain is an often ignored part of Kent. Tucked away at the end of Hoo Peninsula, this is where the waters of the Thames and the Medway mingle. It is hardly fashionable territory, yet in these backwaters there is a surprising sense of remoteness for somewhere that is barely three dozen miles from London.

When I moved to Rochester, I found in the **Isle of Grain** a strange cocktail of rural desolation, industry and engaging scenery – the latter pretty two dimensional, to be sure, but often nicely enhanced by dramatic skies.

LEAVING CHATHAM

The **Pentagon bus station** in Chatham is the starting point. The Pentagon won no awards for its design. It is as uncompromising as the town it serves. Chatham is post-industrial and post-Navy. Yes, you can take in the **Historic Dockyard** to learn something of the town's key role in naval history, but a visit emphasises the gap in Chatham's social fabric which was left when the Royal Navy finally pulled out of the town in 1984.

From Chatham, the 191 heads north to **Rochester**, a town squeezed on to a neck of land surrounded on three sides by the Medway. A town, not a city, for Rochester lost its city status a few years ago when a new Medway unitary authority was created. This demotion remains a sore point with the locals. But it should not deter you from stopping off in Rochester, for the town has a fine Norman cathedral, a castle to match and some first-rate domestic and civic architecture (see box below).

Town scenes dominate as the bus crosses the **Medway** to unexciting **Strood** and you may be forgiven for thinking that the 191 is an urban road warrior, condemned to traverse for ever endless streets in and around the Medway towns. But beyond Strood the character of the route changes. Our bus purrs north through Chattenden to Hoo – effectively the 'capital' of the peninsula – and **High Halstow**.

After High Halstow, bus route 191 serves the tiny village of St. Mary Hoo, and then runs north to **Allhallows-on-Sea**. There was a time when Allhallows fancied itself as a rival to busy Southend-on-Sea, seven miles distant from Allhallows on the opposite bank of the Thames. The day trippers from London never arrived, nor did the London commuters who were predicted to find sanctuary in this obscure spot. The railway closed for want of trade, and Allhallows is now a small village with a large caravan park

ROCHESTER NOTES

The **visitor information centre** in Rochester High Street (☎ 01634 843666) is a good place to start your explorations of Rochester. The town is full of connections with Charles Dickens, who set some of his novels in and around Rochester. There is a good Dickensian walking trail, described in a leaflet available from the visitor centre. For refreshments, try **The Deli** (28 High St; ☎ 01634 841009) and **The Garden House Café & Deli** (98 High St; ☎ 01634 842460).

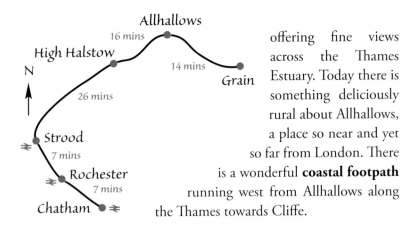

offering fine views across the Thames Estuary. Today there is something deliciously rural about Allhallows, a place so near and yet so far from London. There is a wonderful **coastal footpath** running west from Allhallows along the Thames towards Cliffe.

THE ISLE OF GRAIN

Finally our bus reaches the Isle of Grain, divided from the **Hoo Peninsula** by Yantlet Creek. Blink and you may miss it! Indeed, you'll find a lot of folk who contest Grain's claim to be an island, and it is hard to believe that Yantlet Creek, nowadays no more than a dribble of water, once provided a high-water route for barges bound for the Medway from the Thames.

The isle is a conundrum for visitors – a real mixture of industry (and industrial dereliction), remote rural housing, and some great views of the Thames (especially if you happen to be seated at the

SMUGGLERS AND MALARIA

High Halstow has a fine setting on a low hill – that's a rarity in these parts. Visit the 10th-century St Margaret's Church, and take a short walk to **Northward Hill RSPB nature reserve**, which offers great views across the Halstow marshes, including the now derelict former smugglers' inn called Shades House. Dickens captured something of the history of this area in *Great Expectations*. Life wasn't easy on these marshes. Indeed, until the start of the last century there were often severe outbreaks of malaria. The **Red Dog** (☎ 01634 253001) in High Halstow is a reliable watering hole.

GRAIN: AN OPPORTUNITY MISSED?

It is hard to credit that the industrial complexes on the Isle of Grain hide the site of one-time **Port Victoria**. This was a grand scheme of Victorian railway magnate **Sir Edward Watkin**, who dreamt of developing a new Thames Estuary port for London, less prone to fog and congestion than the docks upstream. Watkin found a fan in Queen Victoria who used the entrepreneur's port at Grain for journeys to the continent. In the early 20th century, the Port Victoria facility was used by royal delegations from Germany and Norway. No trace of Port Victoria remains.

front of the upper deck of a double-decker bus). First impressions of the Isle of Grain are not inspiring. There are great sweeps of containers in a complex called **London Thamesport**, and there are power stations towering over squat gas and oil storage tanks. But look again, and you will also see marshes and wetlands, and if you take time to linger, you'll find birdlife and insects aplenty.

Bus 191 now reaches its *ultima Thule*: the village of **Grain**. Alighting from the bus, well might one wonder why Grain is worth a journey. But a short walk along High Street brings you to the lovely Norman church of St. James, and further along the High Street, you arrive at a beach, the newly christened **Grain Coastal Park**. This is a magic spot, completely unadorned with the usual British seaside paraphernalia – just a pebbly beach with lovely views across the Thames, north to the pier at Southend-on-Sea, and east – just a short hop across the mouth of the Medway – to the busy port of Sheerness-on-Sea, on the Isle of Sheppey. Clamber up on to the remains of the former Fort Grain for a splendid view of the abandoned tower, which lies in the mouth of the Medway, between the Isles of Grain and Sheppey. ∎

ABOUT THE AUTHOR | **PAUL WREN** has lived in Rochester for 12 years. As a self-confessed travel addict he is happiest when exploring offbeat places – whether by bus, train, plane, ferry or on foot.

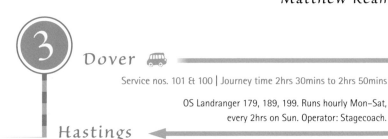

Exploring the Cinque Ports

Matthew Reames

3 Dover 🚌

Service nos. 101 & 100 | Journey time 2hrs 30mins to 2hrs 50mins

OS Landranger 179, 189, 199. Runs hourly Mon–Sat,
every 2hrs on Sun. Operator: Stagecoach.

Hastings ←

This cruise along the coasts of Kent and East Sussex is two bus routes rolled into one. For Stagecoach's bus number 101 quietly morphs into the number 100 on its 50-mile journey from Dover to Hastings. Along the way the route takes in four of the five original **Cinque Ports** – the 12th-century confederation of maritime towns that were granted special privileges in return for providing ships and men in service to the king. As if to emphasise the Englishness of the venture, the word 'Cinque' is pronounced 'sink', not at all like the French 'cinq' (or the Italian 'cinque').

CHALK CLIFFS AND MARSHES

Our journey starts in **Dover** not far from the castle. She or he who holds the position of Constable of Dover Castle is accorded the grand title Lord Warden of the Cinque Ports. Recent incumbents include Sir Winston Churchill and Queen Elizabeth The Queen Mother who between them held office for almost half-a-century. The burdens of office are evidently not very taxing.

The route out from Dover follows the A20 road, where most car drivers speed along, hardly aware of the remarkable chalk

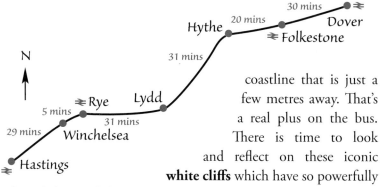

coastline that is just a few metres away. That's a real plus on the bus. There is time to look and reflect on these iconic **white cliffs** which have so powerfully shaped the English imagination. There is a quick glimpse of the Battle of Britain memorial before the bus drops down towards **Folkestone** with fine views of a broad sweep of Channel coast. Next stop is **Hythe**, one of the Cinque Ports, and suddenly the whole demeanour of the coast has changed. No more chalk cliffs, but rather a shingle coastline with marshland beyond. And Hythe, backed by Romney Marsh, made a decent living from smuggling.

Beyond Hythe, the road hugs the coast down to Dymchurch before turning inland to **New Romney** where the Cinque Port Arms pub is one of the few tangible reminders of the town's important historical role in maritime defence and commerce. The fate of New Romney is a reminder of the fragility of this stretch of coast. A huge storm in 1287 reshaped the shoreline, leaving the former port of New Romney high and dry – stranded inland without access to the sea. Then it's south to **Lydd**, a town that, though never one of the Cinque Ports, played a supporting role in the confederation, which had a network of 'antient towns' and 'limbs'. Lydd was one of the latter.

Rye Bay and beyond

Stagecoach styles this route 'The Wave', a name that nicely reflects the journey's intimate association with the sea. The scenery is at its most remarkable in the stretch beyond Lydd. The route skirts the wetlands of Walland Marsh to reach **Rye Bay**. The bus is quiet, the upper deck almost empty. This is country that inspires quiet

RYE

The historic town of Rye occupies an enviable site presiding over the **River Rother** and the surrounding marshlands. Its former defensive role in the **Cinque Confederation** is evident in the Ypres Tower and remnants of the old town wall. There is a maze of cobbled streets, pretty cottages and gardens and perhaps the greatest density of tea shops anywhere in southern England. Rye has rich **literary associations**, from Henry James to Joseph Conrad, H G Wells to G K Chesterton. The town has a good tourist information centre (4/5 Lion St; ☎ 01797 229049, www.visitrye.co.uk).

reflection. We skirt Camber's famous sands to reach Rye, one of the two so-called 'antient towns' in the Cinque Confederation. The other is Winchelsea, where our bus stops just ten minutes beyond Rye. Both are lovely Sussex towns, and each just begs to be explored.

From Rye, the bus follows the old Royal Military Road to **Winchelsea**, entering the latter through the Strand Gate. Then on over low hills with beautiful views of the Brede Valley to the north, to Guestling, now no more than a small village but once a place that demanded great respect. It was in **Guestling** that one of the main courts of the Cinque Confederation would pass judgement. Beyond Guestling, the density of housing increases as **Hastings** comes into view. This was once one of the five main ports, but today better known as a place for seaside amusements. Most passengers alight at the rail station. The bus continues on through Hastings, serving suburban estates and schools on its way to its final destination at Conquest Hospital. The very name is a reminder that, from Norman times to the present day, this stretch of coast has played an important role in English history. ■

ABOUT THE AUTHOR | **MATTHEW REAMES** lives in Virginia (USA) where he is studying for a PhD in maths education. Until mid 2011, he lived in Canterbury (England) where he taught mathematics.

THE SUSSEX COAST: TOWNS AND DOWNS

Jenny Jones

4

Brighton 🚐

Services nos. 12, 12A, 12X or 13X | Journey time 70–90mins

OS Landranger 198, 199. Daily, 4 to 6 times per hour.
Operator: Brighton & Hove (B&H).

Eastbourne ◄

The augustly named Brighton and Hove Bus and Coach Company (B&H) runs the frequent buses that link Brighton and Eastbourne on the Sussex coast. This journey, dubbed the Coastal Trail by B&H, is a serene progression from the Regency splendour of Brighton to the sedate resort of Eastbourne. And it is my favourite bus route, offering a chance to savour some stunning coastal and downland views. To make the most of it, I always like to sit upstairs at the front of the bus.

LEAVING BRIGHTON

Brighton is chic, cosmopolitan, Bohemian even, and the first part of our journey takes in a medley of classic **Brighton sights**: the gold-topped Clock Tower, the town's iconic pier and the striking 19th-century Italianate aquarium. Brighton has always been a place for fun, and though the days of vaudeville are long gone, you'll still find fish & chips and fortune tellers aplenty. From the bus there are good views of Brighton's hallmark Regency architecture – notably Royal Crescent with its black mathematical tiles and Lewes Crescent with its elegant garden enclosures. As the road starts to climb uphill, we see the **Volk's Electric Railway**

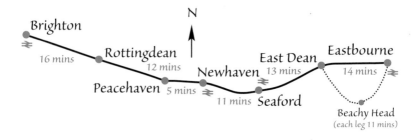

N

Brighton
16 mins

Rottingdean
12 mins

Peacehaven 5 mins

Newhaven

11 mins Seaford

East Dean
13 mins

Eastbourne
14 mins

Beachy Head
(each leg 11 mins)

running along the beach, and have a bird's-eye view of the yachts, shops and restaurants at Brighton Marina.

Standing slightly aloof on the left is **Roedean**, the famous girls' public school founded in the 1880s. A secret tunnel runs under the road to link the school with the beach. Standing guard at the next roundabout is the striking Art Deco St Dunstan's Centre. It was constructed in 1938 as a rehabilitation centre for blind ex-servicemen and women, and still serves that purpose today. As the bus approaches **Rottingdean** a restored black smock windmill built in 1802 stands in proud silhouette against the Sussex sky. Rottingdean is a pretty spot and certainly warrants a wander (see box opposite). With buses running so frequently along this route, it is easy to hop on and off at will.

Following the contours of the chalk cliffs, the road climbs steeply out of Rottingdean, then drops down sharply into

Brighton Pier (photo © Martinturzak / DT)

Saltdean. At the bottom of the dip is **Saltdean Lido**, built in 1937 and one of the few 1930s lidos still in use. It is a classic piece of Art Deco architecture. Over the next couple of miles Saltdean merges into Telscombe Cliffs which in turn morphs into **Peacehaven**. Here we cross the **Greenwich Meridian** (longitude 0°) – a monument on the cliff-top path marks the exact line. Peacehaven has a curious history, having grown very quickly in the early 1920s when a local property developer offered free plots of land to Londoners looking to relocate to sunny Sussex. For many years, folk lived in improvised accommodation such as huts and converted railway carriages, which were eventually replaced by an unremarkable scatter of bungalows. Modern Peacehaven might not look too interesting, but it does have a hidden secret visible only at low-tide (see box on page 24).

ROTTINGDEAN

Rottingdean village has many quaint old cottages faced with local **Sussex flint**. This one-time farming community became a smugglers' haunt, then in the 19th century attracted an artistic and literary set. The house on High Street where the eminent Victorian artist **Edward Burne-Jones** lived is marked with a blue plaque. He designed the stained-glass windows in the lovely 13th-century church of St Margaret's, entered through the lychgate opposite the village pond. Rudyard Kipling's former home, The Elms, is near the church – he wrote *Kim* and the *Just So* stories here. Next to The Elms are the **Kipling Gardens**, open to the public. Continuing round the pond we reach The Grange, the former home of painter Sir William Nicholson, now a library, museum and art gallery.

The **Olde Cottage Tea Rooms** in High Street is a reliable spot for coffee, light lunches or cream tea (☎ 01273 303426; open 09.00–18.00 Mon–Fri, 10.30–18.00 Sat & Sun). The **Plough Inn**, next to the village pond, offers a traditional pub menu (☎ 01273 390635).

Now we are east of Greenwich, bowling along the A259 towards the cross-Channel ferry port of **Newhaven**, still served by ferries from Dieppe in France. As the road swings inland, a great sweep of Sussex downland opens up before us. We cross the swing bridge over the **River Ouse**, views upriver to the fishing boats and downriver to the modern commercial port. Beyond Newhaven, alight at the Denton Corner bus stop for the Ouse Estuary Nature Reserve. This is a valuable wetland where you might spot teal, moorhens, shelduck and mallard. And on a good spring or summer day, listen out for skylarks.

Just by the road sign announcing the start of Seaford, there is access through a small car park to **Bishopstone Tide Mills**, where once great waterwheels were powered by the Channel tides. There are the remains of a village that once housed 100 workers.

THE SEVEN SISTERS

Seaford won't detain you, but immediately after the town comes some of the best scenery of the entire journey – starting with a panoramic view of the Cuckmere Valley and Friston Forest. The road soon descends steeply to a sharp bend, with the **Golden Galleon pub** on the right (☎ 01323 892247). This is a great place to stop for refreshments, with excellent views from the terrace. Through the pub car park is a path to the beach – about a mile away. Bear right and go up the hill, past the coastguard cottages, for a memorable view of the Seven Sisters cliffs.

The next bus stop is **Seven Sisters Country Park** – one of the highlights of the route (see box below). Looking back during the steep ascent up from the valley floor we are treated to wonderful views of the meandering river, glistening as it snakes its way towards the sea. Don't blink now, or you'll miss the village of Friston, with its duck pond and 11th-century church. Nestling in the wooded valley beyond is its sister village, **East Dean**, where back in the 1800s locals made a decent living from smuggling gin.

Next we can enjoy a stretch of totally unspoilt downland – just us, the sheep, the cows and the views. In the distance to the right is the former Belle Tout lighthouse, now a hotel, perched seemingly precariously atop the cliff. Built in 1832, the lighthouse was decommissioned in 1902 when the new Beachy Head lighthouse was built at the base of the cliff. In 1999, due to coastal erosion, the whole building was lifted on to rollers and moved 17 metres inland – quite a feat!

SEVEN SISTERS COUNTRY PARK

Taking its name from the Seven Sisters chalk cliffs between here and **Beachy Head**, this scenic area is part of the **South Downs National Park**. The River Cuckmere meanders lazily through open chalk grassland, eventually reaching the sea at a shingle beach flanked by steep cliffs. The wonderful and varied scenery makes this a very popular place for walking, cycling, birdwatching and canoeing. The **visitor centre** adjacent to the bus stop has local information and maps to help you make the most of your visit. Other amenities include the **Bike Hire Centre** (☎ 01323 870310), the **Exceat Farmhouse Restaurant and Tea Gardens** (☎ 01323 870218) and toilets.

Behind the visitor centre you can walk or cycle into **Friston Forest** to explore the woods and wildlife along various waymarked routes.

SEASONAL SIDETRACKS

Much of the bus route from Brighton to Eastbourne follows the main A259 coast road. But buses numbered 13X make **a splendid deviation**, leaving the main road at East Dean to serve a dramatic stretch of chalk coast that includes **Birling Gap** and **Beachy Head**. The 13X runs at weekends from mid April to mid September and daily for an 11-week summer season. It makes little difference to the overall journey time to Eastbourne, but that digression is really something special.

Don't worry if you don't have a bus pass. B&H fares are reasonable. A **saver ticket** purchased from the driver costs just £5 and gives the freedom to roam on all B&H buses for a day. The company's network features a number of **attractive seasonal routes** from Brighton to the heart of the new South Downs National Park. They include the 79 to Ditchling Beacon and the 77 to Devil's Dyke. Open-top buses are often used on the latter route in July and August. The 77 and 79 are both part-funded by the National Trust. The canny folk at B&H have grabbed what is surely a prize internet domain: www.buses.co.uk. You can find maps and schedules for all B&H services there.

We pass the turning where the seasonal 13X bus turns off south to Birling Gap and Beachy Head – a very scenic diversion which is perfect for walkers. Over the crest of the next hill **Eastbourne** springs into view. The bus winds its way down, past the Old Town and the shopping centre, then on to the seafront, ending its journey at Eastbourne Pier.

Compared to its livelier neighbour Brighton, Eastbourne may seem like a place for respectable maiden aunts, but don't underestimate it. The pier has a camera obscura – an original 360 degree Victorian projector; the bandstand offers a lively programme of outdoor concerts and the **Towner Art Gallery** (College Rd; ☎ 01323 415470; www.townereastbourne.org.uk; open 10.00–17.00 Tue–Sun) has a fine collection of 19th and 20th-century art. It is a place to linger. ∎

ABOUT THE AUTHOR | **JENNY JONES** is a freelance writer, editor and proof-reader. She has lived in Brighton for over 25 years.

Country Lanes to Guildford

Sylvia Cole

⑤ Aldershot 🚐

Service no. 46 | Journey time 80mins

OS Landranger 186. Runs hourly Mon–Sat. No Sunday service.
Operator: Stagecoach.
Connects with Journey 6 in Guildford.

Guildford ◄

There are plenty of fast buses from Aldershot to Guildford. Bus number 20 speeds between the two in just 40 minutes. But if time is not important, then opt for the 46 which shuns main roads and meanders gently through **Surrey lanes**. This is a slow travel diversion, a beautiful journey at any time of the year but at its best in autumn, when the trees are clothed in their autumn shades of russet and gold, or in early spring with daffodils and bluebells along the way. For forty years, working in solicitors' offices, I caught the fast bus and missed the simple rural appeal of the slower services.

The 46 is rarely busy. It is a bus used by villagers exchanging pleasantries and local news. Leaving **Aldershot**, the route studiedly ignores the road signs that point east towards Guildford and heads off in the opposite direction.

The Wey Valley

Before long, we slip over the county boundary, swapping Hampshire for Surrey, and arrive in **Farnham**. And it's here in Farnham that we catch our first glimpse of the River Wey. No great torrent, but we cross it half a dozen times on the journey to Guildford.

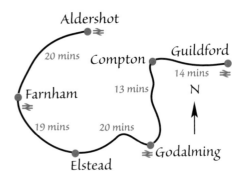

From Farnham we head more decisively towards Guildford, the ruins of **Waverley Abbey** on our right. This was the earliest Cistercian foundation in England, dating back to 1128. Entrance is free and you can visit any time in daylight hours. Then the bus runs east to **Elstead**, a village with a handsome mill (now a well-known gastro-pub), a fetching church and one of those oversized village greens that are so typical of Surrey.

We wend our way along lanes, winding through beech woods. There are views of downs and farmland and we pass Shackleford and Hurtmore to reach one of the most striking pieces of architecture on this journey. **Charterhouse School** moved to this Surrey hilltop in 1872, having outgrown the central London site where the school was founded in 1611. The main school buildings are high Victoriana. The school's name – Charterhouse – is taken from the old Carthusian monastery which had once occupied the school's original London site. From Charterhouse, we drop back

WATTS GALLERY

The Watts Gallery in **Compton** is a highlight of this journey and certainly warrants a stop. The gallery is devoted to the work of the Victorian artist **George Frederic Watts** and opened in 1904. It happily reopened in mid 2011 after a three year restoration period (☎ 01483 810235; open 11.00–17.00 Tue-Sat, 13.00–17.00 Sun, closed Mon; admission charge). The **tea shop** serves good English seasonal fare and tasty Welsh rarebit. Even when the gallery is closed, you can visit the extraordinarily ornate **Watts Cemetery Chapel**. It is breathtaking, magical and utterly inspiring.

down into the **Wey Valley** to Godalming. This is a place that exudes a sense of quiet affluence, and it's a good place to pause for an hour or two. There is a striking octagonal town hall, a feast of Arts and Crafts architecture, and a good range of boutiques and cafés.

GODALMING AND BEYOND

After a steep climb out of Godalming we drive through Farncombe and Binscombe and reach the village of **Compton** with timbered cottages and antique shops inviting us to rummage amongst their treasures. On the outskirts of the village is **Watts Gallery** (see box opposite). From Compton, the route joins the A31 for the final run into the cathedral city of **Guildford**. There are fine views of the red-brick cathedral with its distinctive green roof before our bus stalls in Guildford traffic on its way to the **Friary Bus Station**. This sounds like a religious endgame for the 46 from Aldershot. We've had hints of Cistercians and Carthusians on our twists and turns through Surrey lanes. Now it is the chance of the Dominicans, who settled here in the 13th century. But the friars are long gone, and the only hints of their stay in Guildford are in the name of the bus station and nearby shopping centre. ■

ABOUT THE AUTHOR | **SYLVIA COLE** discovered this beautiful bus route upon her retirement. The slow bus to Guildford has since inspired her to use her bus pass for further adventures.

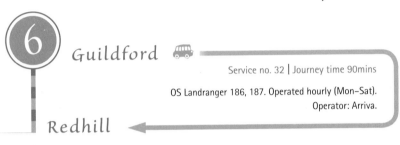

Along the Pilgrim's Way

Nicky Gardner

6

Guildford

Service no. 32 | Journey time 90mins

OS Landranger 186, 187. Operated hourly (Mon–Sat).
Operator: Arriva.

Redhill

Happy was the day when the M25 motorway eventually opened, so suddenly relieving the old A25 road of the burden of traffic it had shouldered for far too long. Surrey villages that nestle in the shadow of the **North Downs**, places like Gomshall and Buckland, learnt to breathe again. No longer were they pummelled relentlessly by heavy trucks heading east towards the Kent ports.

This route below the scarp of the North Downs has long been a traditional thoroughfare from west to east across the **Weald**. Chalklands to the north, wooded sandstone hills to the south. The **Pilgrim's Way** followed this natural vale. And nowadays bus 32 follows the A25 east from Guildford through a string of Surrey villages to Dorking, Reigate and Redhill.

Surrey may boast no great mountains, but such modest relief as there is has long determined transport patterns. I catch a sense of that as the Arriva bus heads out of **Guildford**, its route following a narrow gap between chalk hills carved by the River Wey. Not five minutes out of town, and we cross the line of the Pilgrim's Way. Then east along the foot of the North Downs to pretty **Chilworth**, a village that for 300 years made a good living through manufacturing gunpowder. Albury is next, an estate village with a handsome crop of mock Jacobean cottages, all extravagant chimneys and fussy brickwork.

This is pretty country, green and pleasant in a way that only England can manage, with a strong sense of history. No surprise, perhaps, that a dozen or more villages along this bus route featured in the *Domesday Book*.

Under the Hammer

Abinger Hammer, a half-hour out of Guildford, is not a place you can easily miss. Traffic on the A25 slows to edge round the wooden clock that juts impertinently out over the main road. It's certainly not the quaintest of the villages on this run, but I like it for its homely feel. Less pretentious than Albury, more coherent than Shere. Abinger Hammer is a place to wander. Like many of the communities on this route, it has an oversized village green. But the green at Abinger Hammer is made all the better by the little **Tillingbourne stream** that flows across its middle. It always reminds me that for over seventy years, bus services hereabouts were run by the Tillingbourne Bus Company. Ten years ago Tillingbourne folded, making way for the big national operator which quickly muscled in to pick up Tillingbourne's former

---

ABINGER HAMMER

Abinger Hammer village store doubles as the local café. Look for the sign **Abinger Hammer Tea Rooms** (☎ 01306 730701; open 10.00–17.30 daily). It's a homely spot, much less fussy than many of the cafés along this route. Great bacon sarnies, or try the Abinger Lunch. Watercress abounds, a reminder that the hammer ponds along the **Tillingbourne Valley** which once powered the Wealden iron industry now make admirable watercress beds. Walk up to the farm shop at the east end of Abinger Hammer village to see the watercress beds. The village pub, the **Abinger Arms** (☎ 01306 730145), is an honest red-brick place just west of the clock.

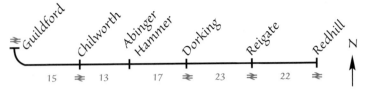

Numbers above show travel time in minutes between marked way stations

routes. Today this is solid Arriva territory, with a fleet of modern single-deckers sporting shades of cyan and spring green.

Not many bus routes can boast such distinguished **literary associations** as the Arriva 32 through Surrey. Lewis Carroll lived in Guildford, E M Forster in Abinger Hammer and John Evelyn in Wotton. Look out for lovely St John's Church on the left as the bus cuts through hilly Wotton just east of Abinger Hammer. It is in an impossibly picturesque setting, a rich ochre Bargate stone building with a Horsham slate roof picture perfect against the backdrop of the Downs beyond.

Next comes **Dorking**, one of the few Surrey towns to be dominated by its church. Dorking has an appealing main street, remarkable not for any lovely buildings but more for its curves and slopes, the south side being appreciably higher than the north. From here it is an easy run east under the shadow of **Box Hill** to Brockham, with its distinctive triangular green. The route continues east through unremarkable **Reigate** to end in prosaic Redhill, where travellers wanting to continue further east along the Pilgrim's Way can connect on to the Southdown 410 service which heads along the foot of the Downs through Godstone to Oxted. Or return west to Guildford by train. For much of that rail route, at least as far as Shere, the train line is slightly higher in elevation than the A25, giving a different perspective on the villages through which the Arriva bus passed on our outward journey from Guildford to **Redhill**. ■

ABOUT THE AUTHOR | **NICKY GARDNER** is co-editor of *hidden europe* magazine and also co-editor of this book. She last travelled this route with her dad (a bus-pass holder) in early 2011.

A Meander through Beds, Bucks & Herts

Brian Grigg

7 Luton 🚌

Service no. 61 | Journey time 1hr 40mins to 2hrs

OS Landranger 166, 165. Runs hourly Mon–Sat.
Operator: Arriva.

Aylesbury ←

B us routes change over the decades. When I was growing up, the bus from Luton to Aylesbury was always the number 16. Nowadays it is the 61. But whatever the number, whatever my age, I have always enjoyed the ride to Aylesbury. It is a route that touches three counties, along the way playing cat and mouse with the Chiltern Hills.

Starting point for the 61 is **Luton Airport**, from where the run into town passes the Vauxhall Motors factory, a reminder that the fate of Luton over the last century has been much bound up with the car industry. After stops at the town's rail station and the Galaxy Centre (less extraterrestrial than it sounds), the 61 is soon bounding west on **Hatters Way**. Before it threw in its lot with automobiles, Luton was one of the premier hat manufacturing towns in England. And here on the right is a reminder of the hat trade: Luton Town Football Club is still affectionately known to locals as 'The Hatters'.

Our bus heads west through urban sprawl across the M1 to **Dunstable** and the more open countryside beyond. Dunstable Downs are striking, the scarp of the Chilterns presiding over the vale below. If you fancy a breezy walk in open country, you can

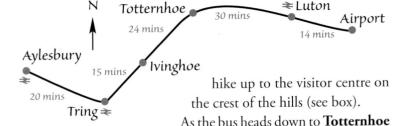

hike up to the visitor centre on the crest of the hills (see box).

As the bus heads down to **Totternhoe** there are glimpses to the south of a white lion carved in the chalk to mark the presence of **Whipsnade Zoo**. I like Totternhoe, and as a boy would often come out here by bus with my family. It's a good location for butterflies and birds. If time permits, take a break at the **Cross Keys** (see box on opposite page).

THE ICKNIELD WAY

Now comes the most rural stretch of the run to Aylesbury, as the bus follows the ancient Icknield Way along the Downs. Entering Buckinghamshire, we skirt **Ivinghoe Beacon**. Pitstone Windmill is the next local landmark. It is a beautifully restored 17th-century post mill which once provided flour for both Pitstone and Ivinghoe. The bus pauses in both villages and then crosses over the main railway from London to northwest England. It was not far from here that in 1963 the so-called 'Great Train Robbery' took place. Gangsters audaciously planted a false red signal to halt a southbound train carrying used banknotes.

CHILTERNS GATEWAY CENTRE

The centre (☎ 01582 500920; open daily 10.00–17.00, closes earlier in winter) is in a splendid location, and is a popular spot for kite-flying and hang-gliding. There is a good café at the centre where you will often find the famous Bedfordshire clanger on offer. A one-time staple dish in these parts, farm workers would take a clanger out to the fields with them for midday sustenance. It is an elongated dumpling, savoury at one end and sweet at the other.

We cross the **Grand Union Canal** and, now in Hertfordshire, cruise through flatter country to the pleasant market town of **Tring**, which – a little improbably perhaps – has a branch of the **Natural History Museum**, the museum's only outpost beyond the capital. It is worth taking a look at the world-class collection of stuffed mammals, birds and reptiles (☎ 020 7942 6171; www. nhm.ac.uk/tring; open daily 10.00–17.00, Sun from 14.00; free entry).

From Tring it is an easy 20-minute breeze along the A41 to **Aylesbury**. Although the bus continues through the centre of Aylesbury to the bus station, I suggest alighting in High Street. In nearby **Market Square**, you'll find one of England's finest old coaching inns. Nowadays, the King's Head is a National Trust property. The town's tourist information centre is in the pub courtyard.

The 61 is a great run through an unsung part of the Home Counties. Hope to see you on it one day! ∎

ABOUT THE AUTHOR | **BRIAN GRIGG** grew up in Dunstable in the 1950s and 60s, developing an early interest in public transport. He now lives in London, travelling by bus and coach all over England.

SOUTH & SOUTHWEST ENGLAND

It was the unbridled enthusiasm of Hilary Bradt for one particular bus route, namely the **X53 Jurassic Coast** service from Poole to Exeter, which really convinced us of the clear potential in a book celebrating Britain's favourite bus routes. You don't need to have Hilary's commitment to bus travel to realise that south and southwest England is ideal for exploring by bus.

If you have an English bus pass, you'll ride for free of course. And if you don't, the regular fares won't break the bank. For example, a **Day Explorer ticket** costing just £7 is all you need to make the journey on the X53 from Poole to Exeter and back – that's nine hours of bus travel.

We give the Jurassic Coast route its due in *Bus-Pass Britain*, it being the only journey we have split into two sections. Hilary introduces us to the western section of the route, then in Lyme Regis hands over the baton to Ron Lee to escort us eastward to Poole. Other journeys in this region cover **coastline and moors**, market towns and prehistoric settlements. We roam from the chalk country of Hampshire to the far tip of Cornwall.

Yet still there were routes for which we had no space. Western Greyhound's 510 service from Exeter to St Columb Major (near Newquay) on the north Cornwall coast is a very useful long-hop from east Devon into deepest Cornwall.

Other **West Country spectaculars** that you may like to try are the two-hour journey from Barnstaple to Bude via Hartland using Stagecoach 319 from Barnstaple, connecting in Hartland to Western Greyhound 519 for the onward journey to Bude. Through fares are available. ■

The Secret Delights of North Hampshire

Pauline Phillips

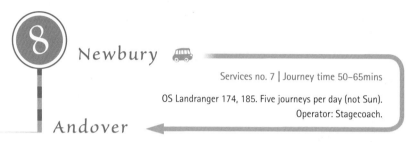

8

Newbury

Services no. 7 | Journey time 50–65mins

OS Landranger 174, 185. Five journeys per day (not Sun).
Operator: Stagecoach.

Andover

The historic market town of Newbury is just 60 miles from London. It is a thriving place situated at the junction of the A4 and the A34, and served by direct trains from London. It lies at the hub of a wonderful network of local bus routes that include three really first-class journeys: the number 4 over the Berkshire Downs to Lambourn, the 13 that serves villages south of the Kennet Valley on its run west to Hungerford, and the journey south into Hampshire on the number 7 – the one described here. This last route crosses beautiful, untroubled scenery sheltering **hidden delights** that tempt you to alight and explore, and with five buses a day there is scope for stopping off along the way. The trip begins in Newbury (see box on page 38), at the bus station situated in Market Street, next to the West Berkshire Council offices and opposite the splendid new cinema.

Newbury to Highclere

Climbing out of the **Kennet Valley**, we follow the A343 southwards, under the busy Newbury bypass, and continue through **Great Pen Wood**. This is a good spot for forest walks. A couple

NEWBURY

The River Kennet flows through Newbury, running east to join the Thames at Reading. In the late 18th century the new **Kennet and Avon Canal** provided a waterway through Newbury linking London with Bath and Bristol, later to have its fortunes clipped by the arrival of the **Great Western Railway**. You can follow the old canal towpath west to Bath and east to Reading. Newbury has a good range of shops, from smaller independent stores to the larger high-street brands, eating places galore and a famous racecourse served by its own railway station. The **open-air market**, dating back to 1204, is held on Thu & Sat and a Farmers' Market on the first and third Sunday of each month.

of buses each day detour along the Enborne Valley to serve the villages of Ball Hill and Woolton Hill.

This is border country, the territory where Berkshire quietly slips into Hampshire. **Highclere** is the first place of any size in Hampshire. The village is noted for its extraordinary castle, in truth more a palace than a castle. It is a fine piece of Renaissance Revival architecture, adapted in the early Victorian period but styled in a manner that affects to be much older. The architect responsible for this dramatic remodelling was none other than Charles Barry who moved to the Highclere project after reconstructing the Houses of Parliament in London. It is interesting to compare the two buildings. And if Highclere seems a little familiar, it is probably because you have seen it on television. It served as the fictional Downton Abbey in the popular period drama of the same name which was aired in 2010 and 2011.

Note that public openings at **Highclere Castle** are very irregular, with about 60 public days scheduled for 2012 (a spell around Easter, one weekend in May, a week in early June and then Sundays to Thursdays in July and August; details on www. highclerecastle.co.uk). Even if the castle is closed, Highclere warrants a stop. The Red House, on the main road, is a reliable spot for lunches (☎ 01635 255531; closed Mon).

Highclere to Hurstbourne Tarrant

Beyond Highclere, our bus climbs gently to **Three Legged Cross**, a former pub but now a private residence. This is a place for keen walkers to alight (see box overleaf).

Bowling along the road surrounded by green rolling hills, we pass a turning on the right beckoning to the secluded village of Ashmansworth, where the composer Gerald Finzi once lived. One bus a day makes a little detour into the village, a reminder that for those without cars the local bus really is a lifeline link with the wider world.

The next highlight is **Hurstbourne Tarrant**, a charming village surrounded by high chalk downland, threaded by the Bourne, a stream which only flows in winter. A plaque on the **George and Dragon pub** (☎ 01264 736 277) reveals that Hurstbourne Tarrant was the home of the famous Shakespearean actor Donald Wolfit. The village was a favourite of William Cobbett, author of *Rural Rides*. 'This, to my fancy, is a very nice country,' wrote Cobbett. 'It is continual hill and dell.' And we get a sense of what Cobbett meant as the bus climbs steeply out of Hurstbourne Tarrant on the main road towards Andover.

Views over the downland and meadows surrounding Andover dominate as we approach **Enham Alamein** (rivalling Three Legged Cross as the oddest place name on this bus route). The name alone is an incitement to alight at the thatched bus shelter. The place has an interesting history. In 1919 a consortium of London businessmen purchased Enham Place, a country house that then dominated the tiny hamlet of Enham, and started a rehabilitation centre for ex-servicemen with disabilities arising from World War I.

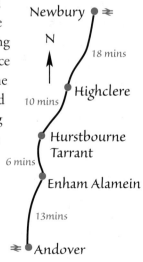

WALKS ON THE WAYFARER'S WAY

At Three Legged Cross our bus route crosses the **Wayfarer's Walk**, a well-signed footpath that meanders for 70 miles through the chalk vales and downlands of Hampshire. The five-mile walk northwest to **Walbury Hill** and Inkpen Beacon is superb, but choose a good day, for it can be formidably windy up on the high downs. Walbury Hill has an **Iron Age fort**. From the ridge there are stunning views over Hampshire and Berkshire, and hang-gliders and kites (the feathered kind and the recreational variety!) can often be seen here. **Inkpen Beacon** is close to the prominent landmark of **Combe Gibbet**. The original gibbet was destroyed many years ago and has been replaced several times. Walking southeast from Three Legged Cross along the Wayfarer's Way another splendid vista opens up across **Beacon Hill** (accessible to the public from the A34) to Watership Down, the location of Richard Adams's eponymous book.

Enham Place was demolished in 1939, but the village had established a reputation as a community that helped those with disabilities reach their full potential. Purpose-built housing, much of it in a style redolent of the early garden cities, makes Enham somewhere special. The village became Enham Alamein in 1945 following a substantial gift by King Farouk on behalf of the Egyptian people in gratitude for Allied help in the victory of the Battle of El Alamein. The entire village today still continues its mission of helping folk with disabilities. You can find out more at www.enham.org.uk.

After Enham Alamein, a village so brimming with noble aspirations, **Andover** might seem like an anticlimax. But it is the end of the road for the number 7 and time to alight. It is worth strolling round the town before making the return journey to Newbury. ∎

ABOUT THE AUTHOR

Originally from the Potteries, **PAULINE PHILLIPS** has lived in Newbury since 1973 and seen it grow from a quiet market town to a prosperous, bustling place. Pauline is a dedicated walker through this lovely countryside.

MOONRAKER COUNTRY

Vicki Messam

9 Trowbridge

Service no. 49 | Journey time 1hr 25mins to 1hr 40mins

OS Landranger 173. Runs hourly Mon–Sat, 5 journeys on Sun.
Operator: Stagecoach.

Swindon

I awoke one night three years ago with one of those Eureka moments. I realised that I really know more about Wiltshire bus timetables than one might sensibly admit to. Indeed, I knew some timetables off by heart. The Wilts & Dorset bus to Salisbury… the APL Travel link to Marlborough… and a dozen more besides. Armed with this deliciously eccentric intelligence, I founded a little group composed of folk who, like myself, love both walking and bus journeys. This Devizes-based group operates under the aegis of the University of the Third Age (U3A).

And if you are based in Devizes there is one bus route which is truly a mainstay of everyday life: the Stagecoach 49, often called the **Trans-Wilts Express** which links Trowbridge with Swindon via Devizes and Avebury. Don't be misled by the title. This bus journey is hardly an express. Occasional trains will speed you from Trowbridge to Swindon in 40 minutes. The Trans-Wilts Express is a bus option geared to those who like to travel slowly. Our U3A group has explored various sections of the 49 on many occasions this past year or two, and it has always been memorable, whether we have rain, sun, wind, sleet or snow. Perhaps the secret is that we always meet in a local pub *before* setting off.

DEVIZES

The local Council styles Devizes as 'Wiltshire's hidden gem'. Being bang in the middle of the county, and at the intersection of two major routes across Wiltshire, Devizes can hardly claim to be hidden. The name derives from the Latin *castrum ad devisas*, meaning 'the castle at the boundaries', alluding to the place where three manors met. The first castle was built in 1080 and the town's road layout still follows the lines of the inner and outer baileys of that early castle. It is good to find a town that is still shaped by history.

The **Market Cross** bears an interesting inscription commemorating Ruth Pierce, a local resident who, in 1753, claimed that she could not pay her dues for a bag of corn. When accused of not paying she said, 'I am honest, I will drop down dead if I am not.' She promptly dropped down dead with the money in her hand!

Wadworth Brewery, famous for brewing 6X beer over the last 125 years, has an excellent visitor centre on New Park Street, open daily from 09.30. Beer is delivered to local pubs in the town by dray and on most days of the week the brewery's two shire horses, Max and Percy, can be seen pulling their welcome loads around Devizes.

Devizes visitor centre, in Market Place, has leaflets and guidebooks and is open daily (find out more at www.devizes.org.uk).

EAST FROM TROWBRIDGE

Trowbridge is Wiltshire's county town, a little surprisingly perhaps. Sedate Salisbury and upstart Swindon both think they have better claim to the privilege. But Trowbridge it is. The bus starts at the local Tesco supermarket – but don't judge Trowbridge just on that detail. Wiltshire's county town, once famed for its textiles, has more to offer. The first 30 minutes of the journey are a pleasant run east with, at several points, good views north over the **Kennet and Avon Canal**. There are place names that ooze history: Semington Turnpike and Seend Cleeve. Approaching Devizes, **Caen Hill locks** are on the left. This spectacular series of locks, over two dozen of them packed into a short stretch of canal, was judged an engineering miracle when completed in 1810.

Arriving in **Devizes**, the bus stops in the marketplace – so much better than relegating buses to supermarket car parks. The **Black Swan Hotel** serves as a very comfortable waiting room for the buses. With its welcoming staff, this old coaching inn is a pleasant place to linger over a coffee and watch the world go by. The bay windows are popular with locals waiting for the 49, especially on Thursdays which is market day in Devizes. 'Here she comes,' says a keen-eyed observer in the bay window and suddenly all the world is on the move as shoppers gather up their bags and head out to the bus. There is no need to rush; the timetable always allows the bus a five-minute pause in the market square.

A STORY ABOUT SMUGGLERS

The stretch of route from Devizes to Avebury is the finest of the entire journey. Grab one of the front seats on the upper deck if you can. These seats offer the best view of the unfolding journey into the Wiltshire landscape. Sit comfortably, off we go!

Leaving Devizes the bus travels along Long Street, a beautiful conservation area with tall 18th-century town houses. The **Wiltshire Heritage Museum** and the 12th-century St John's Church are on your right. The church retains much of its Norman architecture and was the place where General Hopton and the Royalists took refuge when surrounded by the Roundheads during the English Civil War in 1643. Three medieval churches stand in Devizes, and two of them still show the cannonball holes sustained during the bombardment of the town.

Swindon

15 mins

Wroughton

12 mins

Avebury

6 mins

Beckhampton

20 mins

N

Devizes

34 mins

Trowbridge

A couple of bends later and to your right is **Crammer Pond**. There is a lovely local tale about this pond. Wiltshire folk lived well from smuggling and they would stash their contraband in Crammer Pond for safe keeping. When returning one moonlit night to retrieve their liquor, a policeman passed by and enquired curiously of the smugglers 'What's going on here then?'

'We're fishing for cheese' said the men, pointing to the moon's reflection in the pond. Evidently bemused but satisfied by the explanation, the policeman continued on his way, reflecting on the utter stupidity of these country locals. Those born and bred in Wiltshire are now often dubbed Moonrakers.

Crossing the Kennet and Avon Canal, the road climbs very slowly up on to the downs. The prominent hill to the left is **Roundway Down**, site of a major Civil War battle. A marked trail (called Battle Walk) tours the hill, with an elevated viewpoint and signs giving vivid, bloody accounts of the battle.

The **Millennium White Horse** is carved into the chalk here. A local farmer gave land to the local Council and the horse was carved into the hillside by volunteers to mark the millennium in 2000. The horse is one of a number of Wiltshire White Horses, most of which face to the left. This one is unusual, for it gallops to the right.

SACRED SPACES

We detour off the main road to serve **Bishops Cannings**, a village with a church that boasts a dramatic slender spire. And now four miles of sheer magic, a journey through the rolling Marlborough Downs into a prehistoric landscape. We pass Wansdyke, a strange earthwork defence built in the 5th or 6th century, and Shepherds Shore, the site of an old coaching inn.

You may be able to count the bell barrows that stand on each side of the road. These little round burial mounds, some individual and others in clusters, are easy to make out. They are a reminder that, for the prehistoric residents of Wiltshire, the downs were sacred territory.

To the left on the hilltop is the **Lansdowne Monument**, built by Lord Lansdowne of Bowood House to remind himself that there were not many more miles to go on his homeward journey. At Beckhampton the Swindon Road crosses the A4 Bath Road. It is said that Beckhampton gave rich pickings for a notorious gang of highwaymen who robbed the mail coaches. Locals recount that the last highwayman to be hung in Wiltshire met his death in the middle of what is now the A4 roundabout.

From the junction we continue straight on towards Avebury. To the left are Adam and Eve, two distinctive longstones that act as heralds for Avebury Stone Circle, still about a mile away.

Silbury Hill (see box on page 44) stays a companion on our right for a mile as we continue towards Avebury, a village at the heart of a great complex of Neolithic monuments which in 1986 was inscribed (along with Stonehenge, 30 miles away to the south) on the UNESCO World Heritage List. **Avebury Henge** contains three stone circles, one of them the largest in Britain. The bus follows the road that goes through the middle of a stone circle. But seeing the stones is not enough. Definitely plan to stop for an hour or two. The village is justifiably popular in the tourist season. But if you can contrive to visit on a quiet midwinter day, you are in for a treat. Mysterious Avebury at its best. Take a walk around the stones. There are well-maintained pathways. Try some stone cuddling if you wish. I've been tree and stone cuddling for years and it is very therapeutic. Many of the individual stones have names and some I feel I know like old friends. You can find out more in the museum (open daily from 10.00 till dusk).

What a bus ride! Where else can you view from a double-decker such great sweeps of chalk downland and such a feast of prehistoric burial sites? And ride through the centre of a World Heritage Site? It is no surprise perhaps that the final leg of the journey on to Swindon is something of an anticlimax. But it is not without interest. There are pleasant north Wiltshire villages with a liberal dose of thatched roofs. And then, as the bus drops down from the hills towards **Swindon**, one of Britain's most important libraries: the archives of **London's Science Museum** are kept in Wroughton and are open to the public. Shortly after Wroughton, the bus crosses the M4, from where it is a few minutes through uninspiring suburbs to the end of the journey. Ride the whole route from Trowbridge to Swindon, and then you can say you have seen the best of Wiltshire – the land of the Moonrakers. ∎

ABOUT THE AUTHOR | In 2007 ex-potter **VICKI MESSAM** formed the 'Bus-Pass Walking Group' for Devizes U3A. The twice-weekly walks involve using public transport. The Trans-Wilts Express journey is a firm favourite.

LAND OF THE SUMMER FOLK

Pat Robinson

10 Wells 🚍

Service no. 29 | Journey time 1hr 25mins

OS Landranger 182, 193. Runs hourly Mon–Sat. No Sunday service.
Operator: First.

Taunton ←

I n one of England's smallest cities – Wells in Somerset – the bus station isn't hard to find. I stroll across the Cathedral Green, taking in the moated Bishop's Palace, and on through medieval streets to catch my bus for Taunton, Somerset's county town located some 35 miles away to the southwest. It's a familiar journey for me, but these days sitting high in the bus I can see and enjoy everything as the **Somerset countryside** unfolds. Maybe I'll catch a few words of the local dialect. Somerset folk still throw in phrases that reveal the West Saxon origins of their unpolished language. And even if the bus is empty, I will still enjoy spotting elaborate church towers, the blossom of the cider orchards or the rich bird life. Sometimes I just sit back and dreamily enjoy the **ever-changing cloudscapes** of Somerset's wide horizons.

THE LEVELS

A few interesting detours apart, the bus travels mostly on main roads through the wetland heart of Somerset before reaching the higher land of south Somerset. In my younger days, these wetlands were called 'the moors'. Modern maps show them as the Somerset

Wells

20 mins

Glastonbury

8 mins
Street

N

55 mins

Taunton

Levels. Since Neolithic times men have fought hard to keep their land and built their homes above the 50-foot-contour to protect them from the greedy sea of the **Bristol Channel**. The battle never ceases, from the bus I can see the constant effort to manage the water levels in these wetlands. Rivers, rhynes, drains and pumps all have to be carefully maintained to prevent uncontrolled flooding. In winter dark, pollarded willows stand out above the flooded, icy fields. In summer life is full again, as livestock is brought down from the hills to enjoy the amazing green of the pastures. This is a Somerset ritual, as the summer folk reclaim their land.

GLASTONBURY AND STREET

Leaving the cave-laced limestone **Mendip Hills**, passing by old mills and villages, the bus soon gets down to the first of the Levels. Now the road follows an old causeway linking Wells and Glastonbury on the slopes of the Isle of Avalon, dominated by **Glastonbury Tor** which can be seen from three counties. Nestling on the slope below are the proud ruins of Glastonbury Abbey.

The bus continues over the old causeway and crosses the River Brue to the Quaker village of **Street**. The local Blue Lias stone used for the shoemakers' homes gives a coherent feel to the village where the Quakers James and Cyrus Clark founded the Clarks shoe empire. It is a story well told by the **Shoe Museum** in Street (High Street; for opening times phone ☎ 01458 842169; free entry).

South from Street, the bus makes an engaging detour along the little ridge of the Polden Hills, affording magnificent views of the Levels. Then we drop back down on to the flatlands, and pass

MYTH AND LEGEND

Glastonbury is the stuff of legends. It is said, probably without any firm evidence, that Joseph of Arimathea founded **Glastonbury Abbey**. Throw in tales of holy thorns, and the Holy Grail too, and you have a lot of fodder for local myths. Glastonbury claims key roles in the spread of Christianity through Wessex and in the **Arthurian legend**. You can see what is alleged to be King Arthur's tomb at the abbey. The bus stops very conveniently by the abbey gatehouse. The abbey is open daily from 09.00 till dusk (☎ 01458 832267; www.glastonburyabbey.com). Today, of course, Glastonbury is most noted for its annual **music festival**.

the **Isle of Athelney**, the modest hill where legend tells of King Alfred burning the cakes. A monument marks the site. The next landmark, on the bank of the River Parrett, is Burrow Mump, crowned by a ruined church. The Levels are at their lowest here, inhabited by mute swans and birds. Villagers have long grown withies for basket making.

But now the road rises. Dramatic changes in geology and landscape, and suddenly there are large farms on rich farmland before we reach the edge of **Taunton**. We detour through some unhappy urban sprawl and cross the River Tone to reach the centre of Taunton. The bus station is within the sturdy fortifications of Taunton Castle so a short walk across Castle Green and through the gatehouse will bring me into the centre of Somerset's busy county town.

And yet I've hardly started to tell you of life on the **Somerset Levels**. I've told no stories of the villages, said too little of the summer folk, and not even hinted of the Battle of Sedgemoor. There is so much more to be discovered on future bus rides. ∎

ABOUT THE AUTHOR	**PAT ROBINSON** has been making this journey across Somerset for over 50 years. Latterly, travelling the route by bus has opened up a new fascination for the county's history and landscape.

THE PURBECK BREEZER

Angela Simpkins

Bournemouth

Service no. 50 | Journey time 1hr 20mins

OS Landranger 195. Hourly in winter, every 20 to 30mins in summer.
Operator: Wilts & Dorset.

Swanage

The Purbeck Breezer is aptly named. For during the spring and summer months it is operated by open-top buses, so here's a chance to cruise the coast cabriolet-style. For the best seats, board the bus at **Bournemouth station** where the route starts. The atmosphere on the top deck is one of excitement and holiday fun, which nicely infects even those who are merely making routine journeys to work or the local shops.

It was an inspired moment when local bus operator Wilts & Dorset decided in 2009 to swap time-worn old vehicles for brand new open-top buses on the route to Swanage. Suddenly, folk started to ride the route for fun. Rebranded the **Purbeck Breezer** (for Swanage is on the Isle of Purbeck, which oddly is not an island at all), this is a British bus success story. It happens also to be the only bus route in this book where you get a ride on a ferry as part of the journey.

TOWARDS SANDBANKS

Travelling through Bournemouth you will get a first glimpse of the sea. The bus heads out through the smart residential areas of

Westbourne and Canford Cliffs. At **Branksome Chine** you might be tempted to hop off to enjoy the beautiful beach, but stay aboard for this is a route that just gets better and better. At Sandbanks Road, there is a splendid panorama over **Poole harbour**. 'That's the second largest natural harbour in the world,' says the bespectacled young lad in the front seat. Who knows if that is really true, but Poole harbour is certainly lovely. It is blessed with several islands, the most celebrated of which is Brownsea Island (see box below).

The road out to Sandbanks takes us along a little thread of land with the sea on both sides. At the end the ferry awaits, ready to take our bus and its passengers on the short voyage across the mouth of Poole harbour.

PURBECK BOUND

Well, an ocean cruise it is not, but the five minutes afloat on the **Sandbanks ferry** are always interesting. The sheer density of shipping is remarkable so the ferry master has to be very attentive. There are yachts and motorboats, even a huge catamaran leaving Poole harbour to travel to the Channel Islands.

The ferry docks at **Shell Bay**, starting point of the South West Coast Path. 'At 630 miles, the longest national footpath

---

BROWNSEA ISLAND

The largest of Poole harbour's several islands, Brownsea boasts 500 beautiful acres of woodland, heath, shore and wetland. Unusually for southern England, it has a thriving colony of **red squirrels**. Dorset Wildlife Trust manage a **nature reserve** on the island. The island as a whole is under the care of the National Trust, which levies a small landing fee on visitors arriving on Brownsea. You can **catch a boat** from the jetty next to the Sandbanks ferry (Brownsea Island Ferries; ☎ 01929 462383). The island has many striking buildings, including a fine Victorian Gothic church, a fake castle and picturesque clusters of cottages.

---

in the United Kingdom,' intones the boy with the professorial demeanour in the front seat. Should you fancy a shorter walk, it is about two miles along glorious sands to **Knoll Beach** where you can get refreshments at the National Trust café (open daily, ☎ 01929 450259).

For something a little different, pause for a swim at the naturist beach on the way. Don't worry – even if skinny-dipping is not for you, the naked souls on the beach will not mind you wandering past. And, if you want, there is an alternative walk to Knoll Beach leading over heath and sand dunes. Known

Steam survives on the Isle of Purbeck: the Corfe Castle to Swanage railway (photo © Nick Stubbs / DT)

as the Heather Walk, this well-marked trail is a riot of colour when the *Calluna* is in flower.

The bus rolls south over Studland Heath – Brand's Bay on your right – to **Studland** village (see box opposite) which is worth a wander. There is a fine Norman church and plenty of tempting walks. Ballard Down, immediately south of the village, is one of my favourites. From the crest, you can survey the entire Purbeck Breezer route, with views over a great sweep of coastline north to Bournemouth. Then turn and look south to Swanage.

Bournemouth

15 mins

Branksome Chine

15 mins

Sandbanks

Shell Bay

8 mins

N

Studland

15 mins

Swanage

SWANAGE

Back on the bus, it is a pleasant 15-minute journey from Studland to **Swanage**. This is a classic seaside town, and in the main tourist season the town's many bars, cafés, and fish and chip shops can be full to overflowing. My favourite Swanage diversion is **Chococo** (Commercial Rd; ☎ 01929 421777), a place that is dedicated to chocolate lovers. Try their ice cream sundaes (my top choice is the sensually named 'When Harry met Sally'). For winter days, they do scrumptious hot chocolate, and good tea, coffee and homemade cakes.

Swanage has a lot to offer: another wonderful Dorset beach, a Victorian pier, a steam railway for excursions to nearby **Corfe Castle**, and plenty of boat trips. At the end of the day, just hop on the Purbeck Breezer for the ride back to Bournemouth. ∎

ABOUT THE AUTHOR | **ANGELA SIMPKINS** retired to Dorset in 2004 and has been lucky enough to spend much of the time since exploring this beautiful county – on many occasions with the aid of the Purbeck Breezer.

The Jurassic Coast: West

Hilary Bradt

12 Exeter

Service no. X53 | Journey time 1hr 30mins

OS Landranger 192, 193. Daily, every 2hrs. Operator: First.
Connects with Journey 13 in Lyme Regis.

Lyme Regis

This is a bus with attitude; it squeezes cars up on to the pavement in the narrow streets of Beer and Lyme, and persuades even pushy Land Rovers to reverse out of its way. The X53 is justifiably self-confident; it's the **Jurassic Coast bus**, a double-decker with ammonites painted on its sides. And it's my local bus. As it slows to the bus stop I check whether my favourite seat at the front of the top deck is still empty and clamber up the stairs to join shoppers, walkers and sightseers. We all want to sit where we can watch the Devon countryside slowly unfold. This is, after all, an Area of Outstanding Natural Beauty, and there's plenty to see (for information on the Jurassic Coast see www.jurassiccoast.com).

Heritage

The Jurassic Coast was accorded **World Heritage** status in 2001 and several towns have scrambled for the honour of being its 'gateway'. Perhaps Lyme Regis deserves it most since the town has long been known for fossils (helped by the success of *The French Lieutenant's Woman*) but Exmouth and Seaton can justly make the

claim – and do. All along the coast there are noticeboards explaining the geology, and a careful search along the pebble beaches may yield an ammonite or two. And for all to view are the giant ones embedded in the rocks between Seaton and Lyme Regis.

This is a route made for walkers, and between Exeter and Lyme Regis are some of the best stretches of the **South West Coast Path**, varying from the easy 30-minute stroll from Beer to Seaton to the much more challenging hike through the Undercliff to Lyme. My favourite is the cliff-and-village walk to Branscombe (see box page 57).

LEAVING EXETER

The administrative centre of East Devon and famous for its splendid cathedral and river views, Exeter was thoroughly bombed in World War II and suffers from 'clone Britain' shops and architecture. To

EATERIES

The **Cathedral Café** in Exeter, just a couple of steps from the cathedral, has very good food/snacks (☎ 01392 285988; open 10.00–16.45 Mon–Sat). The **Mason's Arms** in Branscombe (☎ 01297 680300) is a 14th-century pub which served to slake the thirst of the quarrymen at the nearby Beer Caves. The **Anchor Inn** in Beer has outdoor seating in the summer and cosy fires in the winter plus good food (☎ 01297 20386). Or try **Hix Oyster and Fish House** in Lyme Regis (☎ 01297 446910), a nationally famous seafood restaurant.

escape the glass and metal of the high street head for the quayside where small traditional shops and workshops front the river, and life is led at a slower pace. The cathedral deserves at least an hour's visit. The bus station is not at all bad, well organised and with a nice café if you arrive early for your bus. The first stretch from **Exeter** is pretty dull. Doze if you like, but wake up before Newton Poppleford for one of East Devon's eccentricities. In a garden to your right, opposite the first cottage of the village, is a large clock face set into a red telephone box. It's the work of Ken Woodley, a local clockmaker. The village itself is typical inland Devon, with a pleasing collection of cob-and-thatch cottages, including what is arguably the oldest toll house in the country (1758).

STOPPING ALONG THE WAY

Sidford is next, squeezed into the valley of the River Sid which

reaches the sea at the Georgian resort of Sidmouth. The next bus stop serves the area's most famous attraction, the **Donkey Sanctuary**. Spending two hours visiting the donkeys and having coffee in the tea room is enjoyable at any time of year, and although the place is free, any money you spend in the shop goes to a good cause. The sanctuary works with impoverished donkey owners in Africa to help them improve the care of their animals.

Retro-style on the Seaton Tramway
(photo © Darrensharvey / DT)

COASTAL WALKS

Weston Mouth to Branscombe and Beer (7 miles)
For the best mix of cliff views, coves and cottages, take the path from the **Donkey Sanctuary** to Weston Mouth, then eastward along the South West Coast Path towards Beer. A footpath leads off to Branscombe, one of the loveliest villages in **East Devon**. It is strung out along a deep valley, with blossom-covered thatched cottages, an interesting church and gourmet pubs. Occasional buses run from Branscombe to Seaton but you'll probably need to continue along the cliff path to Beer to pick up the bus again, making this a seven-mile walk.

Beer to Seaton (2 miles)
Just about anyone can do this walk – the path is even paved – and it is justly popular, providing as it does some lovely views of Seaton and its bay, as well as meadows, white cliffs, and a bird's-eye view of Beer.

Seaton to Lyme Regis (7 miles)
This is a serious undertaking since there is no escape route – once committed you must keep going. The path takes you through the other-worldly jungle of the **Undercliff**, a unique woodland of ash and hazel which has gradually taken hold after a mighty landslip in 1839 reshaped the coastline. But be warned, it is often muddy, there are many steep hills, and in the summer the sea is hidden from view so it can feel monotonous.

A mile or two beyond Sidford the route starts to get more interesting as the bus plunges into the network of narrow lanes that lead to Beer. Buses are not permitted to reverse, so we passengers on the top deck watch with some relish the discomfiture of the oncoming drivers as they weave their way backwards to the nearest passing place or try to squeeze by on the grass verge. It gets worse in the narrow streets of Beer itself where drivers find themselves between a bus and a hard place.

Beer is a delight, a working fishing village with boats drawn up on the pebble beach and a curving bay dominated by the white chalk cliffs; these are an anomaly along the Jurassic Coast where the older, **red Triassic rock** dominates. Beer is the perfect place to pause: two hours is just right to browse the art galleries, have a meal or drink at the Anchor pub, then walk to Seaton along the coast path.

Compared with its neighbours on each side, **Seaton** is undistinguished but we residents like it that way. The long expanse of beach is cut by the River Axe, which brings birdwatchers flocking to the estuary. Walkers will find that two hours is not quite enough time to accomplish the ups and downs of the coast path to Lyme Regis so better to dawdle and have a cream tea as a reward when you get there. Non-walkers can take one of the colourful old **trams** up to Colyton, breaking the return journey to pick up the bus at Colyford.

Lyme Regis is the most famous town along the Jurassic Coast so in the summer its charms are rather swamped by the number of visitors. Parking is never easy, so arriving by bus is a double benefit. You can sit back and admire the sweep of ocean as you start your descent, and peep into upper-storey windows as the big double-decker squeezes through narrow gaps between buildings before depositing its passengers with a sigh of relief at the seafront. But why not continue eastward? The X53 runs on to Poole, and that eastern section of the route is described in Journey 13. ∎

ABOUT THE AUTHOR | **HILARY BRADT**, MBE, is founder of Bradt Travel Guides and has rejoiced in bus travel since the introduction of the all-England bus pass in 2008.

THE JURASSIC COAST: EAST

Ronald Lee

13 Lyme Regis

Service no. X53 | Journey time 3hrs 10mins

OS Landranger 193, 194, 195. Daily, every 2hrs. Operator: First.
Connects with Journey 12 in Lyme Regis.

Poole

The previous journey in this volume is the run from Exeter to Lyme Regis on the famous X53 Jurassic Coast bus route. 'A bus with attitude,' wrote Hilary Bradt in her account of that route. But it is also a bus with stamina for the stretch from Exeter to Lyme Regis is merely the first third of the long X53 journey from Exeter to Poole. So why not stay aboard the X53 and join me on the continuing journey as we head east from Lyme Regis along the **Dorset coast**? Climb aboard and let me show you the stretch of coast I now call home.

BRIDPORT BOUND

Lyme Regis post office is good for more than stamps. Here, at the top of Broad Street, you join the **Jurassic Coast bus** for Poole. Front seat passengers may fear they are heading for an unfortunate encounter with the local tourist information centre, but worry not! The X53 drivers are adept at managing Dorset's challenging roads, and our bus makes a very tight left turn without harming buildings that are merely inches away. An earlier generation of Dorset architects didn't reckon on modern buses having to navigate

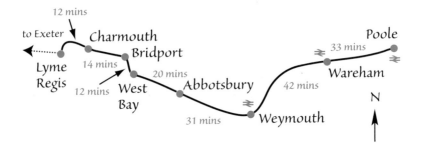

12 mins

to Exeter

Charmouth

Poole

33 mins

Lyme
Regis

14 mins

Bridport

Wareham

20 mins

12 mins

West
Bay

Abbotsbury

42 mins

31 mins

Weymouth

N

between their buildings, and first-timers on the X53 are often in awe of the bus driver's skill in avoiding the medley of architectural hazards that jut out assertively into Lyme's narrow streets.

Charmouth is the first spot on the route along the coast. Everyone in Charmouth cheered in 1991 when a bypass was opened, so relieving the town of the heavy traffic that had so afflicted it for years. Twenty years on, and Charmouth is a quiet little town that makes the most of having been the place where Mary Anning, the early 19th-century fossil collector, made her most celebrated discoveries. Charmouth vies with Lyme in claiming to be the **fossil capital** of the Jurassic Coast.

The tourist images of Dorset may have seduced you into thinking that this is a county of quaint cottages, cobbled lanes and beautiful vales. But the X53, heading east from Charmouth, reveals another side of the Dorset coast: ugly caravan sites. Lots of them. I am afraid you cannot miss them. But let's agree to look the other way and I'll not mention them again.

Beach huts at Charmouth
(photo © Mark Eastment / DT)

ABBOTSBURY

Abbotsbury demands a stop. It is a picturesque village, well known for its subtropical gardens and its swannery. **Abbotsbury Swannery** is a sanctuary for wild swans. It is a place to see these beautiful birds at close quarters. **Abbotsbury Gardens** were founded in 1765 and host a spectacular range of exotic flora. The village website at www.abbotsbury.co.uk is a model of good information provision that other Dorset communities might usefully emulate. You'll certainly not starve in Abbotsbury. The village boasts two decent pubs and has no less than four tea rooms.

Back on the main A35, we climb to **Morecombelake**, the original home of Moores Bakery, the dark building which you will see on the right. Devotees of good old-fashioned biscuits make pilgrimages here to see the place where, way back in 1880, the Dorset Knob was invented. Nowadays this acclaimed Dorset delicacy is baked in a modern Bridport factory, but happily they are still packed in very retro-styled tins – a nice deference to tradition.

And here we are cruising down towards Chideock. Suddenly on the left there are signs announcing an 'escape lane' – hopefully not used too often, but no doubt a lifesaver when drivers of heavy trucks (or even buses) suddenly find their brakes have failed. With Chideock behind us our next stop is **Bridport**. The town is noted for the manufacture of rope and nets. And for its traditional market, which in truth is what prompted me to settle in Bridport. The market is as good as ever, and if you are passing through on a Wednesday or a Saturday, do stop. You'll be in for a treat.

After leaving the bus station the road rises to the red-brick **Georgian town hall**, supported on pillars, with a butcher's shop below, built in 1786 for £3,000. It is a gem of a building, refurbished in 2011 with some much-needed tender loving care. We turn right at the traffic lights and down to the left we see Bucky Doo Square, not a square at all but a triangular area of granite setts. It is Bridport's equivalent to the village green, but without the burden of having to cut the grass. As we continue east we see **Palmers Brewery** – the only thatched brewery in England.

CHESIL COUNTRY

We ride south, the River Brit on our right, to **West Bay**, a place that until the mid 19th century was known as Bridport Harbour. But West Bay wanted to be something more than merely an adjunct of nearby Bridport and asserted its own identity. And when the tide is in, the harbour is still a busy spot. West Bay marks a dramatic change in the character of the Dorset coast, as rugged cliffs give way to the long shingle ridge known as Chesil Beach.

We then go through Burton Bradstock and Swyre, skirt Limekiln Hill and then, far away to the left, we get a glimpse of the **Hardy Monument** – in honour of Vice Admiral Thomas Hardy, flag captain of *HMS Victory* at the Battle of Trafalgar, not Thomas, of literary fame. Then comes one of the most magnificent vistas on the entire X53 bus route. As we drop down towards **Abbotsbury** (see box on page 61), there is superb panorama that takes in Chesil Beach, the stretch of water behind the beach known as West Fleet, and the starkly beautiful ruins of St Catherine's Chapel. In the distance is the Isle of Portland.

From Abbotsbury, we continue southeast with occasional views of West Fleet and East Fleet, and Chesil Beach beyond, until we reach **Weymouth**, where the bus stops by a striking statue of King George III. It was the king's patronage of Weymouth that brought fame and fortune to the seaside town.

THE FINAL ACT: POOLE

Skirting Weymouth Bay, we pass through **Osmington**, a busy place in smuggling days, and turn inland past Poxwell Manor House on our left (reported as 'faire and newe' in 1625), sheltered behind its walls and an attractive gatehouse. The scene is idyllic

Dorset, with little ponds, a gentle river and four Purbeck stone cottages with impressive thatched roofs.

But now we have a sharp change in mood. Modernity intrudes with a light-green building in the distance, just prior to the small town of Wool. This is **Winfrith Atomic Energy Research Establishment**, now in the process of being decommissioned. We pass signs to Lulworth to the right, a famously beautiful village with its castle and cove. In the distance are the Purbeck Hills.

Continuing east via Wareham, it is a short run to **Poole**, with a large inlet called Holes Bay on our right. At low tide Holes Bay, which is really an extension of Poole harbour, is dreary mudflats. But the twice-daily tides bring Holes Bay to life, subtly transforming it into an appealing stretch of water. The final approach to Poole shows two sides of the community. Busy working docks and, by contrast, a boatyard that builds luxury yachts. So there is still some money out there. But I doubt whether the yacht owners take time to ride the X53. ▪

ABOUT THE AUTHOR

Born in Plymouth some seventy-plus years ago, with chemistry and history interests, the Dorset coast has everything that **RONALD LEE** needs. He hopes it brings pleasure and challenge to others who travel the route.

WIDECOMBE FARES

'There'd normally be more people,' explained the bus driver as I settled into my seat, 'but the ladies from Holne and Scorriton are away at some village function today.' The only other passenger nodded in agreement; a mound of bulging carrier bags around his feet suggested he'd been making the most of Newton Abbot's bustling weekly market.

This chunky little minibus (service no. 672 operated by Country Bus) runs only on Wednesdays, carrying shoppers to the market from **Widecombe in the Moor** and a handful of other remote **Dartmoor villages**, then rattling them back home later with their purchases. A Saturday service that runs along part of the same route is geared more to tourists; it features as Journey 16 in this volume.

I'd picked the route for the beauty of the 75-minute ride: through **hidden valleys** where streams meander and trees form a lacy ceiling overhead, across open moorland with dramatic rock formations, past tiny hamlets, round steep, gear-grinding hairpin bends, along single-track roads and over ancient stone bridges too narrow for larger vehicles. At one such bridge, our minibus squeezed by with only inches to spare.

I was **entranced by the view**. The scenery unwound like a film strip – alternating frames of woodland, moor, rocky outcrops, thatched stone cottages, distant landscapes – to a soundtrack of chatting by the driver and my fellow passenger. They explained the value of the bus to the **local communities**, not just as a means of transport but as a social focus. On their weekly market trip, passengers from different villages can meet and exchange news. It's an outing for the elderly. The driver keeps a lookout for the more infirm or overloaded and drops them off as near as he possibly can to their front doors.

But – they told me – local Councils and bus companies are **feeling the financial pinch** badly. Smaller companies may close. Passengers, mainly pensioners, on this route are so concerned to keep the service that most are voluntarily paying the full fare rather than using their free bus passes. This stayed in my mind long after the end of my very scenic journey: the concession exists and is generous, but it's up to us whether or not we use it. I like having the choice. JB

THE EXMOOR ROLLER COASTER

Pam Johnston

Minehead

> Service no. 300 | Journey time 55mins
>
> OS Landranger 181, 180. Runs Easter to October only, 4 times daily Mon–Sat, thrice daily Sun. Operator: Quantock Motor Services.

Lynmouth

J ust one glimpse of the open-top double-decker bus speeding across Exmoor is enough to bring a smile to the faces of young and old alike and send us all rushing to the nearest bus stop to see when the next bus might be due. For this is an exciting ride through the **glorious Exmoor countryside**, much of the route along the A39 coast road (which as A roads go is decidedly rural and features some famously steep hills). Thanks to Quantock Motor Services' initiative, and some welcome financial support from Somerset County Council, summer bus travellers can enjoy spectacular views of coast and moorland. There is plenty of historical interest and easy access to a variety of walks – and all this in addition to one of the best roller-coaster rides in England.

THE EDGE OF THE MOOR

The route starts in central **Minehead** at the terminus of the **West Somerset Railway,** which gives us a nostalgic glimpse of Victorian travel before we leave. This is a traditional seaside town with buckets and spades, ice creams and family fun; it is also the gateway to Exmoor and prides itself on its well-kept parks and floral displays. The **South West Coast Path** begins here, marked by an enormous sculpture of a pair of hands holding a map. So, if you are game for a long walk, it is just 650 miles to Shell Bay in Dorset, where you can connect on to Journey 11 in this volume. But let's take the bus today. There is something very special about climbing aboard an open-top bus, and the sense of adventure and excitement in the air is shared across the generations.

We must choose our **seats on the top deck** with care. The notices on the seats warning of overhanging branches have to be taken very seriously! This is one reason why a seat on the off-side is best. Not only can we laugh at the people on the nearside when they have to keep ducking their heads as we go along, but we also get the best coastal views further along the route. The very best seats are the eight that are under cover right at the very front. They offer the best all-round views and protection from the sun, wind and rain, but we'll have to be there early to be sure of one of those.

The bus pulls away. It takes a while to adjust to the brisk fresh air and the swaying motion, but as the bus wends its way through the busy town streets, we gradually acclimatise, so that by the time it has finished the gradual climb to the A39, past the majestic bulk of North Hill rising up on the right, we are ready for the adventure ahead. You'll find a sketch of our route on page 69.

The bus turns right on to the A39 and is soon speeding westwards through the heart of the Exmoor countryside. This is the 12,000-acre **Holnicote Estate**, given to the National Trust by Sir Richard Acland in 1944. It consists of picturesque villages, moors,

THE DUNSTER CONNECTION

The first Service 300 of the day actually **starts in Dunster** and the last bus returns there. Dunster lies east of Minehead, so that extra leg adds an extra 20 minutes on to your open-top bus journey. Details about the service are available from **Quantock Motor Services** (☎ 01823 430202, www.quantockmotorservices.co.uk).

heathland, woods and farms and is the English countryside at its very best. **Dunkery Beacon**, the highest point on Exmoor, and Dunkery Hill dominate the landscape to the left and the picture-book villages of Selworthy, Allerford and Bossington lie to the right. These are places with Exmoor's hallmark ancient packhorse bridges and honey-coloured thatched cottages, all good fodder for photographers shooting images of rural England.

The bus presses on towards the sea through the **Vale of Porlock**. This place has delighted visitors for centuries. Successive generations of the Acland family apparently loved it here so much that they called it 'the happy valley'. How right they were!

THE VILLAGE OF PORLOCK

Our claret and cream bus stops twice in **Porlock** to pick up passengers, giving those already on board an opportunity to admire the thatched cottages, note the *real* shops, and perhaps choose an inn or tea room to visit later on. The second stop is outside the parish church of St Dubricius, with its truncated steeple. We must make a note of this because local folklore has it that its top may be found hidden away in the woods further along our route.

MAKING THE MOST OF THE ROUTE

There is so much to see and do along this route that it could easily be the focus of a short holiday. **Porlock** is well situated to enable the route to be easily explored in either direction. Take time too to sample the Quantock Motor Services no. 39 single-decker bus that runs every two hours between Minehead and beautiful Porlock Weir (not Sun).

There is a **wide choice of accommodation** in the village, ranging from a popular campsite to a delightful small luxury hotel that is a great personal favourite, **The Oaks Hotel** (☎ 01643 862265; www.oakshotel. co.uk). A free local accommodation booking service is offered by the helpful staff at the **Porlock visitor centre**, situated near the bottom of Porlock Hill (☎ 01643 863150; www. porlock.co.uk; open 10.00–12.30 Tue–Fri and until 13.00 Sat). This is also the best place for information about the places of interest along the route.

REFRESHMENT STOPS

There is a wide choice of refreshment stops along the route to suit all tastes. In Minehead, **The Turntable Café** (☎ 01643 704996), on the station platform, gives a good view of the steam trains whilst waiting for the bus. The **National Trust Periwinkle Tea Rooms** (Selworthy; ☎ 01643 862769) serve splendid cream teas in an idyllic setting. The **Whortleberry Tearoom** (High St, Porlock; ☎ 01643 862337) serves excellent light food and sells a wide range of local jams and chutneys. **The Ship Inn**, at the foot of Porlock Hill, is an old smuggling inn serving local ales and food (☎ 01643 862507). Four miles along the A39 west of Porlock, The **Culbone Stables Inn** (☎ 01643 863334), recently refurbished, has a pleasant beer garden.

The bus then continues along the village street to the foot of **Porlock Hill**. This famous hill has been challenging motorists since cars were first invented. It climbs 725ft in just under a mile at a gradient of 1 in 4 in places. The local museum, housed in a medieval manor house in High Street, has a fascinating photographic archive of the incidents that have occurred on Porlock Hill over the years and this is complemented by a splendid little motor museum that opened a few years ago in old garage premises in High Street.

The main road narrows to a single lane for a short stretch near the picturesque 13th-century **Ship Inn**. A first timer on the top deck looks ahead and gasps. 'Surely this bus can't go up there,' he says with evident anxiety. *Oh yes it can!* As the vehicle chugs round the outside edge of the first hairpin bend, we have our first view of the magnificent sweep of Porlock Bay. We see the distinctive oval-shaped pebbles that form the mile-long shingle ridge stretching out below.

This ridge was breached by the tide in 1996 and since then nature has been allowed to take its course. This has created a tidal lagoon on the salt marshes that lie between the village and the sea. It is a good spot for birdwatching.

We can also see the little port of **Porlock Weir** lying far below. Many of the cottages there date from the 17th century and it is a fine place to sit on a summer afternoon and watch the rapid rise of the tide in the tiny harbour.

But there is no time now to continue admiring the view because the bus hoots and abruptly turns away as it negotiates the second hairpin bend – on the inside this time! Children shriek with delight here, whilst adults of a nervous disposition look anxious and pray that the bus makes it. But rest assured, it always does. Everyone wonders how much higher we have to climb and many are torn between looking up at the hill, or just relaxing and looking back at the stupendous view below. The bus climbs on and on across Porlock Common towards the old grade-2-listed AA phone box at the top of the hill – a nostalgic reminder of motoring as it used to be.

Then all of a sudden it seems we are on top of the world. There are breathtaking views across the rolling Exmoor hills towards Dunkery Beacon on the left and panoramic views across the **Bristol Channel** to Wales on our right.

Across Exmoor

We settle back in our seats and soak everything in. This is a dramatic and rugged coastline of headlands with high cliffs falling away sharply to the sea. The bus passes **Culbone** where, hidden amongst the woods to our right and accessible only on foot, is reputedly the smallest parish church in England. Culbone Church dates from Saxon times and has a tiny spire – and yes it *does* look as if it might fit on top of St Dubricius in Porlock.

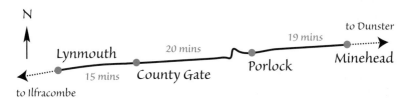

The bus trundles on over the gorse and **heather-clad moorland**, past grazing sheep and if we are lucky, the occasional red deer and Exmoor pony. Down to the left lies the **Doone Valley**, immortalised by R D Blackmore in his classic tale *Lorna Doone*. Just ahead is County Gate, which marks the Somerset/Devon border. This is a favourite spot for walkers who want to stride out over the moors or along the South West Coast Path.

Once in Devon the bus soon reaches the top of Countisbury Hill, not quite as steep as Porlock Hill, but steep enough. It doesn't bother us though – we are old hands at this game now. The bus descends confidently down into **Lynmouth**, which nestles attractively in a deep ravine at the confluence of the fast-flowing East and West Lyn rivers. Peaceful now, but the scene of devastating floods back in 1952. There is a small exhibition about the flood not far from the Glen Lyn Gorge, where a fine display about the power of water is to be found. On the esplanade is the famous Victorian cliff railway that rises 500ft up to the twin town of Lynton on the cliff top above. From there it is two miles west to the celebrated Valley of the Rocks, a striking natural landscape that is a major tourist attraction.

So now it is time to leave our trusty bus, smooth our windswept hair, stretch our legs and go and explore. But what a glorious bus journey. ■

ABOUT THE AUTHOR | **PAM JOHNSTON** is a retired schoolteacher from Guildford. She loves Exmoor and visits the area as often as she can.

John Deacon

15 Plymouth 🚍

Service no. 93 | Journey time 2hrs 15mins

OS Landranger 201, 202. Hourly Mon–Sat, 4 Sunday journeys.
Operator: First.

Dartmouth ◀

This route takes us through the rolling countryside of the **South Hams** with its old thatched cottages – an exploratory transect, if you will, across the southernmost portion of Devon. It takes in dramatic headlands, attractive coves, and some seductively beautiful inlets before culminating in the lovely ancient town of Dartmouth. The thing I like about the 93 is that, Sundays apart (when the service is sparse), it runs sufficiently frequently that one can break one's journey on a whim. The next bus always comes along an hour later for you to continue your journey.

Hop on the top deck and map the progress of the Devon seasons – from lambs and primroses in spring to pheasants and blackberries in autumn. And the great plus of the upper deck is that one can see over the thick Devon hedges into fields and gardens along the way.

Old Mother Hubbard and more

Our journey begins at Plymouth's Bretonside Bus Station and after crossing the **River Plym** we head east out of the city to Yealmpton. Old Mother Hubbard's thatched cottage is on the right, opposite the Rose and Crown (☎ 01752 880223), one of the new generation of gastro-pubs. Look for tasty Devon fish specialities. Food is served daily from noon.

Yealmpton takes its name from the River Yealm, which we cross just east of the village. The old toll house by the bridge nicely records the toll charges of yesteryear. Then it's on through fields with red soils and reddish cattle to Modbury and **Aveton Gifford**, both spots where our bus squeezes through narrow roads. The top deck is great for people-watching in these little communities. There is a good view west along a road open only at low tide (running beside the River Avon) from the long bridge just beyond Aveton Gifford. More often than not, the bus will stop at the end of the bridge to drop off or pick up hikers. It is a good spot for walkers wanting to connect on to the nearby South West Coast Path.

Devon's rivers certainly make a dramatic impact on the county's topography, so it is a long climb up from the River Avon to Churchstow and Kingsbridge. The timetable is such that passengers normally need to swap buses at **Kingsbridge Quay**. Both vehicles are numbered 93, and the connection is usually guaranteed. But take the moment to pause for an hour for Kingsbridge has a lot to offer.

KINGSBRIDGE

Kingsbridge is the centre for the local area with a wide variety of shops, pubs & cafés. But the real attraction is the **Cookworthy Museum** in the old Grammar School in Fore Street (☎ 01548 853235, www.kingsbridgemuseum.org.uk, open 10.30–1700 Mon–Sat, but shorter winter hours). The museum charts the history of the entire South Hams area. Kingsbridge has a very good **tourist information office** (☎ 01548 853195) on Kingsbridge Quay just near the spot where the bus stops. Those of the bus-pass generation will find a welcome smile and good cup of tea at the **Pensioners' Rest Room** (open 10.00–12.00 daily), reached through the gate marked 'Kingsbridge UDC' beside the bus stops at the quay.

I sometimes use a break in Kingsbridge to make a little side diversion down Kingsbridge Estuary to Salcombe. The beautiful named **Tally Ho Coaches**, a Kingsbridge-based bus operator, run an hourly service (not Sundays) down to Salcombe, just 25 minutes away. Even better, take a boat to **Salcombe**. Services depart twice or thrice daily in the season, but the times do vary with the tides. The tourist information centre will have current times.

On to Dartmouth

The scenery changes, becoming less hilly as we head east out of Kingsbridge and cross over the single-track bridge to follow the head of the estuary, passing more traditional **Devon thatched cottages**. We get a chance to admire the skill and patience of the driver as he manoeuvres his vehicle along these twisting and narrow roads. On the way through the villages of Charleton, Frogmore and Chillington there are road signs pointing the way to little hamlets and ancient churches hidden away in the deep Devon lanes. After passing through Stokenham, where a right turn would take us south towards the isolated communities around Start Point and Prawle Point, we finally emerge on the coast at **Torcross**.

On leaving Torcross, the bus runs for about two miles between the beach and the freshwater lake of Slapton Ley, a popular spot for birdwatchers. Then on through the straggly village of Strete to the beautiful cove of Blackpool Sands. The latter is worth a stop. It has a Blue Flag beach and the Venus Beach Café (☎ 01803 770209; open daily 09.00–17.00, shorter hours in winter), which

TORCROSS

This little village with the **Start Bay Inn** (☎ 01548 580553) and several cafés is at the southern end of the sweep of Slapton Sands. It is a good jumping-off point for several **fine walks**. One of the best is south through Beesands and Hallsands to the lighthouse at Start Point and then on to Salcombe. These paths are all marked with the acorn symbol of the **South West Coast Path** and more information regarding them and the rest of the route can be found at www.southwestcoastpath.com.

is open in even the worst of winter weather, is good for snacks or a light meal.

From **Blackpool** it is 20 minutes of hill and dale, lots of changing of gears, until eventually we drop down into Dartmouth. But if you want a more dramatic finale to your journey, alight from the bus at the Village Hall in Stoke Fleming. From here it is possible to walk around the top of the cliffs following the signed coast path through Little Dartmouth. There are glorious views of the River Dart and the Day Mark navigation tower on the opposite hill, before you descend through the woods, full of bluebells in season, to reach **Dartmouth Castle** (☎ 01803 833588; open daily 10.00–18.00 in summer, but shorter hours otherwise). From here there is a choice of a ferry or the road for the mile into town.

Dartmouth is the ultimate town for boat lovers. Dartmouth harbour is effectively the town's main street. Don't miss the Cherub Inn (☎ 01803 832571) and surrounding Tudor buildings in Higher Street and The Butterwalk. One of the great pleasures in Dartmouth is just to take a seat along the **waterfront** and relax while watching the action on the river, with ferries and pleasure craft always on the go. ■

ABOUT THE AUTHOR | **JOHN DEACON** is a retired engineer from Plymouth who has travelled along this road for 50 years, watching the changes along the way.

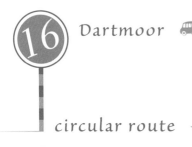

The Haytor Hoppa: A Dartmoor Delight

Hilary Bradt

16 Dartmoor 🚐 circular route

Service no. 271 | Journey time 1hr 40mins

OS Landranger 191. Easter to late October,
4 times daily on Sat only. Operator: Country Bus.

This book wouldn't be complete without including Dartmoor, the highest land in England south of the Pennines, and often described as England's last wilderness.

Everywhere here is granite: rocks as large as cars scattered randomly or piled on top of hills to form the tors that define **Dartmoor**, quarried and dressed granite in the walls of ancient village churches, or rough-hewn and arranged in circles or rows by the first humans who made the moor their home. The low-lying perimeter is another world, however, networked by deep narrow lanes and footpaths meandering through gentle, flower-filled meadows.

The **Haytor Hoppa**, unashamedly a bus for tourists, was introduced in 2009 to reduce visitors' dependence on their cars. It starts and ends in Newton Abbot (good for train connections), and from Bovey Tracey it makes an anticlockwise circumnavigation of Haytor, returning to Bovey Tracey and then to Newton Abbot. That circular route provides wonderful views of Dartmoor and, for a mere £5 (or £10 for families), travellers may hop on and off as often as they want. The two-hour gap between buses is just right for a variety of walks or for a leisurely lunch.

Gateway to Dartmoor

The first leg from **Newton Abbot** to Bovey Tracey is along a main road and is nothing special. But there is always a happy air of expectancy from the people waiting at **Bovey Tracey.** This is one of Dartmoor's 'gateway towns' and a personal favourite (see box opposite). Once aboard I found the passengers twittering with anticipation, and I soon joined in; the Haytor Hoppa is that sort of bus – people talk to each other.

But it's hard to talk and look at the scenery, and the views from the large windows were gorgeous. 'I love that,' said my neighbour. 'Our first glimpse of Haytor.' This is probably Dartmoor's best known landmark, having the advantage of being relatively close to the road. We were now on the high moor, with ponies grazing among the gorse, sheep dozing by the roadside,

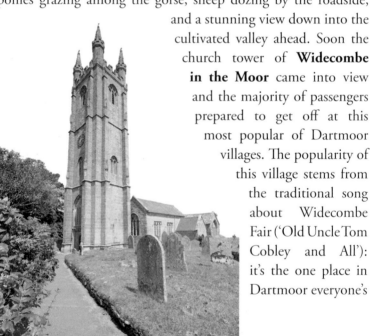

and a stunning view down into the cultivated valley ahead. Soon the church tower of **Widecombe in the Moor** came into view and the majority of passengers prepared to get off at this most popular of Dartmoor villages. The popularity of this village stems from the traditional song about Widecombe Fair ('Old Uncle Tom Cobley and All'): it's the one place in Dartmoor everyone's

The 'Cathedral of the Moor' at Widecombe in the Moor (photo © Moorfam / IS)

heard of. The village sits in a hollow, with the extraordinarily high tower (350ft) of the church giving it the popular name of the 'Cathedral of the Moor'.

Mixed up with all the **legends of Widecombe** is the fact, that during a dramatic thunderstorm in October 1638, the church was struck by lightning and four people were killed when the tower crashed through the roof. Legend tells us the devil tethered his horse to the tower while he went about his mischief with some local lads. He remounted in a hurry, forgetting that his black steed was still tethered, and toppled the tower as he galloped away.

Next to the church is the headquarters of the local National Trust, with a good library and information centre. On the spacious green is a **Millennium Stone** under which are buried photos of every house, and every family in the parish. However, they are on CD/DVD so whether the people who unearth it centuries hence will be illuminated or puzzled remains to be seen.

From Widecombe the bus toils up the hill to the high moor again, heading for **Hound Tor**. The stop here, at Swallerton Gate, gives walkers access not only to Hound Tor but Bowerman's Nose, both examples of what can happen if you disturb a coven of witches when out hunting: the hunter, Bowerman, and his hounds were turned to stone. The hunter with his serene smile is one of Dartmoor's iconic images so it's worth paying him a visit and then continuing across the moor to Manaton to pick up the bus again.

Half a mile beyond Swallerton Gate my neighbour said: 'Keep looking to your left, and you'll see Jay's grave. Look, there are the flowers!' The grave belongs to Kitty Jay, a girl who took her own life after being seduced by a local lad in the early 19th century. As a suicide she was buried outside the parish boundary, but exhumed in 1860 and reburied in a proper grave in its current position at a cross roads. Fresh flowers are put there each day – but by whom, no-one knows. Then we were down in the trees and greenery of **Manaton**, on a narrow winding lane. 'I don't like this bit,' the driver told me. 'I have to go so slowly and it's hard to keep to the timetable.'

MANATON AND BEYOND

Manaton is another beguiling place for a stop. A spacious green sets off the fine church of St Winifred, dressed in traditional Devon white, with a row of thatched houses behind it. One splendid house, Wingstone Manor, was for a time the home of **John Galsworthy**, who wrote *The Forsyte Saga*. The interior of the church has a fine wooden screen which is notable in that it was literally defaced during the Reformation. Every carved saint and angel has had its face chiselled away. A helpful explanatory sheet

---

EATERIES

Rugglestone Inn (Widecombe in the Moor; ☎ 01364 621327) is a small and very popular old inn on the outskirts of the village that has been a favourite with locals and visitors for many years. Good food and a sublime location. Open all day at weekends; reservations essential during the high season.

Kestor Inn (☎ 01647 221626) is in a little hamlet called Water, a half mile outside Manaton. Nice views from the conservatory area, and a mix of locals and hikers.

---

tells us what we should be seeing. For instance St Margaret of Antioch being swallowed by a dragon, with just her red dress visible as she disappears down its throat. She cut her way out of the beast's stomach with her handy sword, so has become the patron saint of women in childbirth. The view from the churchyard, across the moor to Haytor, must be one of the best in Dartmoor.

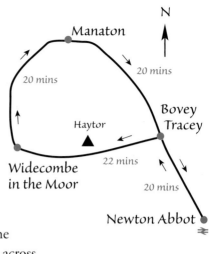

A little over a mile to the southeast are **Becky Falls**, a place of water and mossy quietness. It's good for birdwatching too: I spotted a dipper bobbing about on the rocks. This is the last official stop before the Haytor Hoppa meanders its way along the tree-lined lanes back to Bovey Tracey and Newton Abbot. However, the bus will usually stop for anyone who hails it, whether at a bus stop or not, and it guarantees not to leave you stranded on the moor. If the last bus back is full they'll send a back-up vehicle. ∎

ABOUT THE AUTHOR

HILARY BRADT, MBE, is founder of Bradt Travel Guides and has rejoiced in bus travel since the introduction of the all-England bus pass in 2008.

DARTMOOR SUNDAY EXCURSION

Journey 16 makes the perfect Saturday excursion to Dartmoor. A **summer Sunday bus service** gives the chance to travel across the middle of the moor. Service 82 (branded Transmoor Link) runs from Exeter via **Princetown to Plymouth**, for much of the route following the very rural B3212. Buses run five times in each direction. In 2011, the Transmoor Link operated from mid May to mid September.

THE MAGIC OF MOUNT'S BAY

Marilyn Cliff

17 Helston

Service nos. 2 or 2A | Journey time 50 to 60mins

OS Landranger 203. Hourly Mon–Sat, every 2hrs Sun.
Operator: First.

Penzance

Cornwall is a beautiful county and a great way to see Cornwall at its best is from the top of a double-decker bus. You'll catch glimpses of the sea beyond lush green fields. There are ancient menhirs, sturdy stone cottages and the engine houses that were once so important in the local mining industry.

My journey to England's most southwesterly town, Penzance, begins outside the **Blue Anchor** in **Helston**. It is a rugged, simple pub, ably managed by Kim and Simon Stone (☎ 01326 562821). The pub has its own brewery. And, best of all, it is a hub not just for drinkers but also for bus passengers. Yet Helston is a difficult spot to leave. It is a pleasant little town, one noted in particular for the **Furry Dance** (called 'The Flora' by some) held in early May each year. It is a celebration of the passing of winter and the arrival of spring. There are several dances throughout the day, the main one being at midday when the men wear top hats and tails and the ladies wear beautiful gowns and hats. The dancers make their way through the town, even passing through some of the houses, accompanied by the Helston Town Band.

There is the usual mix of folk on the bus today. A few shoppers bound for Penzance and tourists heading to **Mount's Bay**. We leave town, passing the **Coronation Lake**, which was opened in 1912 to recall (a little belatedly) the coronation of King George V in June 1911. It made a big difference to Helston, ushering in a tradition of water sports and water carnivals, and it is still much valued today.

Penrose Estate is the next big landmark. This area is looked after by the National Trust. Its prime feature is The Loe (An Logh in Cornish), the largest natural freshwater lake in Cornwall. It is believed to have been created in the 12th century after violent storms caused the formation of a huge bank of sand and shingle, which cut off the valley (through which flows the River Cober) from the sea. This bank is known as Loe Bar. The **variety of habitats** around the area – such as woodland, marsh and open water – encourage a wide range of wildlife. The Loe is reputed to be the lake where Sir Bedevere cast King Arthur's sword Excalibur.

From Helston the bus climbs up the hill with pleasant woodland on either side, before the long descent into **Porthleven**, a part of the journey that in spring is made all the better by great spreads of daffodils. Porthleven is quintessential Cornwall. Boats bob gently on their moorings on warm summer days or thrash wildly on stormy ones. Work by local artists is displayed in shops and galleries around the harbour. It is a good spot to break your

PORTHLEVEN EATERIES

There are two good pubs by the harbour which both serve food: the **Harbour Inn** (☎ 01326 573876) and the **Ship Inn** (☎ 01326 564 204). Both are open daily. The Ship Inn has the edge when it comes to decent seafood, nicely declaring itself to be a no-go zone for pasties and chips. But you may want to skip the pubs for **Roland's Happy Plaice** (☎ 01326 562723; open 12.00 till early evening, closed Jan & Mon exc Jul & Aug), judged by many locals to be the best chippy in Cornwall. Roland is Roland Lowery who, with his wife Lindsey, moved from Barnsley five years ago. So you can even get good **Yorkshire-style mushy peas** to accompany fine Cornish fresh fish.

journey. Enjoy the screech of the gulls, take a look at the harbour and then pause in one of Porthleven's many good eateries (see box on page 81).

Shortly after returning to the main Penzance road and passing through the villages of Breage and Ashton, **Tregonning Hill** comes into view on the right. It has an interesting history that dates back to the Bronze Age. The remains of a Celtic stronghold, Castle Pencaire dating from around 250BC, can be found on the hilltop. Nearby there is a quarry where John Wesley is alleged to have preached. This is also the place where William Cookworthy first extracted china clay in the mid 18th century.

I love to walk along the crest of this hill where, on a clear day, there are magnificent views across the whole of Mount's Bay on one side and over towards St Ives on the north coast to the right. There is a topograph showing the distances to a number of landmarks on the hilltop close to the site of the Celtic remains.

The bus soon turns left and heads down the hill to **Praa Sands** (but take care for it is only number 2 buses that make this engaging diversion; the 2A takes a slightly different route). Praa is the ancient Cornish word for 'hag' or 'witch'. As the bus descends down the hill Pengersick Castle comes into view. This is supposedly one of the most haunted buildings in Britain and there is a strange eeriness about the place.

Praa lies in a sheltered depression and the beautiful stretch of golden sand is very popular with families and has lifeguards during the summer months. The bus toils up the hill on the western side of Praa to return briefly to the main road. After taking a sharp right turn the journey continues into the pretty village of Goldsithney.

The bus meanders along narrow lanes towards Marazion. This town on the shores of **Mount's Bay** is a favourite with tourists.

A TRIO OF MARAZION PUBS

The **Fire Engine Inn** (☎ 01736 710562) offers an extensive menu as well as a fabulous view of Mount's Bay. Or sit outside the **Kings Arms** (☎ 01736 710291), a fine 18th-century pub in The Square and just watch the world go by. You can also try the **Godolphin Arms** (☎ 01736 710202; www.godolphinarms.co.uk), a family-run inn perched on the sea wall at the end of the causeway leading over to St Michael's Mount. They offer accommodation as well as a delightful beachside terrace and a varied menu.

There are stunning views across to the **Lizard Peninsula** and Land's End. In my opinion this is the best part of a lovely journey.

There are tantalising glimpses of **St Michael's Mount** between the higgledy-piggledy cottages as the driver negotiates the narrow road leading down into Marazion, before culminating in the full panoramic view of the mount rearing majestically out of beautiful Mount's Bay. There is a causeway linking the mount to the mainland at low tide, offering visitors the novel experience of appearing to walk on water! At high tide visitors to the mount are ferried over in small boats.

If you want to work off the effects of an over-indulgent **Marazion** lunch, there is a level footpath from Marazion passing through Long Rock to Penzance which is an easy and pleasant walk of about three miles with sea views all the way. For the final part of the journey, the bus from Marazion to Penzance also runs parallel to the beach for a while with super views across to Mousehole and Newlyn. Buses on the 2 and 2A route end in Penzance, but it is not the end of the road. You are not quite at the end of Cornwall. You can continue to Land's End, with both Western Greyhound and First offering services on to this farthest tip of the English mainland. ■

ABOUT THE AUTHOR | **MARILYN CLIFF** changed city life for a rural retreat eight years ago. She now lives in Helston, Cornwall.

WALES

L et's not beat about the bush. Wales, and more particularly the rural parts of the Principality, are God's gift to the bus traveller. Explore **three national parks** in Snowdonia, Pembrokeshire and the Brecon Beacons, a great variety of coastal resorts and, in the hills of mid-Wales, some of the most sparsely populated terrain in Britain – all very accessible by bus.

Thanks to sensible planning co-ordinated by Cynulliad Cenedlaethol Cymru (the National Assembly for Wales), long-distance services in Wales and local routes dovetail very well into each other. The main network of long-distance services, for many years known as TrawsCambria, will be relaunched in early 2012 as **TrawsCymru** (www.trawscymru.info), ushering in an era of high-tech coaches on some routes. Yes, on-board Wi-Fi as you cruise through the Cambrian Mountains. And the great thing about Wales is that Welsh bus passes are generally valid on these longer-distance routes.

But don't despair if you don't have a bus pass. Exploring Wales by bus can be remarkably cheap. For example, we recently travelled by bus from Aberystwyth to Holyhead at the northern tip of Anglesey. The one-way fare for the five-hour journey was just £6 per person, using an Day Saver ticket which we purchased from the driver on boarding the first bus. No need to pre-book.

We have a foursome of Welsh routes in the pages that follow. Together these routes capture the **diversity of the Principality**, yet they also reveal a common theme. Wales is very palpably a different country from England. It has its own language, culture and traditions. Tread gently, travel slow, take time to stop off here and there, and you will find places that are very special. Join us on Journey 18 (on the opposite page) as Tim Locke escorts us over the border into Wales. ∎

Border Crossing

Tim Locke

Hereford

Service nos. 461 or 462 | Journey time 1hr 50mins

OS Landranger 149, 148, 147. Every 2hrs Mon–Sat.
Operator: Sargeants Brothers.
Connects with Journey 22 in Hereford.

Llandrindod Wells

The two-hour ride by bus from Hereford to Llandrindod is a perfect cross-section of some of my favourite countryside, giving a most satisfying sense of crossing a national border. Here England metamorphoses into Wales spectacularly abruptly: one moment you are in a gently pastoral, rolling, quintessentially English landscape.

Then comes the 'Welcome to Wales' sign and the landscape changes dramatically as moors, bracken, gorse and crags appear. Herefordshire's half-timbered villages give way to scattered sheep-farming communities and grey-stone hamlets. Accents also change along the way.

This is an easy route to access, with rail stations at either end of the journey. And there are several places along the journey that make good stopping-off points. I have known this area for many years, and have a second home on the Welsh side of the border. But until recently I had never ventured on the little red bus that takes a meandering, utterly rural route from Hereford to Llandrindod Wells. It was a rewarding way to appreciate how the area might look to a newcomer. I sat at the back – the rear three rows on the 31-seater bus are raised enough to get grandstand views over the ubiquitous hedgerows. The convoluted route isn't one I had ever followed in its entirety before.

CIDER COUNTRY

Hereford's a big place compared to everything else on this route. Don't be deterred by its nasty inner ring road, too often clogged with serious traffic. From the bus you get little idea of Hereford's many charms. The city has many gracious partly Georgian brick streets around the cathedral, which is home to the medieval Mappa Mundi. This is a quite remarkable 13th-century map that plots the world as seen through the eyes of scholars of those times. Just outside the cathedral stands a life-size statue of the composer Sir Edward Elgar, on whom this region's landscape made such a profound impression. The statue depicts Elgar about to mount his beloved bicycle, known as Mr Phoebus.

The starting point for the bus journey to Wales is Hereford's exuberantly **Gothic railway station**, and there are glimpses of Herefordiana as you travel – a chunk of the medieval city wall, then, opposite the Bulmer's Heineken depot, a retired cider press poses as street sculpture. After Victorian suburbs give way to semis, the whole urban scene evaporates and is replaced by the most gorgeously rural Herefordshire scenery. Lush greenness, deep red

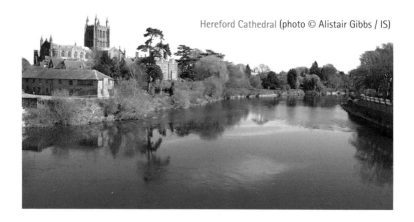

Hereford Cathedral (photo © Alistair Gibbs / IS)

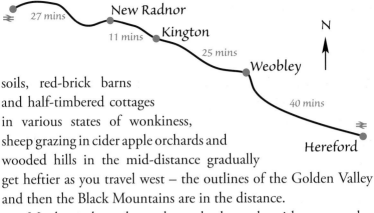

Llandrindod Wells
27 mins
New Radnor
11 mins
Kington
25 mins
Weobley
N
40 mins
Hereford

soils, red-brick barns
and half-timbered cottages
in various states of wonkiness,
sheep grazing in cider apple orchards and
wooded hills in the mid-distance gradually
get heftier as you travel west – the outlines of the Golden Valley
and then the Black Mountains are in the distance.

My bus edges along sleepy back roads with cow-parsley
verges; at **Mansell Lacy** a double-decker 461 meets us coming the
other way. I spot an oast house to the south, a reminder of the hop
industry, though the cider orchards are nowadays much more in
evidence than hop gardens.

Weobley looks like a film set for some idyllic chronicle of
rural life, with an extraordinarily rich array of half-timbered houses
gathered around a knot of streets, centred on a long triangular
space and still real village shops, including a butcher's whose
signboard of a Hereford bull promises the famously wonderful

HERGEST RIDGE

Entry signs announce **Kington** as 'the centre for walking', and even
though that might sound like marketing speak the town has some
vintage walks leading from it – notably on the **Offa's Dyke Path**.
This cuts through the town: in a couple of gentle miles for example
you could stroll along it up the road signposted to **Hergest Croft**
(itself a wonderful garden open to the public) and on to Hergest
Ridge for a sublime stroll on carpet-like turf up to a strangely
incongruous group of monkey-puzzle trees, looking out over the
Black Mountains and the twin peaks of the **Brecon Beacons** – the
highest land in Wales outside Snowdonia.

local beef which in itself is a reason for venturing to this county. Aptly for such a riot of black and white, the magpie is the village's symbol, hence the magpie sculpture erected in 2001 on the tiny green.

Beyond Lyonshall, the bus drops down the A44 to Kington, with a hint in the distant hills of the drama to unfold shortly. **Kington** itself looks handsomely urban, in the nicest retro way (see also the box on page 87). You may want to check out the free volunteer-run Kington museum in Mill Street (☎ 01544 231748; www. kingtonmuseum.co.uk; open 10.30–16.00 Tue–Sat) with its entertaining miscellany of bits and pieces, including the remains of a circus elephant buried here and later exhumed.

ACROSS THE BORDER

At **Stanner Rocks**, the hills loom up suddenly and sternly as Radnorshire, the central part of Powys, begins. Our bus slips across the border and now the bare moorland tops contrast completely with the mellowness that ushered us gently through Herefordshire. The bus deviates past **Hindwell Farm** – where William Wordsworth frequently stayed with his relations – and

NEW RADNOR WALK

Water-break-its-neck, a couple of miles out of the village and a level mile's walk from the A44, might be one of the most memorably named **waterfalls** anywhere. A century or so ago, this was a popular charabanc excursion from Llandrindod, and I can remember finding it in the 1970s when I stumbled on a Victorian finger-signpost saying simply 'To the falls'. Its signposting is now more prosaic but the atmosphere still quite magical: you walk for a quarter of a mile along the stream at the foot of a mossy precipice, with ferns and trees clinging to near vertical slopes. It has the scale of a cathedral aisle, with the high altar, invisible until the last moment, being the waterfall which sprays down impressively after prolonged rain.

'Cycles – motors – aircraft' is the intriguing motto sculpted into the great Art Deco façade of **Llandrindod's Automobile Palace**, a relic of the days when the same blacksmith-derived skills must have been needed for repairing all these novel forms of transport. It's now home to a memorable collection of **historic bicycles**, including bamboo-framed machines from the 1890s and the 'Eiffel Tower' advertising cycle where the rider sits eight feet up, along with bikes and memorabilia from great cyclists such as Land's End to John O'Groats record breaker Eileen Sheridan and Italian champion Fausto Coppi.

round a back road that skirts the southern side of Radnor Forest, an austere, bleak, exposed upland that often gets snow when everywhere else around remains green. **New Radnor** (Maesyfed in Welsh) has nothing much 'new' about it – it's a rare medieval planned town laid out on a grid plan within walls that are now reduced to sheep-nibbled grassy humps; the castle mound above the church provides the best views over it all. Now shrunken to village size and recently minus shop and post office, it's amiably sleepy, and beautifully placed among the hills; a preposterously grandiose (and alas sadly crumbling) Gothic memorial to the Victorian statesman and local politician George Cornewall Lewis soars at the southern approach.

West from New Radnor the road contours round the western flanks of Radnor Forest, with a grand bus-seat view of mid-Wales as you drop to Llandegley, where **Llandegley Rocks** loom impressively along a wild-looking ridge – actually they're much smaller than they look and you can climb up in a matter of minutes from Llandegley Church.

Just past Penybont station on the north side of the road is one of Wales's great visual jokes – an official-looking sign that solemnly advertises 'Llandegley International Airport Terminals 1 & 3' a few miles up the road. There's nothing there except sheep pasture, of course, but this spoof sign has somehow survived official

FOOD ALONG THE ROUTE

You'll hardly starve on the bus ride to Llandrindod. The Herefordshire villages bristle with pubs and cafés, though things are a little sparser once in Wales. Here is a trio of cafés on this route that I like. In **Hereford Café@Allsaints** (All Saints Church, High St; ☎ 01432 370415; open 08.00–17.00 Mon–Sat) is in a converted church. It's a nicely unpretentious, bright and airy place for a light lunch or coffee. On the far east side of **Kington**, the **Olde Tavern** (22 Victoria Rd; ☎ 01544 230122) is a gloriously unsophisticated alehouse where nothing much has changed for well over a century; let's hope it stays that way. No food. Closed weekday lunchtimes. Finally, in **Llandrindod** head for **Powell's Café Bar** (Spa Rd; ☎ 01597 824737) where you'll find decent-value light lunches and snacks in a spotless Victorian house opposite the National Cycle Collection.

attempts to get it removed. Were there really airport terminals in these remote hills, I wouldn't be surprised if they were subject to closure during the lambing season.

Finally, the ultimate visual surprise: **Llandrindod Wells** itself (invariably shortened to Llandrindod, or even Llandod). I know of no other quite such richly late-Victorian and Edwardian streetscape in Britain, even though it's hardly a bustling resort nowadays: Art Nouveau shop fronts, frilly iron canopies, lavishly built spa hotels of railway-age brick all jut out unexpectedly into the green pastures of mid-Wales. Llandrindod's railway station still has some of its original signage, and an ancient signal box that is open to the public on some days. A wander around town brings you to **Rock Park**, where you can sample the rusty-tasting chalybeate spring water that brought the health-seekers here in those halcyon spa days. It doesn't taste too great, which is why I take it people thought it is good for you. ∎

ABOUT THE AUTHOR | Travel writer **TIM LOCKE** lives in Lewes in Sussex and has a long-standing affection for the Welsh borderland. He is author of *Slow Sussex*, published by Bradt in 2011.

East to West across North Wales

Tony Hopkins

(19) Wrexham 🚐

Service no. X94 | Journey time 2hrs 20mins to 3hrs

OS Landranger 117, 125, 124. Every 2hrs Mon–Sat, 4 journeys Sun.
Operator: Arriva (Mon–Sat) or GHA Coaches (Sun).

Barmouth ◀

Wales boasts some of Europe's most spectacular scenery and a **great network of bus services**. This 60-mile journey is one of the longer-distance routes branded as *TrawsCambria* or *TrawsCymru* (see page 84). From Wrexham, the largest town in North Wales, our journey tracks south and west, following the delightful valleys of the Rivers Dee, Wnion and Mawddach until it reaches the coast at Barmouth. The railway used to come this way, until, like so many other rural lines in Britain, it fell victim to Dr Beeching's sharp axe. Happily public transport survives in the form of the bus, so take a seat and enjoy!

LEAVING WREXHAM BEHIND

The first leg of the journey is unremarkable as the X94 leaves urban **Wrexham** and runs via Ruabon to the village of **Trevor**. If time allows, do break your journey here, because, although you cannot see it from the bus, you are within a five-minute walk of Thomas Telford's famous **Pontcysyllte Aqueduct**. Constructed between 1795 and 1808, it is the highest navigable aqueduct ever built and carries the Llangollen Canal over the River Dee. There

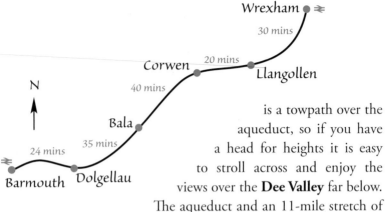

is a towpath over the aqueduct, so if you have a head for heights it is easy to stroll across and enjoy the views over the **Dee Valley** far below. The aqueduct and an 11-mile stretch of the canal from the Horseshoe Falls (which we pass later) to the outskirts of Chirk was granted World Heritage status in 2009.

Following the Dee

From Trevor, we follow the canal into the **Vale of Llangollen** and join the River Dee for the first time. Look up to your right on the approach to Llangollen to see the ruins of the 13th-century **Dinas Brân Castle** perched high above the town. Llangollen clusters around the river, which at this point is very fast flowing. For a closer look at the river, visit the former **corn mill** in Dee Lane. It is now a very comfy riverside pub serving good food (☎ 01978 869555; open daily from noon).

West from **Llangollen**, the surrounding hills close in, and at Berwyn we pass the **Horseshoe Falls** mentioned above. This is not a natural waterfall at all, but a semi-circular weir designed by Thomas Telford to feed into the Llangollen Canal. This is the western end of the World Heritage Site.

On reaching the small market town of **Corwen**, look out for the dramatic life-size statue of Owain Glyndwr, the last Welshman to hold the title Prince of Wales. Owain's ancestral homeland was in these parts and he has left an indelible imprint on local history. Beyond Corwen our bus forsakes the main road to take quieter lanes through the pretty villages of Cynwyd, Llandrillo and Llandderfel. After **Cynwyd** we lose sight of the river for a while as the valley opens out. But soon we are reunited with the Dee which we follow upstream to **Bala**, a town blessed with an enviable location at the northern end of Llyn Tegid (Bala Lake). The town is very much the gateway to **Parc Cenedlaethol Eryri** (Snowdonia National Park), established 60 years ago as Wales's first national park.

Now past Bala, our bus skirts the shores of the lake, with excellent views south over the wild **Cambrian Mountains**. At the end of the lake, we detour to serve Llanuwchllyn, home of the **Bala Lake Railway**, which runs seasonal narrow-gauge trains along the lakeshore to Bala (www.bala-lake-railway.co.uk). By now, the accents and even the language on board our bus have changed. Snippets of Welsh compete with more English voices. And the River Dee is here more commonly alluded to by its Welsh name of Afon Dyfrdwy. It's time to part from the river, though, as we cross the hills to join the valley of the Afon Wnion. Road signs by the main road point the way to tiny hamlets with names that are a happy litany of Welsh Wales. We pause at **Bontnewydd** for half-a-dozen women to join our bus. They are evidently all bound for the market in Dolgellau.

From a tiny village, **Dolgellau** grew steadily on the back of the wool trade in the 18th century. Later a blossoming print industry

WREXHAM

It is easy to dismiss Wrexham as a grimy place shaped around a trio of industries: coal, iron and brewing. But Wrexham has reinvented itself. The modern university town has a **lively buzz**. There are three covered markets and a good **museum** (☎ 01978 297460; 10.00–17.00 Mon–Fri, 10.30–15.00 Sat), where you can learn of Wrexham's earliest-known resident – Brymbo Man. At Bersham, two miles west of Wrexham and easily reached by local bus (no. 6), a **heritage centre** explores Wrexham's industrial past (☎ 01978 318970; open Apr–Oct, 10.00–17.00 Mon–Fri, 12.00–17.00 Sat & Sun; admission free).

and nearby gold deposits added to Dolgellau's prosperity. Today the town has over 200 listed buildings, making it an attractive destination in its own right, its location also ensuring popularity as a great base for exploring the exceptional scenery of southern Snowdonia.

Our bus stops briefly at Eldon Square in the centre of Dolgellau. West from Dolgellau is what many would judge to be one of the finest stretches of bus route anywhere in Britain. The road hugs the north bank of the tidal **Mawddach**. It is beautiful in any weather, but if you ride this route at low tide on a summer evening, you will be rewarded by stunning views of golden sands with **Barmouth Bridge** silhouetted against a setting sun. The bus pauses at Bontddu, a place that in the late 19th century was the scene of a modest gold rush. There are superb views across the Mawddach to the heights of **Cader Idris** as the bus cruises along the north side of the estuary to its final destination in **Barmouth** (see box above). Journey's end is near the railway station, with the tourist office just nearby. ∎

ABOUT THE AUTHOR

TONY HOPKINS, a retired engineer, moved to North Wales 15 years ago, originally to work for the Snowdon Mountain Railway. A public transport enthusiast, he organises regular outings for his local U3A's 'Explore by Bus' group.

Across the
Clwydian Hills

Tony Newman

⑳ Mold

Service no. 2 | Journey time 45mins

OS Landranger 117, 116. Every 2hrs Mon–Sat.
Operator: GHA Coaches.

Ruthin

I have travelled thousands of miles by bus throughout Britain and to me this short journey captures all the delights of bus travel. The hills of Clwyd are the guardians of routes to Snowdonia from Merseyside and northern England. Follow this modest route from Mold to Ruthin and mere ripples in the terrain become ever more assertive and, as we approach our destination, there are stunning views of the main **Clwydian Range** (Bryniau Clwyd in Welsh).

The ancient market town of Mold (Yr Wyddgrug) is home territory for GHA Coaches, a local bus operator that has grown swiftly these past few years through taking over rivals. And GHA dominates the Mold to Ruthin market offering a handful of different routes between the two towns. My first choice is always the bus number 2, which is more adventurous but slower than the rival options (the 1, 1A and X1). The latter stick to the main road, but the 2 boldly explores minor Welsh lanes.

Don't depart from **Mold** too soon. It's a small town with a lot to offer. Its star claim to fame is the remarkable gold ornamental cape, believed to date from the Bronze Age, that was unearthed here in 1833. The original is displayed in the British Museum, but a replica can be seen in the small museum on the first floor of the local library in Earl Road (open daily exc Sun from 09.30). The symbolism of the cape inflects Mold life, even to the extent that a cape-inspired design decorates the exterior of the local Homebase store.

As soon as the GHA bus leaves Mold, we are into a maze of villages and hamlets with typical Welsh names. And if you know a little Welsh it brings the names alive. First stop is **Gwernymynydd** – for English speakers a tongue-twister, but to the Welsh speakers on board our bus the name is a beautiful evocation of the Clwyd landscape. It means 'Mountain of the Elder Trees'.

We take minor roads, many of them barely wide enough to accommodate the bus, to stop at Maeshafn, Eryrys, Graianrhyd, Llanarmon-yn-Iâl and Llanbedr. There are frequent glimpses of **tumbling streams** close by the roadside and always a sprinkling of typical Welsh cottages. Most folk on the bus are regulars and know each other, and a non-Welsh speaker will listen entranced to the steady musical flow of their conversation. At **Graianrhyd** an acute right-hand turn is impossible for a bus, so we make a short diversion either via the old school or the pub car park – the choice is apparently de- pendent on the driver's mood.

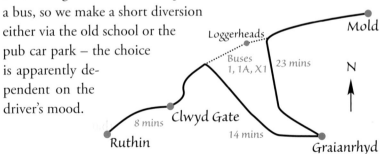

LOGGERHEADS COUNTRY PARK

Buses numbered 1, 1A or X1 all follow the main A494 from Ruthin back to Mold, the fastest buses taking as little as 24 minutes for the journey. All three routes stop at Loggerheads Country Park, which has a fine place in British bus history. The park was created by the **Crosville Motor Company** in the late 1920s. Crosville were big players in the bus business in those days, operating services from the Wirral and Lancashire into North Wales. In a splendid piece of social philanthropy, Crosville's enlightened management purchased land and created Loggerheads Country Park in the **Clwydian Hills**. They encouraged their passengers to take a break to enjoy a walk and some good Welsh fresh air. It is still a fine spot today. **Caffi Florence** (☎ 01352 810397; open daily 10.00–17.00) is in the park and offers a good range of snacks and meals.

Our meanderings through quiet lanes eventually completed, the bus returns to the main road (the A494) and heads more decisively towards Ruthin, cresting a col in the hills and crossing Offa's Dyke at 938 feet. The Clwyd Gate Motel and Restaurant are by the roadside here, and there is a fine view of the Clwydian Range, which is a designated Area of Outstanding Natural Beauty. The bus now descends steeply into the **Vale of Clwyd**, negotiating two hairpin bends to reach the village of Llanbedr-Dyffryn-Clwyd. Soon old and new school buildings face each other across the road and then the bus enters **Ruthin** (Rhuthun in Welsh), a lively and historic little town perched on a small hill. The attractive area around the clock tower seems to be the only piece of level ground in the vicinity. But take a wander for Ruthin, like Mold, is a pleasant town with little lanes, a striking old gaol (now a museum) and an excellent craft centre. ■

ABOUT THE
AUTHOR

TONY NEWMAN is retired. In his working life, he was a buyer for a multi-national corporation. He has a long-standing interest in public transport. A one-time Londoner, Tony now lives in North Wales.

A Taste of
WILD WALES

Nicky Gardner

21 Aberystwyth

Service no. T21 | Journey time 60 to 70mins

OS Landranger 135, 146. Three to four times daily (not Sun) as far as Pontrhydfendigaid; 2 journeys per day continue to Tregaron.
Operator: Evans Coaches.

Tregaron

The average British bus station is an uninspiring spot and the list of bus operators often as dull and repetitive as the architecturally monotonous bus stations that their vehicles serve. Big players like Arriva, Stagecoach and First have extended their networks across the country. So it is always a refreshing change to come to Aberystwyth where local players still hold a little sway.

Richard Brothers (three of them – Marteine, Malcolm and Nigel – and the third generation of Richards in the bus business) still run the bus service down the coast to Aberteifi, though English visitors often still insist that the market town and port on the River Teifi is called Cardigan. Lloyds Coaches operate the hourly X28 north to Machynlleth. They organise these things well in Aberystwyth. Most buses very sensibly depart from outside the train station, and it is there that I find service T21 run by Evans Coaches bound for Tregaron.

The traveller heading for the **Teifi Valley** towns of Tregaron and Llanbedr Pont Steffan can choose between a number of services from Aberystwyth, but the T21 is a local institution, created in a moment of adversity. Just a fortnight before Christmas in 1964, heavy rainfall over the Cambrian Mountains raised the level of the normally placid River Ystwyth. A railway bridge over the river at Llanilar was washed away in the flood. No trains even ran south from Aber after that fateful day, but the locals at least took heart that the railway had succumbed to Welsh weather rather than the terrible axe wielded by the very English Dr Beeching.

If it's Tuesday

The T21 is the lineal descendant of the rail-replacement bus service created in December 1964 to link Aberystwyth with the upper Teifi Valley. J Alwyn Evans is the man behind Evans Coaches, a company which has its modest headquarters in the old station yard at Tregaron. Alwyn and his crews are nothing if not flexible. The **T21 to Tregaron** takes a different route according to the day of the week, sometimes preferring the road via Pontrhydygroes and sometimes not. 'On Tuesdays and Thursdays, I always go through Ystrad Meurig,' explains the driver. 'And on other days, if someone asks then I'll go up to Ystrad. Of course we like them to phone in the day before, but sometimes they forget.'

Aberystwyth Castle
(photo © Shazzelll / DT)

A comprehensive understanding of **Welsh bus timetables** is a privilege reserved only unto a small number of folk in the Principality which is a pity, for these are marvellous social commentaries. The rubric for the T21 carefully defines the limits of J Alwyn Evans's flexibility. 'Stops at Morrison's on request,' reads a footnote which advises how and when the request might be proferred.

We have hardly left the bus stand in **Aber** when the driver's mobile phone rings. Our driver carefully pulls in at an Arriva bus stop, a little impertinence that creates a flurry of expectation among the small crowd of students waiting for the Arriva number 5 up to the University. Our driver answers the phone, speaks briefly and then announces that we will be diverting via Morrison's supermarket to pick up Mrs Lewis.

Mrs Lewis, it turns out, takes her shopping seriously and has evidently purchased sufficient supplies to last for many weeks. 'You know, what with the shortages and all,' she explains as the driver helps her stack three boxes of tangerines on to an empty seat. This is the first I hear of a national shortage of tangerines.

Murder in Llanafan

Before long we and Mrs Lewis's tangerines are bouncing at some speed along a B road, right beside the **River Ystwyth**, with the long-abandoned railway line on the opposite bank of the river. All around are patterned meadows, hedgerows that even in late autumn are lush and green, and stone walls. Each of the surrounding hills is capped with an old Roman fort or ancient earthwork. We pull into **Llanafan** two minutes early and stop outside the church. The village is a spick-and-span place on a little shoulder of land overlooking the River Ystwyth. The church is high Victoriana, a little out of place in this **remote Welsh valley**, yet the graveyard tells the tales of country life and death in rural Ceredigion. There lies poor Joseph Butler, a gamekeeper on the nearby Trawsgoed estate, who was shot dead by a poacher in 1868.

My musings on Butler's fate are interrupted by a toot of the bus horn so I hop back on board and Mrs Lewis recounts the story of Mr Butler's assassin, who is evidently something of a hero in these parts. William Richards stood up to the local bigwigs and his potshot at Lord Lisburne's gamekeeper was judged as being no bad thing. 'It was about time,' says Mrs Lewis, 'that someone stood up for the rights of the ordinary people of Ceredigion.' I hardly expected to run across such revolutionary zeal on the T21. Richards slipped from one cottage to another, protected by publicans and preachers, well looked after by the locals, until one day someone hit on the inspired idea of dressing Richards as a woman and shipping him off to America in disguise. Richards's girlfriend was smuggled out the following year and evidently the two lived happily ever after.

Aberystwyth

N

27 mins

Llanafan

27 mins

Pontrhydfendigaid

15 mins

Tregaron

DRUIDS AND DUTCH CONNECTIONS

Much as I like the Ystwyth Valley, its charms are in my mind greatly eclipsed by those of the Teifi – a valley that for some years was the area I called home. On the T21 it is just a short hop over the watershed that divides the two valleys.

First stop in the **Teifi Valley**, no matter what route the bus takes, is **Pontrhydfendigaid** – a village that while rooted in Welsh Wales has an other-worldly dimension. Mrs Lewis mentions that nowadays it is inordinately popular with Druids and Dutch people, the latter on account of the village having played a bit-part role in a Dutch novel that acquired cult popularity in the mid 1990s. The novel, I subsequently discovered, is called *De Ontdekking van de Hemel*, which means *The Discovery of Heaven*. This seems just right for Pontrhydfendigaid, for if there is a stairway to Heaven from this Earth, I have a hunch that it might well start in the Teifi Valley.

POETS AND PRINCES AT STRATA FLORIDA

There is a **gem of a walk** from Pontrhydfendigaid east to Strata Florida Abbey. With almost four hours between southbound buses from **Pontrhydfendigaid**, you'll have plenty of time to reach the abbey, which is 1.2 miles east of the village. Just follow **Abbey Road**, a lovely lane with little traffic that runs up the Teifi Valley towards the abbey. Amid the lonely ruins of this **former Cistercian abbey** you will find the graves of a dozen Welsh princes and poets.

Pontrhydfendigaid is also a good refreshment stop. The village shop has a **café** (☎ 01974 831202), usually open till about 16.00. But my firm favourite is the **Black Lion Hotel** (*Llew Du* in Welsh), an amiable little inn on Mill Street (☎ 01974 831624; sometimes closed between lunch and dinner, so check ahead). You can also stay at the Black Lion where en-suite singles are £40 and double or twin rooms are £65.

Mrs Lewis and her tangerines decant in Pontrhydfendigaid and from there it is an easy run south to Tregaron, skirting the edge of **Cors Caron** – Tregaron Bog to English speakers. This is a fabulous piece of peaty wetland, home to otters and red kites. A **Welsh drizzle** has set in and today is not good for spotting birds, yet we are rewarded as a lone hen harrier glides slowly over the road in front of the bus. And then, as we approach Tregaron, the sky clears to reveal a rainbow dancing over the hills away to the east. That upland is known as **Elenydd**, a remote and desolate range of hills that is the backdrop to all Tregaron life.

Tregaron connections

Tregaron is the principal market town of the upper Teifi, a laid-back sort of place where buses gather for a chat in the main square. End of the route for the T21 which arrives on time.

I am tempted by the sight of the connecting Mid-Wales Motorways 588 bus that continues down the Teifi Valley on the west bank of the river. What an odd name for a bus company based in a region that is utterly devoid of motorways. But perhaps the A road through Llangybi, narrow and twisty though it is, comes close to the status of a motorway in these parts.

But I pass on the main road option and stick to the **route less travelled**. The 585 school bus, operated by James Brothers, seems much the better choice, for it takes the B road down through Llanddewi Brefi on the east bank of the Teifi. That road runs closer to the hills and it is a chance to ride through the village where once I lived. Wales is like that. Once it gets a grip on you, it lures you back. And happily there is still a plethora of small independent bus operators that will ferry you to even the remotest corners of the Principality. ■

ABOUT THE AUTHOR | **NICKY GARDNER** is co-editor of *hidden europe* magazine and also co-editor of this book. She spent some of the most formative years of her life in the Teifi Valley in mid-Wales.

ARE BUSES BORING?

'Is this the world's most boring blog?' queried a national daily in 2011 when one of the paper's reporters stumbled on Gerald Fletcher's blow-by-blow account of happenings on the X1 Lowestoft to Peterborough bus route. True **devotees of the absurd** need only click through to http://fecx1news.blogspot.com for some fine entertainment.

Yet buses are not boring. History was made on buses. **Rosa Parks** struck a major blow for civil rights in the United States when in 1955 she sat on a seat designated for white passengers while riding home from work on the bus in Montgomery, Alabama.

Even in Britain buses can inspire **revolutionary fervour**. The Bristol bus boycott in 1963 was a protest by Bristolians to contest the Bristol Omnibus Company's refusal to employ non-white workers. For five months the company management held out until at last the company's own workers voted against the ban. That was on 27 August 1963. Just three weeks later, a local Sikh gentleman took up a position as Bristol's first non-white bus conductor. The Bristol protest evoked such considerable public sympathy that it paved the way for the 1965 Race Relations Act.

Nowadays, it seems our revolutionary zeal on buses is directed more at self-interest than the betterment of society. In April 2011, a Gloucester pensioner chained herself to a bus in protest at her local Council's attempt to tinker with the rules governing the use of concessionary bus passes. No, buses are certainly not boring, but they do have a knack of bringing out the best and worst of human emotions. **George Orwell**, a man with such sound socialist credentials that we might have expected him to be a great supporter of buses, was terribly impatient with bus conductors, never seeing them as potential allies in his efforts to denounce capitalism.

They may not be essentially socialist, but buses are essentially social. Ride with **Colin Thubron** on the bus to Samarkand (in *The Lost Heart of Asia*) and you will never forget the ride. Just as we hope the image of Mrs Lewis and her tangerines in Journey 21 will rest with you long after you have finished reading this book. Buses are fascinating. So much so, that we really think that the proverbial Clapham omnibus might well be the most interesting aspect of Clapham. NG

CENTRAL ENGLAND

Our fourth geographical area in this book covers a swathe of central England extending from the Welsh Marches to the North Sea coast and including the one-time industrial hubs of the **English Midlands**. Not always promising areas for local bus journeys you might suppose. But our seven routes in this section tell a more positive tale, and show how even Birmingham's edgy suburbs come to life when viewed from the top deck of the bus.

As in other sections of *Bus-Pass Britain*, there were many near-misses, routes that we were anxious to include which didn't make the final cut. The Sherwood Arrow link from Nottingham to New Ollerton is a nice run through Sherwood Forest. We also know of many superb routes through the **Cotswolds** which are worth exploring; most of these are happily still run by local independent operators. Two of our favourites are the 21 from Moreton-in-Marsh to Stratford-upon-Avon (operated by Johnsons of Henley) and the 853 from Oxford to Gloucester (run by Swanbrook of Staverton).

If you are looking to make long hops on local buses, then the Stagecoach X5 from Oxford to Cambridge was made for you. With half-hourly buses for much of the week, this 100-mile route is one of the longest high-frequency bus services in Britain. Truly dedicated Easterlings can ride from Oxford to Lowestoft on the East Anglian coast with just two quick changes of bus (at Milton Keynes and Peterborough respectively). The overall journey takes nine hours, but we would certainly advise stopping off for an hour at each of the two places where you must change buses. Even we, devotees of local buses though we are, might baulk at the prospect of a nine-hour bus journey. ∎

Through
THE Marches

Victor Chamberlain

Ludlow

Service no. 492 | Journey time 70 to 80mins

OS Landranger 137, 149. Six services daily Mon–Sat (hourly south of Leominster), 3 Sunday journeys. Operator: Lugg Travel (Mon–Sat) or First (Sun). Connects with Journey 18 in Hereford.

Hereford ⬅

The much loved English poet John Betjeman, always a defender of anything with fading charm, once described Ludlow as 'the most beautiful town in England.' And Ludlow's charm has never waned. Indeed, **Ludlow** gets ever better. With a fine range of Georgian buildings, a magnificent Norman castle and a town centre that brims with good locally-owned shops, Ludlow is a gem. And as the first UK town to join the *Cittaslow* (literally 'slow city') movement, Ludlow makes a perfect hub for devotees of slow travel.

You can speed in a car down the A49 from Ludlow to Hereford in just 35 minutes. The bus takes twice that, and for much of the journey it sticks to a quiet B road rather than the main highway. This is essentially a **Herefordshire journey** for, much as Ludlow might be judged to be the quintessential Shropshire town, the border with neighbouring Herefordshire is crossed very shortly after we leave Ludlow.

But there is also much of the flavour of the Welsh Marches about this route. Especially in the first part of the journey, from Ludlow to Leominster, there is a palpable sense that **wilder country** is not so far away to the west. Our route is through the lands of the former earldoms of Shrewsbury and Hereford which were formed in Norman times to control the Welsh.

Radar and radio

Leaving Ludlow through the town's narrow streets the bus passes over picturesque Ludford Bridge. Swirling below are the foamy waters of the River Teme rushing down from Wales. Then it is uphill, skirting the eastern side of **Mortimer Forest** (a fine spot for walks) to the Herefordshire boundary at **Richards Castle**. This may be rural England, but there are many hints of modernity. Looking back there are fine views of Clee Hill, its summit marked by a distinctive golf ball which is part of a radar facility used for air traffic control. It is a mark of Clee Hill's prominence in the local landscape that it features in the famous medieval Mappa Mundi display at Hereford Cathedral.

And away to the left are the masts of the **Woofferton radio transmitters**. Many British readers of this book will probably have never heard of Woofferton, but in parts of eastern Europe the name Woofferton was very well known – at least to devotes of the Voice of America radio network during the Cold War years. VoA broadcasts often started with the call sign 'This is the Voice of America from Woofferton.'

Beyond Woofferton the bus turns into the pleasant village of Orleton with some traditional Herefordshire 'black and white' vernacular architecture. Facilities in the village include two public houses, the church with its shingle-covered timber spire, a post office and a general store. It is a good base for country walks. Then we continue south through Luston and cross the River Lugg, another fast-flowing river that drains down from the Welsh hills, to reach **Leominster**. If you want to make an urban stop on the journey to Hereford, this is your chance (see box below).

HUGGING THE LUGG

It is useful to note that the service frequency on the 492 bus route doubles from Leominster. On Mondays to Saturdays, this means an hourly service, thus making an impromptu stopover a more attractive proposition.

The bus route south from Leominster follows the **River Lugg** for much of the run south to Hereford. A milk depot and a farm cider company are reminders that this is rich farming country. Just south of Newton, where we join the main A49 for the first time on our journey from Ludlow, comes the big surprise of the route. Where the River Lugg makes a big meander to the east, the road continues straight ahead over Dinmore Hill. **Queenswood Country Park** at the summit makes a great stop.

South from Queenswood, the road drops steeply back down into the valley of the Lugg. Some buses leave the main road to

LEOMINSTER

The town of Leominster (pronounced 'Lemster') dates back to Saxon times. Within the town's **compact centre**, just a short walk from the bus station, the medieval street pattern is still very evident. Interesting buildings include the **Priory Church** (founded as a monastery in pre-Norman times) and **Grange Court**, which was formerly the town hall, with an open-air market beneath. There are impressive **medieval overhangs** along Drapers Lane and School Lane and splendid Georgian properties in Broad Street. Leominster was once a wealthy wool town. The **Flying Dutchman** (☎ 01568 612130) on Corn Square is a first-rate delicatessen and café and is a good spot to stop for lunch.

QUEENSWOOD COUNTRY PARK

Queenswood is part of a large **ancient oak forest** that once stretched as far as Wales. It now has a 67-acre arboretum containing over 1,200 rare and exotic trees from all over the world together with 103 acres of semi-natural ancient woodland. There are a variety of **well-marked walks** through the park, superb views, a new information centre and shop (opened in July; ☎ 01568 797853) and a café (closed Mon).

serve either Moreton-on-Lugg or Wellington (though, oddly, never both). Wellington is always a challenge, for the lane to the village is narrow. Last week, we had to wait for a tractor. This week it was a flock of sheep that kept us standing.

CATHEDRAL CITY

As we close in on Hereford, there are excellent views of two distinctive ranges of hills: the **Black Mountains** (which mark the border with Wales) away to the west, and the **Malvern Hills** to the east. But the eye is drawn less to the hills but more to what lies straight ahead. Here are the dramatic spires of the city of **Hereford**, and in their midst the assertive tower of the cathedral. It is a vista of which John Betjeman would most surely have approved.

The final part of the route into the city is interesting. We pass the racecourse, Hereford United football ground and the Courtyard Theatre before following the line of the medieval city wall and ending our journey near the **Shire Hall**. For those who want a train connection, the 492 bus conveniently continues to the city's railway station. ■

ABOUT THE
AUTHOR

VICTOR CHAMBERLAIN is a retired architect who, with his wife, came to live and work in Herefordshire and Shropshire in 1999 and uses the 492 bus regularly.

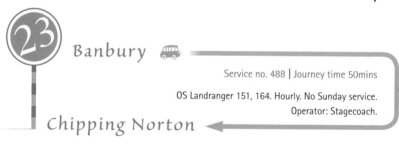

Over the Hills to Chippy

Peter Draper

23 Banbury 🚐

Service no. 488 | Journey time 50mins

OS Landranger 151, 164. Hourly. No Sunday service.
Operator: Stagecoach.

Chipping Norton

The countryside of the northern portion of **Oxfordshire** is surprisingly remote and unspoilt, and service 488 gives ready access to this subtle, pleasing landscape of rippling hills and copses etched with distant spires.

The towns and villages served, from **Banbury** via Bloxham and Hook Norton to Chipping Norton, are all full of interest, and subtle changes in the underlying geology along the way are reflected in the lie of the land and the mix of local building materials. This all adds up to a winning formula, making the 488 a route that is easy to appreciate.

BLOXHAM FOR LENGTH

We start at Banbury's bus station in Bridge Street. Soon we are free of the town, climbing gently to the endearing village of Bloxham. The main street is lined with buildings in warm brown ironstone and dominated by the elegant 180-feet-high spire of the majestic parish church of St Mary. This is one of a trio of notable local church spires, recalled in a rhyme well known to folk in the Banbury area: 'Bloxham for length, Adderbury for strength, and King's Sutton for beauty.'

Visitors to the area might like to use local buses to form their own opinion! **Bloxham church** with its glowing stained glass by William Morris, Edward Burne-Jones and Philip Webb is a fine introduction to the churches of the region.

Leaving Bloxham and passing through the rather isolated community of Milcombe (with a striking final view of Bloxham Church away to the left), the next few miles of the journey have a curiously remote air. Occasional passengers board or alight at isolated farms and there are sweeping views over the neatly hedged country lanes to a pastel-coloured landscape of chequerboard fields, farms and spinneys. This section is a special delight on a clear, sharp spring morning; real, unspoilt Midland England at its best.

HOOKY FOR BEER

We soon reach the large village of **Hook Norton**, known as Hooky to locals. The name Ironstone Hollow on a housing development as we enter Hooky is a reminder that this part of rural Oxfordshire was once home to a flourishing iron trade with blast-furnaces and iron-ore quarries. The pillars of a disused railway viaduct built

BLOXHAM AND HOOKY

You'll find no end of first-class pubs along the 488 bus route. Bloxham and Hook Norton are the two obvious spots to break your journey. With buses generally running hourly, it is easy to pause along the way. But keep an eye on the clock, for last buses on this route are quite early. The **Red Lion inn** in Bloxham High Street (☎ 01295 720352) serves excellent food, and Bloxham has shops and a post office.

Hook Norton Brewery (www.hooknortonbrewery.co.uk) has a visitor centre in the original 1849 maltings building. It is open daily from 09.30. Brewery tours last two hours and must be pre-booked (☎ 01608 73034).

by the Banbury and Cheltenham Direct Railway in connection with this industry form a rather eerie remnant of this period, and can be visited as part of a pleasant walk beginning in Middle Hill, a left turn off High Street near the Sun Inn (☎ 01608 737 570). As well as serving good food, this inn has fascinating sepia photographs of Hook Norton's **industrial past**.

Most visitors to Hook Norton come to see the remarkable traditional **Victorian brewery**. Hook Norton ales are familiar throughout the area and the brewery itself offers tours and has a shop and museum. On a recent journey on the 488 a group of Canadian students alighted for the brewery tour; it was entertaining to see the contrast between their quiet demeanour when alighting in the morning and their noisy chatter when rejoining the bus in the afternoon after sampling the local brew! Definitely a case where taking the bus is a big plus.

Yet another attraction in Hook Norton is the beautiful parish church of St Peter (right by the bus stop), with its striking tower and delightful setting. The 11th-century font at this church draws visitors from far and wide.

CHANGING COTSWOLD LANDSCAPES

After leaving Hook Norton on the Great Rollright road, the tenor of the **landscape changes**. Distant views towards Long Compton have an unmistakably Cotswoldian feel, and we suddenly realise that we have left the brown ironstone strata behind and are into limestone country. This whole area is indeed something of a borderland for the boundaries of Warwickshire, Gloucestershire and Worcestershire are all close at hand.

Banbury
14 mins
Bloxham
14 mins
Hook Norton
18 mins
N
Chipping Norton
Connection
on X8
Kingham

A series of steep descents through Great Rollright and Over Norton villages are a reminder that this route is certainly no sinecure for the bus driver! **Great Rollright** is an attractive village overlooked by the medieval church of St Andrew, but is not in fact particularly near the famed Rollright Stones, Oxfordshire's answer to Stonehenge. For bus passengers, access to this remarkable and mysterious stone grouping of **The King's Men**, The King Stone and (a personal favourite) The Whispering Knights is easier using Stagecoach service 50 (Chipping Norton to Stratford-upon-Avon), which stops on request within a few hundred yards of the Stones.

Bliss Mill in Chipping Norton has been converted into flats (photo © Davidmartyn / DT)

CHIPPY DELIGHTS

Soon we enter the grey-stone town of **Chipping Norton**, known as 'Chippy' to locals. Chipping Norton at about 700 feet is the highest town in Oxfordshire. No wonder it often feels rather windswept. Take a while to get the pulse of Chippy. It has elegant 18th-century stone frontages, a lovely **Neoclassical town hall** and a superb row of almshouses, the latter dating from 1640.

One of the most remarkable buildings in Chipping Norton owes its origins to Victorian industry; on the western side of the town is the former **Bliss Tweed Mill**, which was for many years a major employer. This monumentally impressive building, with its ornate, soaring chimney, has now been tastefully converted into luxury flats.

The imposing parish church of St Mary the Virgin is slightly tucked away from the main West Street to Horsefair axis. This church benefitted from the prosperity of wool merchants in centuries past and contains many individual features of interest, including fine stained glass, well repaying detailed exploration. The building is located adjacent to the mounds of Chipping Norton's former castle, of which no trace now remains; nevertheless, the surviving earthworks are atmospheric enough. The history of the town can be more fully explored at the admirable **museum** (☎ 01608 641712; open 14.00–16.00 Mon–Sat Easter till end of Oct).

Do try this rewarding trip to Chippy – you won't be disappointed. For those travelling onward, the X8 runs at least hourly to Kingham station for train connections to Oxford, London and Worcester. ■

ABOUT THE AUTHOR

PETER DRAPER is a retired lecturer, but spent the last few years of his working life with the Wilts & Dorset Bus Company. He is a lifetime public transport devotee and loves exploring.

ORBITAL DELIGHTS

Nicky Gardner

 Birmingham

Service nos. 11A (anticlockwise) or 11C (clockwise) |
Journey time 2hrs to 2hrs 30mins

OS Landranger 139. Every 8mins Mon–Sat daytime, every 20mins evenings
and Sun. Operator: National Express West Midlands.

circular route

This journey is a bus trip for **urban explorers**. It tracks a route through Birmingham's suburban web, encircling England's second city on a run that is full of cultural colour. As narrated here, it starts and ends in Bournville, but you can of course board the number 11 at any point on its orbit around Birmingham. And, if you grow to like this circular route as much as I do, you might be tempted to stay on board for ever.

Were it not for the complete absence of pubs, I might be tempted to stay in Bournville. It is a happy spot, made all the better by the gentle smell of chocolate from the nearby **Cadbury factory** that drifts from time to time over the park. George and Richard Cadbury – brothers, philanthropists and chocolatiers – knew the ingredients of human happiness: Tudor beams, indoor toilets, decent plumbing, education, the village green and chocolate.

Route 11, often dubbed the Outer Circle, is the boomerang of British bus routes. Climb aboard outside the **Friends' Meeting House** and it matters not if you head north or south. Whichever direction you choose, bus 11 resolutely brings you right back to Bournville. The bus route comes in two flavours: 11A (anticlockwise) or 11C (clockwise), each affording two hours or more of orbital delight as the bus circumnavigates the heart of the city known for chocolate, custard, commerce and culture. Route 11 never touches the centre of Birmingham nor the city boundary, instead maintaining a creative tension between the two as it tracks a circular trail **through the suburbs.**

LOST VILLAGES, NEW SUBURBS

Culture comes in many guises in modern Birmingham and route 11 touches them all. Rachmaninoff and rap, mosques and Sikh temples, halal and hijab, pawnbrokers and bingo, hair weaving and glamour nails. This is a provocative orbit through Birmingham's edgy and neglected territories, a journey that plunges through deepest Yardley and distant Handsworth before returning inexorably and inevitably to the little Utopia that is Bournville.

Birmingham's **Outer Circle bus route** is a veteran among urban bus routes. Brochures in the 1920s extolled the merits of the route. One Mr Baker, in those days general manager of the Birmingham Corporation Tramways and Omnibus Department, put his name to a stylish pamphlet that commanded 'see Birmingham's charming suburbs by 'bus' – if Mr Baker was as good at running buses as he was at deploying apostrophes with precision, then Brummie buses were surely a treat in those days. '25 miles for 15 pence' ran the blurb under a picture of two of the corporation's finest double-deckers sedately processing along an otherwise empty road through leafy suburbs. A distinctly rural finger-signpost pointed down a lane to Yardley and Hall Green, both nowadays dreary suburbs that have impertinently gobbled up the meadows and woodland that once fringed the Cole Valley.

The Birmingham Corporation Tramways and Omnibus Department has been consigned to transport history. It is many years since the corporation's cream and Monastral-blue double-deckers cruised the Outer Circle. Cream and that distinctive dark blue have been supplanted by garish modern buses, happily still double-deckers, but their exteriors strewn by advertisements.

Perry Barr
18 mins
15 mins
Erdington
Handsworth
Winson
Green
8 mins
23 mins
20 mins
Yardley
The Swan
Acocks
Green
11 mins
Selly Oak
7 mins
11 mins
Bournville
14 mins
12 mins
11 mins
Kings Heath
Sarehole
Mill

N

Those who know their buses appreciate that these are Eclipse Gemini models, nicely astronomical names for buses destined to spend their days in orbit. They are operated by National Express West Midlands, a company that evidently has a great sense of irony, for the Outer Circle is anything but an express. These are buses that progress haltingly and often not at all. The fine men and women who are assigned to drive the buses on this route are surely among the most patient souls on the planet as they navigate their Eclipse Geminis through constellations of dense traffic.

From leafy **Bournville**, the anticlockwise bus route tracks south to Cotteridge, where it turns east towards Kings Heath. 'I'm just off to the village,' says a chatty pensioner who climbs aboard at Stirchley and politely asks if he might be permitted to share a seat on the top deck. Ex-Guards, I'd say, but don't have the courage to ask.

The village, it turns out, is **Kings Heath**: urban, choked with traffic, discount perms and not a meadow in sight. The parish church of All Saints presides over a commercial disaster zone. Where once there were the essential ingredients of village life – butchers, bakers and perhaps even candlestick makers – now there are boarded-up premises and a sad row of charity shops.

But the village is something of the mind, and no-one can persuade local residents that Kings Heath is no longer the rural idyll of their imagination. 'Here's my stop,' says the old soldier who reminds me that they do a very passable all-day breakfast at the **Kitchen Garden Café** in the village (☎ 0121 4434725; open from 09.00, from 10.00 on Sun).

ARRIVING IN SAREHOLE

From Kings Heath, the bus drops gently towards the River Cole and Sarehole, a place name that is slowly disappearing from modern maps. No space for the gentle villages of yesteryear that have been gobbled up by the angry city. But **Sarehole** looks like a spot that well deserves a stop.

'Ah, you've come to Hobbiton,' says the elderly woman feeding ducks by the icy River Cole, alluding to Sarehole's illustrious place in literary history. A little improbably, it might seem, unless you know that, as young lads living just a short scamper away to the north, **J R R Tolkien** and his elder brother spent long summer days exploring the meadows and woods around Sarehole Mill. The mill itself is just one of two remaining in a city once famous for

Birmingham: a city of canals
(photo © Tupungato / DT)

SAREHOLE MILL

This is a delightful spot for humans and hobbits alike. The mill and its environs will appeal even to those who have never heard of **Middle Earth**. Yet for Tolkien fans Sarehole will evoke images of the great rebellion as Hobbits united to repel the creeping urbanisation and industrialisation of **The Shire**. Tolkien contributed to the restoration of Sarehole Mill in the 1960s, and today the building houses a small **exhibition** and an excellent tea shop (open daily 12.00–16.00 exc Mondays from early April to late October).

its mills and waterways. Sarehole is a good place to start exploring this little fragment of The Shire.

Kerry, not yet twenty-one and evidently already the mother of three children, is a resident of Springfield, just a short pram-ride from Sarehole. She is a tribute to human fertility and a discerning critic of Tolkien affairs. 'This ain't The Shire. 'Aven't you seen the film? All that stuff the Council says is crap. Those 'obbits all lived in New Zealand.' Kerry's eldest is endeavouring to stick drawing pins into the back tyre of a car parked by the bus stop, but is distracted by the arrival of the Eclipse Gemini that will take us further on our urban orbit. Along the way, Kerry says that she and her flock are heading 'up the Swan'. This intelligence prompts me to reflect that, were George Cadbury on our bus today, he would surely have shared a little homily about the perils of lunchtime drinking, especially setting so poor an example to children of such tender years.

I am mightily relieved when the Swan turns out to be not a pub but a shopping centre in **Yardley**. By the time we reach it, we have seen a decent sweep of suburban Birmingham, resplendent with its tattoo studios, dental laboratories and discount stores. **The Swan**, evidently a local landmark, is not a sight to gladden the heart. Apparently there are plans to redevelop this concrete monstrosity and its inglorious surrounds. I notice that the bulldozers are already in attendance and are busy uprooting the few remaining trees in the area – not a promising start.

Halal and hijab: multicultural Birmingham

From the Swan we have a clear run north, a rare few minutes of light traffic which our driver seems to relish, until we come abruptly to a standstill under the M6 at Bromford. This is **container country**, an eerie territory of railway sidings, canals and industrial parks where the roads are always grimy. Now there are Polish voices on the top deck of the bus as we cruise through Erdington, but Polish is soon eclipsed by Punjabi as we head west through **Perry Barr** towards Handsworth.

Exploring the back streets around the bus route, I could so easily conclude that this northwestern quadrant in our orbit has not made a positive contribution to the human condition. But that would be to overlook the life and work of Oscar Deutsch, the Birmingham-born son of Jewish-Hungarian parents who founded the Odeon cinema empire, which started life as a small chain of local movie houses, many of them in striking Art Deco buildings, in and around Perry Barr.

There is a disconcerting moment as we track down through **Handsworth**. Our driver, a lady this time, turns left on to Soho Road following a sign towards Birmingham city centre. I wonder if our Eclipse Gemini has somehow lost its orbital momentum.

DECODING THE ODEON

It was Harry Weedon, a Handsworth man, who designed many of Bimingham's fabulous cinemas for **Oscar Deutsch**. Sadly, many of Weedon's buildings are now depressively derelict, but around Birmingham they still remember Oscar and his Odeons. 'Ah, yes... Deutsch' said a fellow passenger as we cruised on the top deck through Perry Barr. 'Do you know what Odeon stands for? *Oscar Deutsch entertains our nation.*'

Are we being sucked inexorably into the heart of the city? There are tales told of lesser buses (not Eclipse Geminis of course) that spend their days in gruesome lines around the Bull Ring Shopping Centre and New Street Station. But after just a few yards, the driver, brimming with confidence, makes a right turn on to a minor road that more properly fits our orbital trajectory.

From here on south, it is all 'X-Factor latest' on screaming headlines seen from the top deck. On the streets below, hair weaving and Western Union, teeth whitening 'while you wait', as we glide past mosques and Methodist chapels to Winson Green. Turbans and temples, allotments and community centres and Midland red brick sitting cheek by jowl with grey concrete. Yet there's nothing green about **Winson Green**, one of the forgotten zones west of the city centre. Once home to a large asylum, it now hosts Birmingham's most troubled prison.

'Jesus cares about Rotton Park' proclaims a large banner, seemingly contradicting all the evidence that points to the contrary, before we move south through **Harborne**, once home to W H Auden, and back towards a more middle-class Birmingham. On past Ali Baba's fast food. Ali knows how to hedge his bets, serving both falafel and panini. But soon the Afro hair salons and discount clearance markets give way to dance studios, private nurseries and Italian delicatessens.

Birmingham's Outer Circle is a visual feast and a very fine urban kaleidoscope. The full circle is about the same length as the average feature film. As Oscar Deutsch surely appreciated, all good films can be revisited again and again, each new viewing revealing fresh layers of meaning. Just like this bus route. After a couple of circuits in one direction, hop off and orbit Birmingham in reverse, ever confident in the knowledge that the Outer Circle will always bring you back to chocolatey **Bournville**. ∎

ABOUT THE AUTHOR | **NICKY GARDNER** is a travel writer specialising in Europe's unsung communities. She is co-editor of *hidden europe* magazine and also co-editor of this book.

EXPLORING THE WORLD OF
SAINTS AND TIGERS

Alastair Willis

Northampton

Service no. X7 | Journey time 1hr 30mins

OS Landranger 152, 141, 140. Hourly Mon–Sat, every 2hrs Sun. Operator: Stagecoach.

Leicester

N orthampton's **bus station** enjoys a certain notoriety. When designer and television presenter Kevin McCloud set out to discover Britain's worst buildings, it wasn't long before he turned up in Northampton. This architectural eyesore is not merely gloomy and grimy; it is also hard to find. This is hardly an asset for a bus station. The main entrance is on the first floor of the Grosvenor Centre. Don't be deterred. Persist and you will be rewarded by the X7, a reliable inter-urban route with pretty countryside, appealing villages, and lots of interesting places to stop off along the way.

Northampton and Leicester have a lot in common, including a passion for **rugby union**. Northampton Saints and Leicester Tigers vie for supremacy in the Premiership league. England's manager, ex-Tiger and World Cup winning captain, Martin Johnson, went to school in Market Harborough, the town that marks the midway point of the journey. Fellow travellers, though, are likely to be shoppers and commuters, rather than rugby hunks.

THE LAND OF SAINTS

Northampton and shoes are synonymous. They even fill the local museum and art gallery with footwear-inspired displays. But

my favourite spot in Northampton is the delightful 78
Derngate (☎ 01604 603407;
www.78derngate.org.uk; open
10.00–17.00 Tue–Sun from Feb till
Christmas; entrance £6.20; good small
restaurant). It's best to book a guided
tour. This town house, with its striking interiors, was remodelled by architect Charles Rennie Mackintosh for W J
Bassett-Lowke, founder of a local model-
making business.

Leicester   N

40 mins

Market Harborough

24 mins

Brixworth

16 mins

Northampton

But now it's time to tackle the bus station where stepping
on to the X7 feels like boarding a passing rescue vessel. It takes
a while to clear the suburbs of Northampton, but soon we are
heading north towards Leicester. **Brixworth Country Park** is the
first real attraction. It is a beautiful spot, with easy-to-follow trails
named after various birds: kestrel, skylark, lapwing. It's good to see
the effort made to ensure that everything is wheelchair-friendly.
There is a café, cycle hire and a round-the-reservoir walk of over
seven miles.

The most scenic part of the journey is near aptly-named
Hanging Houghton and Lamport, looking down to the upper
reaches of the Brampton branch of the River Nene. Sir Charles
Isham, the one-time squire at Lamport Hall has a lot to answer

BRIXWORTH WALK

If you want to venture beyond the country park at Brixworth, I suggest
the **Brampton Valley Way**. It follows the route of the old Northampton
to Market Harborough railway and nowadays attracts cyclists and
walkers aplenty. And Brixworth village warrants a stop. In **All Saints
Church** it has one of England's most impressive Saxon churches.
There is a warm welcome at **The Coach and Horses** (☎ 01604
880329) – the fish & chips are among the best I've tasted.

for: in the 1860s he introduced garden gnomes to Britain from Germany.

THE LAND OF TIGERS

Leicester Tiger territory starts at **Market Harborough**. The centre of the town is dominated by the limestone and ironstone 14th-century church of St Dionysius. In its shadow is the old Grammar School, a timber-framed building of 1614, with an open ground floor to accommodate market space. The tall Italianate building behind was part of Symington's factory, a spot that holds an illustrious place in the history of lingerie. Symington's wealth came from making the liberty bodice. The erstwhile factory premises are now the Council offices, library and museum (entrance through the archway and upstairs at the rear). **Harborough Museum** (☎ 01858 821085; open 10.30–16.15 Mon–Sat) has the magnificent Hallaton Treasure on display, one of Britain's most important Iron Age finds of coins, jewellery and pottery.

From Market Harborough, our bus runs northwest skirting Great Glen (not remotely like its Scottish namesake) to **Leicester**, where it terminates at light and airy St Margaret's Bus Station. They should send Northampton architects up here for a little instruction.

To get a feel for Leicester, hop off the X7 at the railway station and head south to New Walk, the stylish late 18th-century traffic-free street. Opposite is the welcoming **Museum and Art Gallery** (☎ 0116 2254900; open 10.00–17.00 Mon–Sat, 11.00–17.00 Sun). The collections range from dinosaurs to German Expressionism and Picasso ceramics. In the city centre, you'll find the market (Britain's largest permanent outdoor market), Leicester Cathedral, and the adjacent medieval guild hall. ■

ABOUT THE AUTHOR │ **ALASTAIR WILLIS** has lived in Northamptonshire and Leicestershire for over 30 years. He is joint leader of a U3A environment group, and a member of rambling clubs, a civic society, and a wildlife trust.

WITH THE
SEA TO YOUR RIGHT

Laurence Mitchell

26 Cromer

Coasthopper service | Journey time 1hr 50mins

OS Landranger 132, 133. Daily (every 30mins in summer, every 1 to 2hrs in winter). Only alternative buses continue beyond Hunstanton. Operator: Norfolk Green.

King's Lynn

The Coasthopper service that runs between Cromer and King's Lynn along the north Norfolk coast must be one of the most useful bus routes in the country – it's even free if you already have a Rover ticket for the Bittern Line rail service between Norwich and Sheringham. Few take the **Coasthopper** for the whole distance though: as its name suggests, it is best suited to short hops along this gorgeous stretch of Norfolk coastline. Eco-conscious (or just plain car-less) birdwatchers use it to get to the wader-rich marshes around Cley-next-the-Sea, Norfolk's birding Mecca; walkers take advantage of a one-way ride in this coastal fringe of linear footpaths that make circular walks difficult; retired locals use it for pension-day outings to King's Lynn or Cromer. Summer or winter, if you look inside the bus you'll find a microcosm of the **north Norfolk community**.

The Coasthopper is perfect for holidaymakers too, passing through many of north Norfolk's best-loved villages – neat, cobble-built clusters like Blakeney, Stiffkey and Brancaster. In addition to Cley-next-the-Sea for birders, there's Morston for seal fanciers, Burnham Market for fine wine and posh nosh, Holkham's beach for bathers and Brancaster for a briny round of golf. And there's

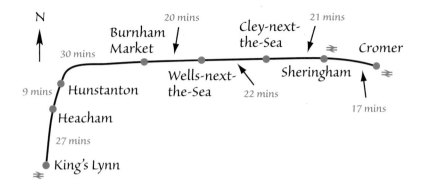

always Hunstanton, Wells or Cromer too for the simple pleasures of fish and chips and a promenade. Agenda-free passengers can simply get on and off as the fancy takes them, tempted by a cosy pub, an appealing stretch of marsh, or tea and scones in a Cley tea room.

West to Wells

I used to visit this stretch of coast a lot back in the late 1970s when I was a bit of a weekend birder. In those days there was no bus service to speak of and so I was obliged to either hitch-hike or persuade my recalcitrant Morris Traveller not to break down *en route* here. So, hats off to Norfolk Green for providing a very welcome lifeline.

Cromer is a possible starting point but coming by train from Norwich I prefer Sheringham as it is a bit more convenient – the bus stops right outside the station.

Once out of town we leave Sheringham's golf course and clifftop caravan sites behind to drop down to Kelling. Immediately, the landscape becomes rather more austere: to our right are tantalising glimpses of sea between sand dunes and pebble banks, while a green swathe of fields with ripening wheat and barley flashes by on the left. Beyond this slopes a ridge of low hills – low, perhaps, but still the loftiest in all Norfolk. At **Salthouse** – so named because of its one-time salt industry – skeins of honking geese rise from the salt marshes to punctuate the sky, a hint of what is to come at **Cley-next-the-Sea** (see box on page 128), our next port of call.

Approaching Cley, a couple of holiday birders, newly retired by the looks of it, dressed in quality camouflage gear and clutching expensive Zeiss binoculars get off the bus. No doubt they will soon be perched on a bench in a hide trying to differentiate their godwits. It is not just birdwatchers of course: the bus is a microcosm of north Norfolk humanity – a real community bus rather than a mere tourist service. Few seem to be riding it for as far as I am though.

We pass the nature reserve's fancy new visitor centre on the left – all glass and eco-friendly pine – before skirting Cley's **windmill**, probably north Norfolk's most totemic building. The road twists through the village past tea rooms, art galleries and a well-appointed delicatessen to pass more marshes and ponds on the way out. In plain view of the bus, slender waders probe the mud for morsels ignoring the stare of birdwatchers on the bank opposite who flick binoculars to eyebrows to check them out.

A pair of walkers, OS maps neatly tucked into plastic waterproof wallets, get off at the Blakeney junction beneath the imposing bulk of **St Nicholas's Church** – the so-called 'Cathedral

NORTH NORFOLK NOSH

Cookie's Crab Shop (Salthouse; ☎ 01263 740352; open 09.00–19.00 daily, 10.00–16.00 in winter) on the green just before the Dun Cow pub and with a nice garden facing the salt marshes is the place to enjoy all sorts of shellfish, seafood platters and smoked fish sandwiches. Cookie's is not licensed but it is fine to bring your own. At weekends it is best to book beforehand.

The **White Horse** (Brancaster Staithe; ☎ 01485 210262) has the perfect location facing out across the marshes. There's even a telescope available for birders. Good local ales and even more local seafood.

ALL OF A TWITTER IN CLEY

'Birdwatching Mecca' might seem a bit of a cliché but **Cley-next-the-Sea** really is the best place in Britain to find rare birds. The Cley Marshes reserve has been looked after by the **Norfolk Wildlife Trust** since 1926 making it the oldest nature reserve in the country. Part of the reason for its impressive range of recorded species is its near-perfect geographical location as a staging ground for migrants and blown-off-course vagrants; a **wide range of natural habitat** also helps enormously. The fact that Cley is so well-watched that any rare arrival is unlikely to slip beneath the birding radar is perhaps another factor to bear in mind. Curiously, Cley has not actually been 'next-the-sea' since the 17th century when ambitious plans for land reclamation by Sir Henry Calthorpe went dramatically awry.

of the coast' – with its curious tiny second tower (a beacon for storm-tossed sailors some have romantically surmised). Then it's **Morston**, barely a village more just a muddy creek with seal trip boats advertising their wares. A schoolgirl gets on here and without so much as a glance out of the window texts her mates as we slip through pebble-built **Stiffkey** (see box on page 131), a curious place that for long dry decades languished without a pub despite no shortage of thirsty villagers. Thankfully, there is a pub here these days – and a handy campsite – an unpretentious base for iodine-charged walks within sniffing distance of the sea.

The girl gets off in Wells, hardly looking up from her phone, as do a few local pensioners who have come here for the shops. After Morston, Cley and Stiffkey, **Wells-next-the-Sea** seems a veritable metropolis.

BUSSING THROUGH THE BURNHAMS

We leave the main coast road for a little tour around Wells, passing in front of the harbour with its granary (now holiday flats), chippie and amusement arcade – the latter a minor concession to the summer holiday trade. A gaggle of enthusiastic dads and kids suspend lines from the harbour wall angling for crabs. For fun not for food, of course – the real industry here was always whelks.

After passing the imposing gates to Holkham estate, we enter the realm of 'the Burnhams', first Burnham Overy Staithe, a haven for sailors, then a turn inland to the pristine Georgian village of **Burnham Market** or 'Chelsea on Sea' as local wags have it. A cluster of tidy allotments line the road up to the village: a breath of workaday normality in the rarefied metropolitan atmosphere of this most untypical of Norfolk villages. They come as a relief, as do the hearty Norfolk accents that board the bus here, unfazed by their village being hijacked by wealthy weekenders from 'The Smoke'. Shiny German cars now seem to be the default here, so a traverse of the village by bus is rewarded by just a hint of smugness.

Leaving Burnham Market behind, we are soon back on the coast road once more. Two more Burnhams follow in quick succession – Burnham Norton, barely a hamlet, with a round tower church but no other facilities, and then Burnham Deepdale.

Burnham Deepdale is home to **Deepdale Camping**, a delightfully green enterprise where it is even possible to stay in a

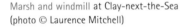

Marsh and windmill at Clay-next-the-Sea
(photo © Laurence Mitchell)

tipi or even a yurt if that is your heart's desire. The camp reception doubles as a helpful information centre, well-stocked with books, maps and goodwill.

Brancaster Staithe comes next, another charming flinty village much loved by weekend sailors that has a small staithe (quay) with a row of attractive 17th-century cottages flanking its entrance. There's a breezy golf course too, right next to the dunes. The bus stops right outside the Jolly Sailors on the main coast road but it is only a short walk from here down to the White Horse where you can gaze over the marshes as you sip your pint and delve into a bowl of mussels.

Brancaster Staithe morphs into Brancaster proper and we drive past the turn off to Titchwell RSPB reserve, another well-respected bird Eden, to arrive in **Thornham**. If Thornham seems a little different in character from what has come before it is probably the appearance of the houses.

Here the vernacular is suddenly transformed from flint and pebble to building with blocks of chalk – a sign of things to come along The Wash. Thornham is a handsome village and the temptation to get off here is quite strong given the proximity of two fine pubs and numerous walking possibilities. If you stay on past Holme-next-the-Sea though, you'll soon arrive at the point where the Norfolk coast abruptly ends its hitherto relentless east-west orientation.

GOING ROUND THE BEND

The sea stays pretty much out of sight until Old Hunstanton where the road makes a sharp turn at the golf course. This marks the bend in Norfolk's coast from where you can watch the sun setting out to sea across **The Wash** – a rare experience in what is primarily an east-facing county. Like Thornham, there's plenty of chalk in the buildings here, as well as carrstone, a local red limestone. Head down to **Old Hunstanton's beach** from here you'll see both in situ in the quite spectacular banded cliffs.

The newer part of Hunstanton is quite nice too, a resort of the Victorian railway age, rather like Cromer. Somehow this feels like the end of the road but the journey does not have to stop here. After a five-minute break for bus and driver to gird their loins, the Coasthopper continues south – or at least alternate services, the ones that arrive at half-past the hour, do.

BEYOND HUNSTANTON

The village of **Heacham** is next, with a stop right by the Norfolk Lavender Centre, which has a tea room and, no surprise, plenty of lavender-based souvenirs in its sweetly odorous gift shop. Then it's the final leg into **King's Lynn**, where the Coasthopper stops conveniently at the railway station before terminating at the bus station.

From here, it is just a short walk to South Quay, by far the most alluring part of the town, nicely restored and with all manner of fascinating maritime connections. ■

ABOUT THE AUTHOR | **LAURENCE MITCHELL** (www.laurencemitchell.com) is a travel writer and photographer based in Norwich, Norfolk. He is author of Bradt Travel Guides to both Serbia and Kyrgyzstan and also *Slow Norfolk & Suffolk*.

View from the Top

As you read the bus journeys in this book, you will surely notice the enthusiasm that many authors share for a British institution: the double-deck bus. The **red double-decker** is a **London icon**, as quintessentially English as the London bobby and the black cab. And although retired London double-deck buses are redeployed in cities around the globe on sightseeing tours, there are few countries where double-deckers are routinely used on regular scheduled local bus services. You will find double-deckers across Britain and, as this book reveals, they appeal to that peculiarly British affection for spying. The view from the top deck is often tantalising, affording as it does the chance to **peek down into urban gardens** from on-high or, on rural routes, to see over the hedgerows.

Beyond Britain, you will find significant numbers of double-deckers in everyday service in just two other European capitals: **Dublin** and **Berlin**. True, you'll see the occasional vehicle that has escaped from its regular habitat and found employment elsewhere. So a lone yellow double-decker of Berlin provenance works in Warsaw. Further afield, double-deckers are important in urban transport in **Istanbul, Hong Kong** and **Singapore**. But the widespread use of double-deckers on local rural bus routes is uniquely British.

The earliest double-deck omnibuses were all open top, leaving passengers who opted to travel 'outside' – as the top deck was dubbed – exposed to the elements. **Open-top double-deckers** are **still used seasonally** on a number of local bus routes in southern England. We have run across them on Wilts & Dorset route 50 from Bournemouth to Swanage, Journey 11 in this book, which also happens to be one of the few British bus routes that includes a ferry crossing. Open-top buses are also used in summer on local routes in Exmoor (see Journey 14), south Devon, parts of Cornwall, in the Brighton area and at Scarborough.

And the **triple-decker**? Well, the only one we know of is the **purple Knight Bus** in the Harry Potter stories. This is a transportation option reserved only unto wizards, so sadly you'll not encounter it on any of the journeys described in this book. NG

This handy rural service plies the **Waveney Valley** area on the Norfolk–Suffolk border, linking villages and market towns on either side of the river. It is an alternative to the more popular routes to the nearest large urban centres, Norwich and Lowestoft. Rather than stick to the main road – the frankly dull A143 – the 580 deviates to follow a slightly meandering route that goes where local people actually live. The 580 service may be aimed primarily at local shoppers and schoolchildren but it's also invaluable for anyone wanting to walk sections of the **Angles Way** that runs between Great Yarmouth and Knettishall Heath near Thetford – a fine lowland route. There's much to be said of this service for non-walking visitors to the region too: Bungay has a castle, a couple of glorious churches and some interesting old-fashioned shops while Harleston and Diss are also worth an hour or two of anyone's time.

DISTANCING DISS

Diss is a town of two halves. There's the delightful old part by the Mere, the reputedly bottomless lake in the town centre.

This is the part of town centred on the market place next to the church and museum – slow, unselfconsciously old-fashioned and quite charming. The other half could be anywhere really – noisy, traffic blighted with a preponderance of bungalows and builders' merchants. The bus station, which to be honest is really just a yard with a shelter and a bus timetable, sits betwixt the two. You can board the 580 here, or catch it three minutes later on the main road close to the railway station (Diss is surprisingly well-connected; being on the main Norwich–London line it's almost commuter territory).

Leaving **Diss** behind there's a quick dash across the busy A140 (a straight-as-a-die former Roman road) to be made before taking the turn off for Scole. Before the re-routing of the main Norwich–Ipswich road years ago, **Scole** was an important way station on what would have been the original Norwich to London coach route. The splendid Scole Inn still stands as testament to this: a huge 17th-century coaching inn that since the demise of passing trade has had to reinvent itself as a posh function centre.

I have fond memories of coming here in the late 1970s when I was a south Norfolk resident. There were regular gigs in the barn out the back that featured local bands like the Global Village Trucking Company. Of course, this was back in the days when we used to knit our own muesli and there was definitely something of a Waveney Valley 'scene'. I like to think something of that spirit lives on in the area. If, as well as a vague counter-cultural atmosphere, there's also an ancient feel to the landscape around Scole, it's genuine enough as the field patterns around here have been shown to be pre-Roman in origin.

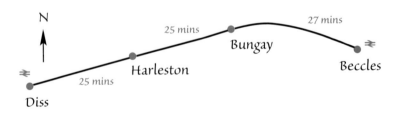

After Scole we follow the main A143 for a short while before dropping down into **Brockdish** – I use 'dropping down' advisedly but, yes, it really is a proper valley, with gently sloping fields and a lazy river at the bottom. Brockdish has a pub, The Greyhound, and a curious Victorian Methodist chapel opposite. There's no shop but oddly enough there is a bric-a-brac place on the main street that has brass candlesticks, paintings of dogs, and souvenir biscuit tins gracing its window – its opening hours are uncertain.

BUNGAY BECKONS

We continue along the High Road, which is actually the low road, to Needham and then on into **Harleston**, a quiet Georgian market town. It is an unaffected sort of place that still has proper hardware stores with men in brown coats serving behind the counter. You might wonder why a place of this size appears to have no medieval church, the reason being that it's not here but in Redenhall, part of the same parish and our next port of call.

After Redenhall, Wortwell and Earsham, we cross a meander of the Waveney to enter the county of Suffolk and drive into **Bungay**. The town's Buttercross – a hexagonal pergola with Justice and her scales atop its dome – is about as close as it gets to a nerve centre in this market town. But Bungay is the sort of place that quietly punches above its weight – it's got a ruined castle,

---

ART AND EATING

Harleston lies pretty much halfway along this route and makes for a convenient place to have a break. The **Gallery & Studio Café** (3 Old Market Place, Harleston; ☎ 01379 855366; open 10.00–17.00 Mon–Sat, 10.00–14.00 Sun) is an independent gallery that exhibits the work of local artists and is also central to the annual **Harleston & Waveney Art Trail** (www.hwat.org.uk). There's also the excellent **Gurney's Bistro** on the ground floor that has great lunches and probably the best coffee in town.

two churches, some fine pubs and even a theatre. Arriving from the villages to the west you can be pretty sure that most of the passengers will decamp here, as teenagers get off to meet up with school chums and pensioners and housewives go shopping or catch up with friends over coffee.

Bungay may well be the 'fine old town' that it likes to portray itself as but it is pretty eccentric too. Ask any one here about **Black Shuck** or the demise of the 'chicken roundabout' and they'll keep you talking for hours. Alternatively, have a look inside the deconsecrated St Mary's by the Buttercross to learn the fearful tale of the legendary black dog.

Back into Norfolk

Once across the bridge from Bungay we are back in Norfolk once more. Ditchingham is distinguished by its enormous, now largely redundant, mill building while Broome is mostly identikit bungalows. Crossing the main Great Yarmouth road at Ellingham we reach Geldeston.

The bus stops at The Wherry, a pub named after the clinker-built barges that used to ply the River Waveney between Lowestoft and Bungay. Getting off here you could elect to walk a mile south across the marshes to reach **Geldeston Locks Inn**, a riverside pub that is a local institution with folk nights, live music and regular beer festivals. Unusually for a pub, although there is easy access by boat or foot, it is located half a mile from the nearest road. Geldeston Locks also marks the point that is the limit of

SUFFOLK BY BUS

Beccles, end point of Journey 27, is a very good base for onward explorations through Suffolk by bus. One excellent journey is to head south from Beccles to **Halesworth** on the 521 (five buses per day, Mon–Sat only, operated by Anglian Bus). From Halesworth, there are good connections to both **Southwold** and **Aldeburgh**.

ST MICHAEL'S CHURCH, BECCLES

The obvious question to ask is why does this **perpendicular Gothic 14th-century church** have a detached bell tower? It does not even seem to be at the right end of the church as the tower is to the southeast rather than the usual west. The answer is simple: if the tower had been built where it ought to be it would be close to the edge of a river cliff – hardly ideal. The near 100ft tower has a clock on all sides but the west one. Local wisdom suggests that the possible reason for this is that Suffolk people are reluctant to give the time of day to their neighbours across the river in Norfolk. Thankfully, tribalism such as this does not seem to have much impact on everyday life in the **Waveney Valley**.

navigation on the River Waveney these days. West of here, you need a canoe.

THE BRIGHT LIGHTS OF BECCLES

Gillingham is next (that's a hard 'g', not like Gillingham in Kent), then it's across the river again and back into Suffolk. Beccles immediately comes into view – the closest thing to a metropolis in this quiet corner of East Anglia. **Beccles** is a town in which the river has always played a significant role; it was an important river port even in Saxon times and until a century or so ago there was a thriving wherry trade in the town. Pleasure boating still provides important revenue. And there is another boating connection: Nelson's parents were married in **St Michael's Church** in the town centre in 1749. The church had only eight bells in those days compared to the ten it has now but no doubt they rang out loud and clear for the happy couple. ■

ABOUT THE AUTHOR | **LAURENCE MITCHELL** (www.laurencemitchell.com) is a travel writer and photographer living in Norwich. His book *Slow Norfolk and Suffolk* was published by Bradt Travel Guides in 2010.

The Road to Skegness

Laurence Mitchell

28 Lincoln

Service Interconnect 6 | Journey time 1hr 45mins

OS Landranger 121, 122. Hourly Mon–Sat.
Five journeys on Sun. Operator: Stagecoach.

Skegness

This double-decker bus route is a lifeline for Lincoln city folk in need of a day out at the seaside. The journey makes a few interesting detours away from the main A138, and with hourly buses and a good-value day ticket available it makes sense to stop off for an hour or two along the way. Walkers might be interested in hiking a section of the **Viking Way** from Horncastle for example. Spilsby, closer to Skegness, is another good place to break the journey. Skegness, often dubbed 'Nottingham on Sea' in the days before cheap package holidays, still gets plenty of East Midlands holiday trade despite the overall demise of domestic tourism. As the old British Rail holiday posters used to say somewhat euphemistically: 'Skegness is so bracing' – it is, so take something windproof. **Lincoln** itself is well worth a look round before you leave so don't just take the bus out immediately – linger and explore awhile.

Leaving Lincoln

Lincoln bus station is an unprepossessing sort of place: a concrete bunker, noisy with thrumming engines and smelling of chip fat,

LINCOLN CATHEDRAL

For two-and-a-half centuries Lincoln Cathedral was reputedly the **world's tallest building**. This record for loftiness ended in 1549 when its central spire collapsed never to be replaced. In terms of ground area it is still the third largest cathedral in Britain and has twice doubled as Westminster Abbey in films: in *The Da Vinci Code* (2006) and *The Young Victoria* (2009).

that has all the charm of an underground car park. Fortunately the city's sights are within an easy walk. Turning left out of the bus station the pedestrianised **High Street** is just a couple of minutes away. Turn right here and you soon reach a narrow street called Steep Hill, which is precisely that. Lincoln is a surprisingly hilly place for somewhere so close to The Fens. Lining **Steep Hill** are cosy cafés and tea rooms and plenty of quirky shops – a bit like York but less touristy. A short stiff climb brings you to the splendidly **Gothic Lincoln Cathedral** (see box above) that looms centre-stage at the highest point in town.

At the bus station I tell the driver that I want to stop off in Horncastle and continue on to Skegness later. Which ticket should I buy? He squints momentarily to mentally calculate the best deal. 'You want to get yourself a Day Out ticket, mate. That's a bit cheaper than the two tickets together and you

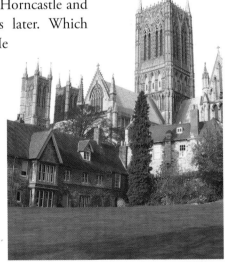

Lincoln Cathedral
(photo © Markwr / DT)

can use it all day.' No contest then. My bus companions are an amiable mix of pensioners and teenagers on their way to their home villages, plus a young tattooed couple with a baby on their way to Skegness for a day out on the seafront.

The bus climbs up through the city to give us a splendid view of the cathedral to the left before passing through a residential suburban quarter. Then it's past the foreboding high walls of **Lincoln Prison** before we traverse an industrial estate that seems to be a car showroom theme park. Leaving the city behind we head east across a low plateau of corn prairie and eye-searing yellow rape. Sudbroke, the first village, is a well-heeled dormitory village spread out along the A138, as is Langworth, another linear village straddling the road. **Wragby**, which comes next, seems to consist mostly of new estates but at least has a centre to it that boasts a couple of pubs and the ubiquitous Chinese take-away.

Beyond Wragby the landscape becomes gently undulating and, approaching Baumber, there are the first views of the southern edge of **the Wolds**, the low hills that lie just to the north. The road seems to follow a ridge, the land dropping away to valleys on both sides with green and yellow fields creating a tapestry effect. It may not be that dramatic, but it is reassuringly pastoral and somehow quintessentially English. Compared to the flat dreary Fens not too far south from here the long descent into Horncastle seems almost vertiginous.

INTO HORNCASTLE

Horncastle life seems to flow around its market square. The bus stops here opposite a memorial to Edward Stanhope, a former town MP and Secretary of State. A few passengers get off while a lot more get on, all seemingly bound for Skegness on this warm late April day. The town has **markets** on Monday and Thursday and is old-fashioned enough for some of its shops to religiously observe half-day closing on Wednesdays. Horncastle's formerly famous horse fair has long gone and the town is better known these days for its antiques and bric-a-brac shops. It is easy to see why – there is a clutch around the market square and even more along the main Skegness road that leads out. There are several **good book shops** too and more traditional butchers than you might imagine a quiet town of 6,000 could support. Horncastle is attractive in a plain, no-nonsense sort of way. It's a twee-free zone – not so much chocolate box, more gravy-powder tin.

FOLDS OF WOLDS

From Horncastle east, the A138 undulates through swathes of ripening corn and the low rise of the Wolds becomes more pronounced to our left. We turn off for Raithby by Spilsby, a hamlet that passes us by in the time it takes to say it. Long, linear **Hundleby** comes next before we cross the main road to enter

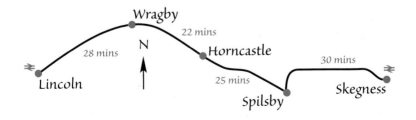

Spilsby. After passing a huge Chinese restaurant and a somewhat incongruous Palladian theatre, formerly a courthouse and jail, we arrive at Spilsby's market square. Pride of place here goes to a statue of local hero **Sir John Franklin**, sea captain and Governor of Tasmania, who was born in the town. The plinth describes Sir John as 'Discoverer of the Northwest Passage' – not strictly true but let's put that down to well-intentioned civic pride.

A few people board the bus who are obviously Skegness-based holiday-makers on day trips out – their shorts and red faces give the game away. 'Are you going to Skeg?' one of them asks the driver, evidently needing more reassurance that the bus's big 'Skegness' destination board can provide.

On to Skeg

Back on the A138, the last stretch to Skegness, the vista ahead shows no sign of the sea. We detour briefly into Partney village, where there's just a church, a pub and a bus stop. Then it's Scremby, after which we take the right turn to **Burgh Le Marsh**, a curious name of mixed linguistic parentage. On the way out there's a roadside windmill that has had a large house built around it. The residents must be the only ones in the village to have a sea view.

Heading into **Skegness** we pass a string of large **caravan parks** and the odd enclave of retirement bungalows – this stretch of coast is not dubbed 'Costa Geriatrica' for nothing. The bus terminus is right next to the railway station, where trains to Nottingham take holiday makers back to the East Midlands. It's still a bit of a walk to the seafront. On the way I pass a mobility scooter emporium right next door to a tanning studio. This, I think, gives a pretty good insight into the demographics of Skegness. ■

ABOUT THE AUTHOR

LAURENCE MITCHELL is a travel writer and photographer based in Norwich, Norfolk. He is author of the Bradt Travel Guides to Serbia, Kyrgyzstan and *Slow Norfolk & Suffolk*. Find out more about his work at www.laurencemitchell.com.

PENNINES & YORKSHIRE

This is a part of England where great conurbations rub shoulders with wild terrain. It makes for a beguiling **mix of communities and scenery**, and presents special challenges for planners keen to facilitate cheap access by public transport for city dwellers wanting to visit their local national parks. The **Peak District** really is on the doorsteps of both Sheffield and Manchester and the **Yorkshire Dales** are but a stone's throw from Leeds and Bradford. And the soft hills of the North York Moors are visible from many parts of Teesside.

In this part of England, bus operators have worked in close partnership with local Councils and the national park authorities to create seasonal services to some of England's most beguilingly beautiful uplands. The result are initiatives like Peak Connections and the seasonal Dalesbus and Moorsbus programmes.

Journey 38 includes a sample route with **Moorsbus**. The other nine routes that we present in this section are all year-round services, all bar a couple of them relatively high-frequency routes that you can sample any day of the week. We should mention a further journey, beyond those included here, that is really well worth making. We really like the Transpeak service from Nottingham to Manchester. Yes, it is a bit of a marathon for a local bus route, with the thrice daily journeys needing over three hours for the full run. But it takes in some super scenery, along the way connecting with Journeys 29, 30 and 31 in this book.

For a dose of bus nostalgia, you might like to try the summer-only 127 from Garsdale to Ripon which uses beautifully restored **vintage vehicles**. Concessionary passes are accepted on this most unusual of British bus services. ■

Hey Diddle Diddle, the Cat and the Fiddle

Ann Clark

29 **Buxton**

> Service no. 58 | Journey time 35mins
>
> OS Landranger 119, 118. Runs hourly Mon–Sat, 5 journeys on Sun.
> Operator: High Peak (Bowers).
> Connects with Journey 30 in Buxton.

Macclesfield

The spa town of Buxton isn't a big place. Small enough for folk to recognise each other. Whenever I get on a local bus, the chances are that I might well know one or more of the other passengers on board. And so friendly are Buxtonians that complete strangers are invited to join in the gossip. Virgin Trains gave a boost to the 58 when, about a dozen years ago, they had the good idea of using Macclesfield station as a gateway to the Peak District. Passengers hopped off the train at Macclesfield, transferring there on to the bus for **Buxton**, Bakewell and Chatsworth House. Nowadays, it is only on Sundays that two buses extend east beyond Buxton, and for most of the week the route is thus essentially a shuttle between Buxton and Macclesfield. It is thus one of the shortest routes in this book. Short and sweet.

Leaving Buxton

Buxton may be located at some altitude – 'the highest market town in England,' we claim – but you often have to go uphill to leave Buxton. Cyclists always moan at this fact of Buxton life. Climbing up from the bowl that shelters Buxton on the bus to

Macclesfield, the first port of call is **Burbage** where the bus makes a short diversion to drop off shoppers. Why not take the bus rather than lug heavy shopping for a mile and a half up a hill? Once clear of the last houses of Burbage, the vista opens up. I see for miles over the **moors** and feel my lungs fill with fresh air and my heart swell with the immensity of the sky.

The chocolate-coloured moors spread out on both sides of the road; to my right are ravines where in the past coal was mined for the Duke of Devonshire's limekilns. Very little remains of the tracks and

Victorian pavilion gardens in Buxton capture the grace and elegance of this Peak District spa town (photo © Stephen Meese / DT)

tunnels that carried the coal but just now and then vestiges can be picked out. Lime production is still a major industry here but hidden from view. On my left I can make out the **deep peat** that covers most of the ground. It's no longer dug for fuel but, even as recently as ten years ago, it was common to see summer turfs being stacked to dry for the upcoming winter.

Our bus driver needs to watch the road carefully as marauding sheep stray from the grazing of heather and bilberry plants to lick the salt from the road surface. Salt is spread over our winter roads to help keep them clear of snow and ice. And the canny sheep have realised that dark road surfaces warm up quickly, even in winter sunshine, and make a more appealing place to lie than rough heather or snowy moors. **Sleeping sheep** are potentially a big hazard to motorists in these parts, so perhaps it's no bad thing that the last bus on this route is off the high moors by early evening.

Over the top

Soon the **Cat and Fiddle Inn** comes into view. I have often wondered how the pub got its name. Although the road is shown on maps as the A537, we locals know it as the 'Cat and Fiddle road'. And it is certainly notorious. It was at one stage dubbed 'the most dangerous road in Britain' by local police because of the number of accidents, mostly caused by motorcyclists racing too fast around the sharp bends and steep inclines.

Beyond the Cat and Fiddle there are **fine views** across open country that I know well from many rambles. The sun glints on

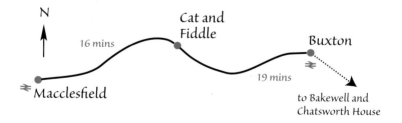

CAT AND FIDDLE INN

Set on the highest point on the A537, this is the second highest pub in England at 1690 feet. The **name is interesting**, perhaps a corruption of the French *le chat fidèle* ('the faithful cat'). Others suggest it recalls Catherine of Aragon, first wife of Henry VIII, who was often called Catherine la Fidèle. I stopped at the **Cat and Fiddle** (☎ 01298 78366) one winter day to find the publican keeping warm by shovelling ten feet of snow from his door. There was no electric power and no beer either. But the welcome was sincere and I made it back in better weather to enjoy a drink. The pub is **open daily** from 11.00, with food served from noon right through to evening (except Mon when the pub closes mid afternoon).

Lamaload Reservoir away to the northwest. The next landmark on our bus journey is Shining Tor, the culminating point of a fine sandstone ridge. Then, as we drop down slowly into Cheshire, the scenery changes. And the mood on the bus changes too. No longer are there just Buxtonians on board, for we stop here and there to pick up other passengers heading for Macclesfield. There are views of **Shutlingsloe**, a fierce spine of rock resembling more the fin of an attacking shark than a hill. But these are the last of the hills. The view ahead is dominated by the lush Cheshire plain.

One distinctive landmark, pointing skyward, is the **Jodrell Bank telescope**. It looks like a huge soup bowl angled towards the heavens. Now, as we near **Macclesfield**, in contrast to the stone houses of Buxton, I see that bricks are king. This manner in which vernacular architecture echoes the underlying geology is endlessly fascinating in England. And the bus gives one the time to take things in. ■

ABOUT THE AUTHOR | **ANN CLARK** has lived in Buxton for over 30 years and is a keen rambler and sometime paraglider pilot. A non-driver and over 60, she now uses her bus pass enthusiastically.

POTTERIES TO PEAK: THE BUXTON FLYER

Patricia Walter

30 Hanley

Service no. 118 | Journey time 65mins

OS Landranger 118, 119. Runs 4 times daily Mon–Sat, 3 journeys on Sun.
Operator: Wardle.
Connects with Journey 29 in Buxton.

Buxton

This route has some of the same flavour as the previous journey in this book, connecting as it does one of the towns along the western flank of the Pennines with the Peak District spa town of Buxton. In that last journey we rode from Buxton to the lowlands. This time we travel in the opposite direction, starting in Hanley and climbing up into the hills.

I love this journey because it takes in two of my favourite towns: historic Leek and elegant Buxton. The landscape shifts from urban to rural as the bus climbs up from the Potteries into the Peak, and the stretch from Leek to Buxton is sheer beauty. No matter how often I travel that stretch, it never fails to impress.

ESCAPE FROM HANLEY

The **Buxton Flyer** carries a variety of passengers from college students and tourists to hikers and shoppers; they are always friendly and chatty. But beware. If breaking your journey, do check the timetable carefully as there are only four buses a day.

Hanley bus station has been on the point of being rebuilt for at least a decade. Now at last the civic authorities are making a start on this long-overdue project. It is a chance to breathe new life into an urban area that really needs some tender loving care. Meanwhile, the 118 is a safe route out of **Hanley**. Although it is a long-established route, the operator has varied. Since August 2011, Wardle Transport has looked after the service.

We travel uphill, leaving the Potteries behind us, twice crossing the **Caldon Canal**, which has happily been restored. The main road is busy, but before long we are in Leek, a town that styles itself 'Queen of the Moorlands'.

Leek came into its own during the Industrial Revolution as a centre for the silk and dye trades. The arrival of a branch of the Caldon Canal certainly helped, and the efforts of James Brindley, the great canal engineer, in putting his home town on the map are recalled in the town's Brindley Mill. It is worth taking a look at this mid 18th-century corn mill even if it's closed, but you can check opening times on www.brindleymill.net. The other name intimately associated with Leek is William Morris, founder of the Arts and Crafts Movement. He visited the town frequently in the 1870s to experiment with organic dyes, textile design and manufacturing improvements.

Leek is rightly proud of its **industrial past**. But it still has a lot to offer today. It has a fine range of independent shops. Check out the boutiques in Getliffe's Yard or wander the town's markets (market days are Wed, Fri and Sat). The tourist information centre in Market Place offers an excellent town trail map. For a relaxing cuppa, try the **White Hart Tea Room** (Stockwell St; ☎ 01538 372122; open 08.30–16.30 Mon–Sat) which also offers beautifully appointed rooms, making Leek the obvious choice if you wish to make an overnight stop.

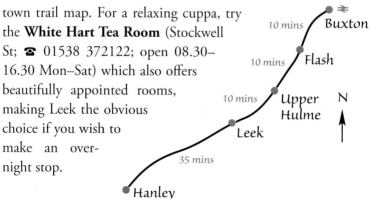

ACROSS THE HILLS

As the bus leaves Leek look for the turning by the Moss Rose pub. This is an old route to Buxton and it winds up to Morridge where highwaymen would wait to ambush stagecoaches. But no-one wants to ambush the Buxton Flyer, which speeds along the modern highway at a cracking pace. As we cross **Blackshaw Moor** there are wonderful views of the Roaches, Hen Cloud (Cloud is the local name for a high hill) and Ramshaw Rocks. These gritstone outcrops, popular with local rock climbers, are great for walking. The road continues to climb steeply towards **Flash** which at 1,518ft is England's highest village. Once a popular haunt for robbers it was the scene of illegal bare-knuckle boxing (called prizefighting) and counterfeit money production. So this modest Staffordshire village is immortalised in the phrase 'flash money'.

Beyond Flash, the Buxton Flyer starts its long descent down Axe Edge, giving the best panorama of the journey. You can see several of the White Peak's limestone tops, and of course the Derbyshire town of **Buxton** where our journey ends. You can connect in Market Place to the waiting 218 bus to Sheffield (run by TM Travel) or return west on Journey 29 in this book. ∎

| ABOUT THE AUTHOR | **PATRICIA WALTER** fell in love with the Peak District many years ago and has enjoyed living in Leek for the past 10 years. |

From Ghost Trains to Glasshouses

Wendy Green

31 Matlock

Service nos. 214 (Mon–Sat) or 215 (Sun) | Journey time 70 to 95mins

OS Landranger 119, 110, 111. Runs hourly Mon–Sat,
6 journeys on Sun. Operator: TM Travel.

Sheffield

The child in the seat behind me is very excited. 'Will we see the train today?' she asks. We have just left **Matlock** and the 214 to Sheffield is racketing along the A6 parallel to the railway embankment only a few feet above the flood plain of the River Derwent. The little girl will be disappointed. There is not even a hint of steam. During the winter the Peak Rail trains only run at weekends and for special events such as Christmas and Hallowe'en. All we catch is a glimpse of the dozens of trucks, carriages, engines and other railway memorabilia in the sidings just before Rowsley.

We turn off the main road near **Peak Village**, which is anything but a village. It is in fact a big retail park – 'a unique shopping experience and great family day out' runs the blurb. We negotiate the narrow twisting lanes by Beeley without hazard and round the sharp bend before the **hump-backed bridge** at the beginning of Chatsworth Park.

'How can this big bus get over that bridge?' enquires the child. I have often wondered the same myself. The occasional grinding sound and the gouges in the road surface suggest that the buses don't always escape unscathed from this encounter with one of the Peak District's famously challenging bridges. But today, many on board focus not on the hazards facing the driver but on the foaming water that tumbles over a nearby weir. There are several herds of fallow deer grazing the **beautiful parkland** landscaped by Capability Brown but the child has spotted something even more special: 'Daddy, look at the reindeer.' 'Red deer,' her father corrects.

SEVENTEEN STAGS AND THE EMPEROR FOUNTAIN

Set against the backdrop of **Chatsworth House** and the Emperor Fountain (which spurts high above the trees) a line of 17 magnificent stags is heading in stately procession towards the road. The driver slows. He is enjoying the sight as much as his passengers. Four stags decide to cross the road. The rest hesitate so the driver takes the moment, a little reluctantly perhaps, and we continue to the main entrance to Chatsworth. Folk say 'cheers' to the driver as they leave the bus to enjoy a day at one of Britain's most popular stately homes. Find out more about Chatsworth (including opening hours and prices) at www.chatsworth.org.

There are no film crews in evidence today but in the four years we have lived in Derbyshire there have been units **filming** everything from period dramas to horror movies here. So you will see Chatsworth on the big screen in films featuring aristocrats (such as the 2008 movie *The Duchess*) or werewolves (for example the 2010 film *The Wolfman*).

Over the brow of a hill a real dowager duchess may occasionally be glimpsed in the village of Edensor. Those in the

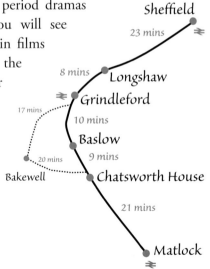

The dotted line on the map (right) shows the Sunday variant of this journey via Bakewell.

know pronounce the name just as the locals do: Ensor. It is the nicest of the Chatsworth estate villages and boasts an improbably grand church for such a small community.

We grumble over the cattle grid, and head north towards **Baslow**. Sunday buses on this route (always numbered 215) make a little detour here, heading west to serve the town of Bakewell in the Wye Valley. But the regular weekday services stick resolutely to the Derwent Valley.

Baslow is the sort of place that devotees of the Peak District inevitably pass through often. It is the meeting point of four main roads and a good spot to break your journey (see box above).

Our bus circles the green at Nether End at one end of Baslow then tracks back past the church, beautifully situated on the bank of the **River Derwent**, its churchyard full of stately elms and yews. Take a look at the clock face where, instead of the regular numbers, letters spell out the name Victoria and the date 1897. Homage to an English queen, to be sure, but it does make telling the time a little difficult.

GRITSTONE, WOODLANDS AND MORE

The road twists along the river towards Calver overlooked by a range of gritstone escarpments to the east: Baslow Edge, Curbar

Edge, Froggatt Edge. We are now within commuting distance of Sheffield and the handful of walkers, tourists, and shoppers are supplemented by students who have seen the magnificent scenery many times before and are busy doing last minute revision.

We cross the Derwent one last time and begin to climb. Here is the turning for **Grindleford station**, good not just for trains but for its decidedly quirky **café** (☎ 01433 63101), renowned for its impressive signs berating customers. These admonishments are cheerfully disregarded by the hungry ramblers, bikers and trainspotters tucking into fry-ups and steaming mugs of tea.

Now comes a very fine stretch as we ride up **Padley Gorge** where waterfalls plunge through ancient oak woodland scattered with gritstone boulders, millstones and troughs left over from the industrial era. This is one of my favourite parts of the journey. It is as magical as Narnia on winter days when the trees are covered with frost or snow.

We emerge from the gorge into open moorland with a vista topped by the gritstone crag of Higger Tor and Carl Wark, an **ancient hill fort**. The family sitting behind me press the bell for the Longshaw Estate stop, the father taking care to ensure that his daughter is warmly wrapped. A wise precaution as this area catches the wind that comes whisking over 'the tops'. One bus driver had a ready answer for the passenger who complained 'it's a bit nippy up here.' 'It's worth it though,' retorted the driver. And he is right. This is a lovely sweep of country. A commemorative plaque records how the Peak District became Britain's **first national park** in 1951. Longshaw Estate is now managed by the National Trust. A visitor centre, in a former shooting lodge, supplies maps and information, instructing visitors on how to identify the rare ants that are found here. There is a tea room (☎ 01433 637904) and across the road the 18th-century **Fox House Inn** (☎ 01433 630374) staves hungry appetites with a selection of meals from light bites to Jamaican stew and roast guineafowl.

A final haul uphill, over the border into Yorkshire, and the view stretches eastwards to Sheffield – a city most famous for its

SHEFFIELD BOTANICAL GARDENS

The gardens are open daily free of charge (☎ 0114 268 6001; www.sbg.org.uk). The lower entrance in **Thompson Road** is only a few yards from the bus stop. Sheffield has a hilly centre, and the garden layout makes the most of the slopes. There are **first-class glasshouses** (some recently refurbished) , herbaceous borders, rock and water gardens, prairie areas and a dozen other habitats. And it is not just a place for flora. There is **wildlife** too. On one visit I was sitting in a woodland area eating a sandwich when a rustling of leaves beneath the bench revealed a Russian hamster searching for titbits, closely followed by a guinea pig emerging from under a rhododendron bush.

cutlery industry. A sign tells us it is only eight miles to the centre of town as the road curves downhill past Sheffield Tigers RUFC to the upmarket suburbs of Whirlow and Ecclesall. On down by boutiques and bistros, florists and fish shops to the roundabout at Hunters Bar and student territory. Another couple of stops and I have reached my usual destination – **Sheffield Botanical Gardens** (see box above).

In truth, I rarely make it to the end of the route, for the Botanical Gardens offer a great distraction. But the bus runs on into town, eventually terminating at **Sheffield Interchange** – which is, just as the name implies, a temple of multimodal transport provision. Once merely humble Pond Street Bus Station, the Interchange has become the focal point of Sheffield transport, with local buses and long-distance coaches converging on this point. The train station and tram stops are just a short walk away. All perfect, one might think, but the Interchange is hardly conveniently placed for the city centre. ∎

ABOUT THE AUTHOR | **WENDY GREEN** is a retired teacher who now lives in Derbyshire.

Stuart Vallantine

Hyde

Service no. 343 | Journey time 55 to 70mins

OS Landranger 109. Runs hourly every day. Operators: Speedwell Bus (Mon–Fri daytime), JPT (Sat daytime) or First (Mon–Sat evenings & all day Sun). Connects with Journey 33 in Mossley and Oldham.

Oldham

So what do we make of a bus service that is shared by three operators, each taking turns to run the service at different times of the week? Is it perhaps a route that offers such rich pickings that the bounty must be shared? Or is it a case of three operators having had their corporate arms twisted to fulfil a public service to the citizens of Greater Manchester? Probably more the former than the latter for the 343 bus, which meanders through unsung territory from Tameside to Oldham, is often well-filled with passengers.

It is a route that comes with a nice dose of local history. In 1899, life in the **Tame Valley** really looked up when the Stalybridge, Hyde, Mossley and Dukinfield Tramways and Electricity Board was formed to provide tramway services and electricity to the four communities identified in the board's cumbersome title. By 1904, the company's trams linked the four towns, later to be replaced by buses, numbered 4 or 4A. That changed to 343 in 1973, and seven years later the route was extended from Mossley over the hill to Oldham. And, apart from a little tinkering with the route here and there, the basic route from Hyde to Oldham has stayed the same for over 30 years.

I have had a lifelong interest in buses. There are grander routes, there are quirkier routes, but I have always had a soft spot for the 343 for its happy mix of industrial heritage and moorland scenery.

FROM COTTON KINGS TO CHARTISTS

Hyde has seen better days. Two hundred years ago, the town had over three dozen working cotton mills. Today there is just one. Cotton was the mainstay of the Hyde economy, and the 343 bus, on leaving Hyde, runs north past the old **Ashton Brothers Mill**. This part of Hyde rejoices in the name Flowery Field, though in truth the place is not quite so delicately rural as the name might imply. But there are parks aplenty, including Hyde Park (take note, Londoners!). It was originally the grounds of Newton Lodge where the Ashton family lived, conveniently close to their mill. Flowery Field blends into Dukinfield, a town whose reputation relied on coal, cotton and Chartism. Yes, there's always been a bit of revolutionary fervour hereabouts.

Now the bus heads more purposefully towards **Stalybridge**, a little place that deserves a look (see box). North from Stalybridge, our route to Mossley is defined by the Tame Valley, and there are frequent views of the river and the **Huddersfield Narrow**

STALYBRIDGE

Stalybridge has more to offer than tater pie and tripe. This town lay at the very heart of the **Industrial Revolution** in Lancashire and elements of the mill and canal landscapes still remain. These are forgotten, dusty spots, full of memories. Stay on the bus beyond the town centre for **Stalybridge Country Park**, where you can wander up the Brushes Valley, past a series of reservoirs on to open Pennine moorland. Back in the middle of Stalybridge, a little gem is the buffet on Platform 1 of the town's railway station. It is a great place just to relax over a beer. It is open daily from 11.00 (noon on Sun).

Canal. It is not for nothing that the latter waterway, which reopened for navigation ten years ago, is called 'narrow'. The hills close in, and one has a real sense of embracing the Pennines. But the 343 is a fickle creature and, having stopped at **Mossley**, our bus now changes direction and heads west to Oldham. We skirt Quick Edge and before long we are entering the heart of Oldham. This journey from Hyde to Oldham is hardly demanding. But it's fun, and it gives some nice insights into the not-quite-urban, not-quite-rural landscapes in a region where industry rubs shoulders with the **Pennine foothills**.

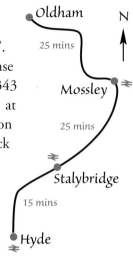

Not yet had enough? Then you can change at Oldham on to the next journey in this book and continue exploring Greater Manchester. But, before you do, take a look at **Gallery Oldham** (☎ 0161 7704653; www.galleryoldham.org.uk; open 10.00–17.00 Mon–Sat, Sun till 16.00). 'A space for people and ideas,' claims the gallery publicity, and it's true. You'll find exhibitions – often with some provocative contemporary art on display – and a café that's good for coffee, snacks and light lunches. If you prefer your refreshments without such arty overtones, then just head to the **Ashton Arms** in Clegg Street where they pull a good pint and serve decent pub food (☎ 0161 7858126; open daily, but hot food served Mon–Fri lunchtimes only). It is a simple, un-fussy place. But don't underestimate the Ashton Arms. It has a fine reputation for its range of real ales. And yes, there's the same name again. The Ashton family. Remember them? We passed the Ashton Brothers Mill as we left Hyde at the start of the route. ∎

ABOUT THE AUTHOR | **STUART VALLANTINE** began his love affair with buses on the 343 in 1984. Nearly thirty years on, he still hasn't lost the habit of sitting on the front seat of the top deck.

In the Shadow of
The Moors

Martin Clark

Oldham

Service no. 350 | Journey time 60 to 80mins

OS Landranger 109. Runs every 30 mins (hourly evenings and Sun).
Operator: First.
Connects with Journey 32 in Oldham and Mossley.

Ashton-under-Lyne

A trip by bus from Oldham to Ashton-under-Lyne may not at first sound very appealing. These two former **Lancashire mill towns**, on the eastern edge of Greater Manchester, are just four miles apart and are linked by a straight road and the frequent 409 bus service. However, our journey will be on the 350 bus route, which provides a longer and more scenic alternative between the two towns by way of villages that lie high on the flanks of the Pennines. Quite a detour, but it's worth the ride.

There are some similarities between this route and the preceding journey in this book, proof perhaps that folk who know this area well concur that the Pennines are like a magnet, always inviting residents of the cotton towns to head east into the hills. And Oldham is a cotton town par excellence. Did you know that in its heyday more cotton was spun in Oldham than in any other town in the world?

THROUGH MUMPS TO DELPH

We head out of **Oldham** through Mumps. Now there's an odd name for you! Locals say it comes from an old dialect word, mumper, meaning 'beggar'. This road is the A62, once the most important road over the Pennines (linking Manchester with Leeds). Nowadays it is much reduced in status, as heavy trucks bound for Yorkshire stick to the nearby motorway. The road climbs slowly to enter the **Saddleworth area**, a cluster of villages that specialised in the wool trade (see box opposite).

The houses gradually thin out and we find green fields on both sides as we reach Scouthead, the highest point on the route at almost 1,000ft above sea level. The bus begins the descent to Delph and we are treated to wide views across the Saddleworth villages to the high Pennine moorland beyond. As the road snakes around the steep hillside, the consistent gradient is testimony to the skills of the builders of this 1790 turnpike road.

At the foot of the hill, we turn off into the pretty village of **Delph**. This is brass-band country and Delph even featured in the film *Brassed Off*. We get a good look at Delph on this route, as the bus turns around and comes back through the village. In order to turn, the bus squeezes up Lodge Lane, probably the narrowest bus route in Greater Manchester.

The bus now takes us along the valley bottom, passing the edge of the village of Dobcross to Brownhill Bridge, where we cross the Huddersfield Narrow Canal. The bus then turns south to take us through the bustling village of **Uppermill**, an excellent place to break the journey.

Heading south we leave Saddleworth and enter the Pennine town of **Mossley**, a place that once had over 40 mills. Crossing the Tame Valley, we climb up towards a nick in the hills ahead before starting the long descent to Ashton. For much of this route, our eyes have been trained on the Pennines to the east. But now, we

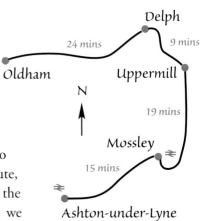

SADDLEWORTH

Saddleworth is a lovely **geographical oddity**, a fragment of land that was long a part of Yorkshire on the west side of the Pennines. It was the reorganisation of local government in England in 1974 that led to Saddleworth becoming part of Greater Manchester – a bureaucratic shift in loyalties that certainly ruffled a few feathers in an area that still values its social and cultural links with the Yorkshire communities that lie just over the hills. Saddleworth is a scatter of a dozen or more villages (none of which is actually called Saddleworth).

All these villages are worth a look but, if you choose just one to break this journey, make it **Uppermill**, which has a super location on a canal, plentiful pubs and cafés, and is home to the **Saddleworth Museum and Art Gallery** (☎ 01457 874093; www.saddleworthmuseum.co.uk; open 10.00–16.00 Mon–Sat, 12.00–16.00 Sun, shorter winter opening hours). **Boat trips** start at the museum and there is an excellent canal-side walk to Brownhill.

look west across Manchester to the Cheshire Plain. On a clear day we may see Fiddlers Ferry Power Station, the Jodrell Bank telescope and the Welsh hills.

After a short detour into the grounds of Tameside Hospital, we arrive in **Ashton-under-Lyne**, an old market town, but now part of the huge Manchester conurbation, so no longer a municipality in its own right. But Ashton still has a spirit of its own. Take a look at the improbably gracious town hall, stripped nowadays of any civic authority, but home to **Setantii**, a museum about the history and peoples of the Tame Valley (☎ 0161 3422812; www.tameside.gov.uk/setantii, open 10.00–16.00 Mon–Fri, 10.00–13.00 Sat). It is a good way of finding out a little more about the area through which you have travelled in following Journeys 32 and 33 in this book. ∎

ABOUT THE AUTHOR

MARTIN CLARK is a retired primary school teacher. Three of the houses in which he has lived have been situated on this bus route. So the 350 has been part of his life and he never tires of the variety offered by the journey.

TRAMS AND TROLLEYBUSES

Journey 32 from Hyde to Oldham (see page 156) reminded us that some British bus routes today still follow **long-forgotten tram lines**. The bus eclipsed the tram in the years after World War II. Although the cable tramway at Llandudno survived, **Blackpool** is the sole municipality that has shown uninterrupted loyalty to its trams. The **Seaton Tramway**, a tourist attraction mentioned on page 58, is newer – it opened only 40 years ago.

Yet trams are enjoying an **English renaissance** with new networks developed in recent years in Nottingham, Sheffield and Manchester. Even within Greater London, there are now trams again in the shape of **Croydon Tramlink**. The West Midlands has a single tram route that links Wolverhampton with Birmingham.

Trams are returning to grace in Scotland too, with an **Edinburgh network** under construction. The first line is expected to open in 2014. Wales, which in 1807 introduced the world's very first public tram service – horse-drawn in those days – nowadays has no urban tram networks. The **Great Orme Tramway** at Llandudno is the Principality's sole homage to a form of transport that has deep Welsh roots.

Britain's ambiguous relationship with trams reflects a broader issue in the history of urban road transport in Britain. Those of a generous disposition may be inclined to read that history as a creative web of innovation as municipal authorities experimented with successive modes of transport. More critical commentators will see it as a story of vacillation, reflecting the lack of purpose and endemic amateurism that has characterised the country's whole engagement with transport issues for 150 years or more. **Sir Benjamin Hall** – the civil engineer, MP and Commissioner of Works, a man most noted for presiding over the installation of Big Ben at the Palace of Westminster in 1858 – fiercely opposed trams in London, worrying that tram lines might impede the passage of his own horse and carriage. Almost a century later, it was a generation of first-time car owners who led the rallying cries for trams to be banned from Britain's streets.

The **trolleybus** first made its debut on Britain's streets in 1911, much later than the tram. The centenary of its birth went almost entirely unnoticed. The trolleybus outlived the great municipal tram networks. But not for long. The last surviving trolleybuses ran in **Bradford** in 1972. NG

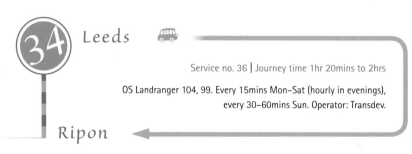

Pearl Lewis

34 Leeds

Service no. 36 | Journey time 1hr 20mins to 2hrs

OS Landranger 104, 99. Every 15mins Mon–Sat (hourly in evenings), every 30–60mins Sun. Operator: Transdev.

Ripon

The city bus station in **Leeds** is the jumping off point for a huge variety of Yorkshire excursions, and if I have a spare day there is a good chance I'll be there setting off to explore my home county. The choice is daunting. There is a raft of Coastliner services for trips to Whitby, Scarborough and Bridlington; the X84 that heads northwest to Ilkley and Skipton; and then my firm favourite, the 36 double-decker to Ripon.

Leather seats come as standard on the top deck. With tinted windows and sensitive lighting, these vehicles have an unusually upmarket feel for a regular British bus. They offer a dash of luxury for a relaxing run to the heart of North Yorkshire. Chatter fills the air on the top deck as we cruise out through Leed's northern suburbs, cross the ring road, and reach open country. Approaching **Harewood**, I spot a pair of red kites circling in the sky. It's only a dozen years since the first red kites were introduced to the Harewood estate, but they have bred successfully and now make a welcome addition to the Yorkshire skies.

There is great little walk if you alight just before Harewood. You can roam through landscaped parkland, see the television set for *Emmerdale*, and skirt a lake to return to Harewood village, where the Harewood Arms is a good spot for a drink. **Harewood House** (www.harewood.org) is of course one of England's most distinguished country houses, a showcase for interiors by Robert Adam and furniture by Thomas Chippendale (who was a local lad). The surrounding parkland was landscaped by Capability Brown.

Over the Wharfe

Back on the bus, it is interesting how dramatically the scenery changes as we leave Harewood village. The main road follows the estate wall down a steep slope, and through the trees there opens out a splendid view of the **River Wharfe** below. There is something so very engaging about the beautiful stone bridge that spans the river. I like this spot. Sometimes I have seen red or fallow deer here, on other trips a fox or a heron. The bus creeps slowly over the bridge, and on through fields of strawberries and soft fruits towards Harrogate. This is 'pick-your-own' country so, at the right season, families carrying luscious baskets of fruit often join the bus.

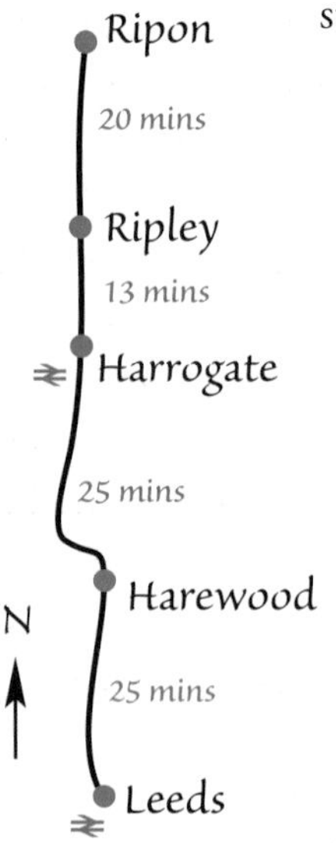

Ripon
20 mins
Ripley
13 mins
Harrogate
25 mins
Harewood
N
25 mins
Leeds

Harrogate, ever restrained and elegant, is a Yorkshire gem. As the bus rolls into town, the Stray spreads out on both sides. It is particularly beautiful in spring with its rows of pink cherry-blossom trees and a rich carpet of crocuses. The frequency of buses on the route makes it easy to break your journey. So stay a while in Harrogate. The West Park United Reformed Church on the Stray has a convenient coffee shop (open Tue & Thu mornings and all day Sat) or make for **Bettys tea room** for more elaborate Harrogate fare. With its distinctive wrought-iron arcade, Bettys (☎ 01423 814070; open daily 09.00–21.00) is a Harrogate

RIPLEY

Rebuilt in the 1830s by the Ingilby family, Ripley is decidedly unusual: a village with buildings styled in a manner common in eastern France but set in the heart of Yorkshire. The **Ingilby family** have lived in **Ripley Castle** for 700 years and still do. Guided tours (☎ 01423 770152) give the chance to see six rooms inside the castle. Ripley is a good place for summer walks. You can wander through the deer park, returning to the village for refreshments. The tea rooms at the castle offer good snacks, or for something more substantial try the **Boars Head Hotel** (☎ 01423 771888). You can find out much more about this estate village on www.ripleycastle.co.uk. It is worth taking time to see the village stocks and the old church, its wall pockmarked by bullet holes – said to have been made by Cromwell's soldiers as they shot at Royalist prisoners.

institution, their fabulous cakes expanding local waistlines for over 90 years. Don't worry if there's a queue when you reach Bettys. It moves quickly, and before long you'll be inside eyeing up the high-calorie choices on offer.

Nearby, the **Royal Pump Room Museum** (☎ 01423 556188; open 10.30–17.00 Mon–Sat, 14.00–17.00 Sun, closes 1hr earlier in winter) has the strongest sulphur well in Europe and tours conclude with a glass of the very smelly water. But now we should rejoin the 36 bus. The route continues north, and crosses another of the rivers that flow down from the Dales. This one is called the River Nidd. Then we turn off through **Ripley** village. The chances are you already knew of Harewood and Harrogate. But Ripley? Probably not. It really is the hidden treasure on this journey. You can read more about it in the box above. From Ripley it is just 20 minutes on the bus into the centre of **Ripon**, a beautiful town with a fine cathedral, and a fitting end to one of Yorkshire's best bus journeys. ∎

ABOUT THE AUTHOR | **PEARL LEWIS** is retired. She records details of her bus journeys in monthly newsletters which she sends to friends and family all over the UK.

A WENSLEYDALE
DOUBLE DELIGHT

Richard Kingsbury

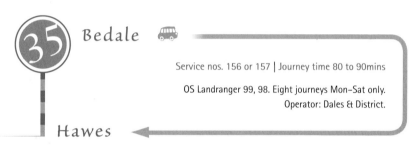

35 Bedale

Service nos. 156 or 157 | Journey time 80 to 90mins

OS Landranger 99, 98. Eight journeys Mon–Sat only.
Operator: Dales & District.

Hawes

Wensleydale lies at the heart of the **Yorkshire Dales National Park**. It is a generous, green, glacial valley, enclosed by Addleborough and Wether Fell. And this gentle sweep of territory is best explored on a magical bus route which, with Yorkshire cunning, operates under two numbers. Dales & District's 156 and 157 services link Bedale and Hawes, offering **magnificent views** from each side of the dale.

Diverting from the main A684, the 156 takes in villages on the south side while the 157 covers the dale's northern hamlets. Picture the legendary Rod of Aaron, in this case the main road, with its entwined serpent: though there is nothing venomous about these Dales & District **scenic bus routes**. Go up the dale one side, come down the other.

Although buses on these routes do not run on Sundays, there is a limited Sunday service up the dale from April till October. It is branded the **Wensleydale Flyer**, running as service number 856, and gives a useful link from the railway station at Northallerton to Hawes. But it sticks in the main to the A684. The Wensleydale Flyer is fast, unadventurous, the Rod of Aaron option, and not a patch on its weekday equivalents.

Up-valley with the 157

In terms of maximising the good views, I recommend going from **Bedale** to Hawes on the 157 and returning with a 156 bus service. And that's a view with which the timetablers evidently concur, for the first departure on which English bus passes are valid, just after nine in the morning in these parts, is indeed a 157 – a journey that favours the north side of the valley.

Starting in Bedale's Georgian marketplace, our bus shows 'Hawes / Gayle' as its destination. Gayle, a tiny hamlet just a few minutes beyond Hawes, has a handy turning space for the bus. If we're smart, we'll occupy seats on the left side for best views across the dale.

Soon after setting off, we go through Crakehall, with its village green and cricket field overlooked by a fine Georgian hall. At **Patrick Brompton**, in whose church (on our right) I was married many, many years ago, the 157 turns right, climbing gently to Hunton. It then winds along narrow lanes and rejoins the A684 in the steep beckside village of Constable Burton. A few minutes later we're at **Leyburn** for a ten-minute breather in the busy marketplace.

From Leyburn, we start to appreciate the sweeping majesty of **Wensleydale**. On the left is the town's hillside cemetery, surely one of the most desirable sites in England in which to be laid to rest, with mighty Pen Hill (1,790ft) brooding over the dale and the River Ure. Like the other Yorkshire dales, Wensleydale was originally named after its river. Thus is was Uredale, or on some maps Yoredale. But in the early 18th century the valley adopted

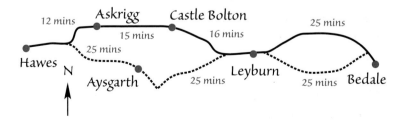

the name Wensley after what was then a significant market town. Nowadays Wensley is just a pleasant dales village – and the spot where the 157 turns right, climbing above Bolton Hall to Preston-under-Scar, giving panoramic views of the dale. We might see a train of the **Wensleydale Railway**, run by volunteers, chugging up the dale from Bedale to Redmire. You can learn more about this train service at www.wensleydalerailway.com.

After Redmire village we climb to **Castle Bolton**, where Mary Queen of Scots was imprisoned 1568–69. Dominating this northern flank of Wensleydale, the castle, dating from 1399, was built by Sir Richard le Scrope, Lord Chancellor to Richard II. Focal point for Royalists, Bolton Castle suffered a six-month siege by Parliamentarian forces in 1645. It remains an impressive bastion, worth a visit, and it's a good starting point to venture out for walks on the surrounding moors.

Still on the northern side of the dale, we come to Carperby, stone-built and slate-roofed, where we pick up villagers heading for the shops in Hawes. With the Ure winding through hay meadows below, we call at **Askrigg**, a favourite spot for walkers. If you like the television series *All Creatures Great And Small* you'll quickly see that Askrigg is the fictional Darrowby of the series. Now the 157 drops down to the A684 at Bainbridge, a broad, open village below Addle-borough's 1,560ft peak. Bainbridge is a popular starting point for a **walk** in the footsteps

Castle Bolton stands sentinel on the north side of Wensleydale (photo © Stephen Meese / DT)

of the Romans (who had a fort at **Bainbridge**) to Semer Water, two miles south, the second largest natural lake in Yorkshire. It is a haven for birds, the surrounding hay meadows a profusion of colour in summer.

For the final lap (four miles) to Hawes on the narrowing A684, we climb towards the head of the dale. We've now left hedgerows a long way behind. This is **drystone-wall country**. Sheep wander over rough fell pastures. In 2001 this was a desolate scene. The tragic spread of foot-and-mouth disease through this part of England meant wholesale slaughter of flocks, bringing despair to already poor hill farmers. It left the countryside bare of livestock, access barred to tracks and paths. The dale was shrouded in eerie silence. If the bus is suddenly halted by wandering sheep or a flock being driven, breathe a prayer for their well-being, daft-eyed and feckless though they may seem.

HEAD OF THE DALE

Hawes welcomes us with its narrow one-way streets. The 157 squeezes over the cobbles between country stores, pubs and tea shops. It has not been a long ride, but the marketplace here feels a long way from its equivalent at Bedale.

AYSGARTH FALLS

Justifiably popular, Aysgarth Falls are not visible from the main road, so ask the driver when to alight. The **way to the falls** is clearly signposted. Allow a good hour here, but do check the bus timetable carefully. Three eastbound afternoon buses stop near the falls. Aysgarth Falls is open daily 09.00–18.00 (19.00 weekends) – free, but be generous at the 'honesty box' by the gate to the upper falls. The artist **J M W Turner** visited the falls in 1816, and William and Mary Wordsworth came here too – on the day after their marriage in 1802.

For the run home from Hawes, I prefer the 156 route (left-side seats are again best for views). Beyond Bainbridge, the 156 leaves the A684 to serve Thornton Rust, with sweeping views of the dale's northern flank, along which we travelled on the outward route. We briefly rejoin the main road at Aysgarth village, and here we are just a five-minute walk to **Aysgarth Falls**.

After Aysgarth, the 156 makes a little foray south into Bishopsdale, before continuing east along the main valley to West Witton, Wensley and **Leyburn**. Then, it's downhill through Harmby into Spennithorne as drystone walls are eclipsed by hedgerows. At **Patrick Brompton**, the bus has one final detour off to the south of the main road, this time to serve little Newton-le-Willows. This Yorkshire village is a world apart from its much larger and very industrial namesake on the other side of the Pennines. When it was announced in 2009 that Newton-le-Willows has won an award as village of the year, many folk must surely have smiled – until they discovered it was the lesser-known Newton that scooped the prize. It is a place I like a lot, not least for being my wife's childhood home. Back in **Bedale**, there's a good choice of pubs and tea shops – and the impressive parish church of St Gregory offers spiritual refreshment. ∎

ABOUT THE AUTHOR | **RICHARD KINGSBURY** is a retired Anglican priest, now living in Bedale in the fair North Riding of Yorkshire.

Abbey to Castle: The Yorkshire Coast

Jill Stuart

36 Whitby

Service no. 93 | Journey time 60mins

OS Landranger 94, 101. Daily: hourly in winter, every 30mins in summer. Operator: Arriva. Connects with Journey 37 in Scarborough.

Scarborough

Arriva's 93 bus service is a route of contrasts. It is a chance for townsfolk to escape from Middlesbrough. And for people on holiday in Whitby, it is a superbly relaxing way of seeing the North York Moors. In this journey for *Bus-Pass Britain*, I focus just on the southern half of the route. Many buses start their journey in Whitby, rather than running right through from Middlesbrough. And it is best to choose a bus with a **Whitby** start if you want to maximise the chance of getting a plum seat with a good view.

So here I am, a sunny spring afternoon, climbing on to the 93 bound for Scarborough. And, true to form, after a couple of stops in Whitby, the bus is pretty well full. This is a hugely popular route. Many of the passengers are holidaymakers. There are walkers complete with backpacks and local villagers returning home with their shopping. The atmosphere is relaxed and happy. I sit back in my seat ready to enjoy what I know is a feast of some of England's most **awe-inspiring scenery**.

We cross the New Bridge spanning the **River Esk**, just upstream from Whitby harbour. From the bridge there is a stunning vista of the whole of Whitby. Then we climb steeply out of the town, leaving the fishing port behind. We turn off to the right through Stainsacre village. From the bridge over the old Scarborough to Whitby railway line there is, looking back, another engaging panorama of Whitby.

A mile or two further along the main A171 to Scarborough we make a left turn through the village of **High Hawsker**. From here the road climbs gradually past fields of sheep with their newly born lambs frisking about as though on springs. Bright green fields of wheat are in abundance, and all the way along, to our left, is the shimmering blue sea. We round a bend and a spectacular view of the whole of **Robin Hood's Bay** appears below us. This unique collage of rugged moorland, green countryside and seascape never fails to captivate me, whatever the season.

After descending steeply down the winding road into Robin Hood's Bay, the bus stops by the Victoria Hotel and several passengers alight. Locally it is just called Bay, and it is one of the most popular and attractive fishing villages on the Yorkshire coast, a place that forms a nice geological counterpoint to the Jurassic coast of Dorset.

The road into the old fishing village is very steep and narrow, and for pedestrians only. My **favourite walk** here is from Robin Hood's Bay along the beach to Boggle Hole and back. It takes just a couple of hours there and back, but remember this is strictly an adventure for low tide.

A TRIO OF FINE PUBS

Three pubs mentioned in the text make good stops, all in the latter part of the journey to Scarborough. The **Falcon Inn** by Harwood Dale Forest (☎ 01723 870717) is the first of the three, serving food daily from noon in summer. The **Blacksmiths Arms Inn** in Cloughton (☎ 01723 870244) is a family-run inn and hotel. Meals are served 12.00–14.00 & 18.30–21.00. The **Oakwheel Inn** in Burniston (☎ 01723 870230) is the most homely of the three. This small village pub has a friendly atmosphere and delicious food is served from 17.30–21.00, Tue–Sat (Sun lunch is 12.00–14.00).

The bus now begins its steep ascent out of Robin Hood's Bay towards the village of Fylingthorpe, a picturesque and hilly place. Several passengers leave the bus here, laden with shopping bags. Now, back on the main road, the moors are resplendent in the sunshine, stretching and undulating into infinity. At times they are as bleak as they are beautiful. In August they are a sea of purple when the heather blooms. There are forests for several miles before we pass the **Flask Inn**, high up on the moors and surrounded by its complex of static holiday caravans and chalets. After several hills and twists and turns we pass the Falcon Inn to our left. It's a good place for tasty good-value food and, with a bus stop nearby, it's a good *en route* stop on this journey (see box opposite).

to Middlesbrough

Whitby

N

19 mins

Robin Hood's Bay

24 mins

Cloughton

17 mins

Scarborough

Now our bus begins its gradual descent from the moors. From our high vantage point we catch a brief distant panoramic glimpse of **Scarborough Bay**, resplendent in the afternoon sun, its castle keep crowning the headland, before we start to drop steeply down the bank into the village of **Cloughton**.

One mile further along the road is the village of Burniston before the bus runs down to terminate outside the railway station in **Scarborough**. But I don't quite stay the course, for I hop off in Burniston and make for the Oakwheel Inn, there to enjoy a convivial pint with friends. And, as at the end of every bus journey, I reflect on just what a privilege it is to have a bus pass. ■

ABOUT THE AUTHOR | **JILL STUART** is a writer who lives by the coast of North Yorkshire. She uses local buses often whilst gathering information for her articles and stories.

TWO VALES: PICKERING & YORK

Jill Stuart

Scarborough

Service no. 843 | Journey time 2hrs

OS Landranger 101, 100, 105. Daily: hourly. Operator: Transdev.
Connects with Journey 36 in Scarborough.

York

Peasholm Park, the unusual oriental park in **Scarborough** which in 2012 marks the centenary of its opening, is the starting point of the smart 843 Coastliner service to York and Leeds. Climb aboard, let's make for the top deck and enjoy an unfolding panorama of **Yorkshire landscapes**. Essentially this is a main-road route, but there are deviations to serve various villages which benefit from having been bypassed by the A64. Along the way we see farms, paddocks, grazing cattle, fields of lavender and gypsy caravans. And there's a medley of colourful Yorkshire village names as we skirt the Vale of Pickering: Ganton, Sherburn, Rillington and then Scagglethorpe, where the timetable announces that we'll stop at the **Ham and Cheese Inn** (☎ 01944 758249). Blessed with a great location, this country pub makes a good stop. There's always another bus in an hour.

By now our bus is already quite full. Locals have long realised that battling the traffic in York or Leeds is no fun. So the bus is a sensible option for shopping trips. We slip off the main road to a leafy lane to serve historic Malton. The designers of the bus timetable appreciate the potential frailty of the human bladder, so they sensibly build in a longer stop at Malton (where there are toilets at the bus station). **Malton**, which has developed around the site of a Roman fort on the north bank of the River Derwent, is a nice place to wander.

Back on the main A64, we catch glimpses of **Castle Howard** in the distance through the trees. It is a really splendid building and one of the first stately homes in England to have a dome. It was designed for Charles Howard, 3rd Earl of Carlisle, by John Vanbrugh and Nicholas Hawksmoor. At this point the River Derwent is tucked away in a wooded valley down to our left. The bus stops at **Whitwell-on-the-Hill** and this is the point to alight for a very pleasing walk (see box page 176).

The A64 is so smooth, and the motion of bus so pacific, that I often nod off on this stretch. But the turn-off for **Stockton on the Forest** always wakes me up. This is one of those straggly linear villages that are so distinctive a feature of the Vale of York. I often wonder how strangers find folk in Stockton. Each house has a name rather than a number. And what an odd assortment of names: reference to agriculture, local landscape features (such as brecks, carrs, riggs or tofts), even mystical allusions.

Beyond Stockton, we get a hint of York approaching. Spires and towers aplenty and then we cross the ring road and cruise through Heworth, an oddly-mixed suburb where fine Georgian dwellings sit cheek by jowl with small modern houses. If you are bound for the shops around the engagingly named Whip-Ma-Whop-Ma-Gate, then Stonebow is the stop for you. And the Coastliner then winds through York's busy streets to the train station, before continuing to Leeds.

Scarborough

48 mins

Malton 12 mins

7 mins Scagglethorpe

15 mins Whitwell-on-the-Hill

26 mins

Stockton on the Forest

York

N

KIRKHAM PRIORY WALK

Seven minutes out of Malton, the 843 bus bound for York and Leeds stops on request at the top of **Whitwell Hill**. Turn left down Onhams Lane which drops down steeply to cross the railway line and the **River Derwent**. On the far bank, less than a mile from the bus stop, is Kirkham Priory. The ruins of this **Augustinian priory** are in a sheltered and very beautiful spot (open daily 10.00–17.00 in summer, Sat & Sun only in winter). Don't expect lavish facilities, but there are loos and you can get hot drinks and snacks at the ticket office.

But **York** is far too good to just pass through. You may like to take in the Minster (pricey with an entrance charge of £9 adult, £8 concessions, but why not attend a service – which is free). For transport buffs, the **National Railway Museum** (well signed from the station) is much less geeky than it sounds. Free entry and open daily 10.00–18.00. And now, surely it's time for a meal. Join me in the Kings Arms (☎ 01904 659435), a lively pub on Kings Staith, where you can sit outside and enjoy river views. They've a decent menu, offering everything from toasted sandwiches to three course meals. And as we are travelling by bus, with no need to drive, there is absolutely no reason why we shouldn't have a drink or two. Buses do have their advantages. Later we can walk the city's ancient walls, see where traitors' bloody heads were displayed and **look at the bars**. No, nothing to do with drinks. York has a wonderful range of local words, and the bars are the old city gates: Micklegate Bar, Monk Bar, Bootham Bar and Walmgate Bar, the latter being the only bar which still has its barbican intact. Walking the walls is a York tradition, as much beloved by locals as by visitors to this most appealing of English cities. ■

ABOUT THE AUTHOR | **JILL STUART** is a writer from North Yorkshire. She finds local buses a very convenient and comfortable way of getting around some of the most magnificent scenery in England.

THE MOORSBUS EXPERIENCE

Marjorie Fossick

Northallerton

Service no. M9 | Journey time 75mins

OS Landranger 99, 100. Twice daily on Sun Apr–Oct (also runs over Easter, on public holidays and every Wed in Jul, Aug & Sep). Operator: Moorsbus.

Helmsley

For a quarter of a century, the seasonal Moorsbus network has ferried travellers into the very heart of the **North York Moors National Park**. Longer routes bring passengers from such cities as Hull, York, Middlesbrough and Darlington, connecting within the National Park to services that take to the narrowest of country lanes. The services generally run from Easter until October and even then not daily. Service patterns do vary from year to year, so it pays to check before travelling. In March each year, the new season's schedules are posted on www.northyorkmoors.org.uk. Alternatively, call the Moorsbus enquiry line (☎ 01845 597000). 2011 saw the usual tinkering with the **Moorsbus** routes and timetables, and this journey follows the M9 which is part of what Moorsbus dub their Western Explorer route. The starting point is Northallerton station on the London to Edinburgh rail route.

There is a mood of happy expectation on the Sunday-morning run east out of **Northallerton**. This is the Vale of York, but all eyes are on the hills ahead. The North York Moors, when approached from the west, present one of the most striking topographical sights in Britain, a sharp escarpment rising from the **Vale of York**. Ahead is heather moorland, but the national park also has some impressive valleys and a wealth of more intimate landscapes: there are becks, woods and dells aplenty.

First stop is **Osmotherley**, a beautiful village that lies on a little shelf on the flank of the hills. What a blessed location – Mount Grace Priory to the north, Cod Beck to the south, and the hills protecting Osmotherley from cold east winds. This village of stone cottages and pretty lanes has impeccable **Methodist traditions**. Indeed, John Wesley preached here on many occasions.

It is a steep climb out of Osmotherley on the road towards Hawnby. We cross a cattle grid that keeps sheep up on the high moor – a nice symbolic reminder that we are entering untamed terrain. Yet there are hints of settlement ancient and modern. There are tumuli, a ruin marked on the map as Solomon's temple and a sheep farm call Chequers. John Wesley followed this route in 1757 when he walked from Osmotherley to Hawnby, describing the countryside as 'one of the pleasantest parts of England.'

We skirt Miley Pike, following the line of an old drovers' road, great views of the Pennines far away to the west, and the distinctive limestone nab of **Black Hambleton** presiding closely over our route. Then we drop down into the headwaters of the **River Rye**. Here, many bridges have suffered in storms. That over Wheat Beck was swept away in 2005, but happily it was rebuilt to restore this pretty road link across the moors.

We cross Blow Beck and Anya's Wood. The latter was named only a few years back in memory of an official of the national park.

THE HAWNBY DREAMERS

150 years ago, some Hawnby tenant farmers, having heard **Wesley** preach, were instructed in a dream to build a non-conformist chapel in Hawnby. For this they were expelled from their homes by their landlord, a staunch Anglican, and had to settle at the bottom of the village close to **Hawnby Bridge**. Although the enmity has long gone, Hawnby is still regarded as a village of two halves, the upper the Anglican and the lower the non-conformist.

Now we reach **Moor Gate**. This spot has perfect views of twin hills, Easterside and Hawnby, matching each other in height and shape, and both decorated with a patchwork of woodland, green meadow and moor. There are plenty of walks from here but the real joy is the proud little ridge walk over Hawnby Hill, dropping down directly from the top into the eponymous village.

Osmotherley

20 mins

Northallerton

32 mins

N

Hawnby

11 mins

Rievaulx Abbey

8 mins

Helmsley

Hawnby, a dreamy little village (see box opposite), is the star of the route. There are good tea rooms (☎ 01439 798223; open daily 08.00–20.00, closed Wed morning) with a lovely sheltered garden, and The Hawnby Inn (☎ 01439 798202; open daily with afternoon break from 15.00–18.00 Mon–Wed) which does excellent food. Check out the old **Methodist chapel** (now private premises) and the Anglican church, where local poets with literary ambition leave their latest scribblings on display.

From Hawnby our bus continues down Rye Dale, detouring to serve starkly beautiful **Rievaulx Abbey** (open daily in summer, weekends only in winter), before arriving in Helmsley. This picture-perfect market town has a fine range of craft shops and cafés, and serves as a hub for the Moorsbus network. You can return to Northallerton via the route by which you came or, to see another part of the region, why not opt for the M11 instead? That route has a late afternoon bus to Northallerton by way of Ampleforth, Byland Abbey and Thirsk. Moorsbus volunteers or park rangers are usually on hand as the bus stops in **Helmsley** Market Place to offer advice about onward travel options. ∎

ABOUT THE AUTHOR | **MARJORIE FOSSICK** is a lifelong walker, a dedicated non-driver and a keen user of her local bus services.

CUMBRIA & NORTHUMBERLAND

England's northernmost counties are a bus traveller's paradise, and our challenge in this section of *Bus-Pass Britain* has been to select just seven routes out of the dozens that begged to be included. We opted for a mix that includes four **year-round routes** and three **seasonal offerings** – two of the latter in the Lake District National Park. Among the near-misses was Weardale Motor Services' route 101 which climbs from the railhead at Bishop Auckland (in County Durham) up lonely Weardale to St John's Chapel and beyond, along the way serving some of the remotest communities in the northern Pennines.

Rural Northumberland benefits from many locally-owned and operated bus services that provide a year-round service to out-of-the-way villages. One of our favourites is the 880 from Hexham to Kielder, the last village in England before the Scottish border – no easy journey on snowy winter days. Howard Snaith Coaches (☎ 01830 520609) operate this route, which runs on Tuesdays, Thursdays and Saturdays. Call in advance and the company will even transport bikes on the run up to Kielder.

At the other end of Northumberland, on the North Sea coast, is one of Britain's most extraordinary bus services: the 477 to **Holy Island**. We have included a short account of this route across a tidal causeway as an optional diversion from Journey 45.

Northern England is blessed with many local bus services that make quite **long hops**. Routes linking Newcastle upon Tyne with both Berwick-upon-Tweed and Carlisle feature here. But take time to **explore the region's byways**. If we had a week to spare, you would most likely find us exploring some of the deliciously rural bus routes in the Alston area of east Cumbria. ∎

THE HONISTER RAMBLER

Michael Holmes

Lake District 🚐

Service nos. 77 or 77A | Journey time 1hr 35mins

OS Landranger 90. Runs 4 times daily in both directions from mid Apr to late Oct. Operator: Stagecoach. Connects with Journey 40 in Keswick.

circular route

This journey is a fine circuit through some of **Lakeland's best scenery**, starting and ending in Keswick, and including along the way two mountain passes (Whinlatter and Honister) and a ride along the shores of three beautiful lakes (Crummock Water, Buttermere and Derwent Water).

Keswick makes an excellent base for exploring the Lakes. Open-top buses run down the east side of Derwent Water. The double-decker bus to Windermere is also a popular choice (and described in Journey 40 in this book). But my favourite is the **Honister Rambler**, a seasonal circular bus service that is a real delight. And you don't have to be a bus-pass holder to enjoy this route at a reasonable price. A Honister and Borrowdale Dayrider ticket costs just £6.50 and allows unlimited travel on both the Honister Rambler services (routes 77 and 77A) and on the open-top Borrowdale Rambler buses (route 78).

ROUND TRIP THROUGH A NATIONAL PARK

So let's join the steady stream of **ramblers** boarding the first anticlockwise service of the day, the no. 77. That's a detail you need to note with the Honister Rambler. A bus with an 'A' makes the circuit clockwise, while one without an 'A' travels the route anticlockwise. No doubt there's some logic tucked away in there somewhere, but it's certainly confusing to many first-time users of this bus service.

Once on board, all the chat is of plans for the day. Some travellers are bound for the fells. There is talk of Lakeland landmarks like **High Stile** and **Haystacks**. One couple, dog-eared Wainwright and old OS map in their hands, have lofty Grasmoor in their sights. Some are making the journey for the first time, others are revisiting old haunts. And a few are clearly here just for the ride, waiting to see how the day unfolds.

We leave Keswick to the northwest with imposing **Skiddaw** to our right. At Braithwaite the first serious climb of the day begins. We are soon into Forestry Commission territory, with dense plantations on both sides of the road. There are inviting gaps in the trees, giving sight lines to distant fells and, at one point, a fine view down to Bassenthwaite Lake far below.

The road climbs to **Whinlatter Visitor Centre** at the top of the pass, just 15 minutes out of Keswick, and a good spot to learn about Forestry Commission work in the area (see box above).

The area is exceptionally rich in **wildlife**. The combination of forests, open heathland habitats and the nearby waters of **Bassenthwaite Lake** encourages variety – so there are crossbills, siskins, merlins and even ospreys. The latter had not been seen in

England since 1842, so when a pair was spotted at Bassenthwaite in 1997, it created huge interest. With support from RSPB, nest platforms were provided and to great excitement the first chick was reared in 2001. Red squirrels are a common sight around the visitor centre at Whinlatter, and the surrounding forests are home to many roe deer.

Whinlatter is a fine introduction to the area, but now the hills beckon, so travellers are back at the bus stop to continue their Lakeland circuit on the next Honister Rambler. The 77 bus comes into view, and we climb aboard to a cheery greeting from the driver. We head west down into **Lorton Vale**, all eyes on a buzzard that lazily circles in the sky ahead. With the farming communities of High and Low Lorton behind us, we turn south to follow the rugged shoreline of **Crummock Water**. Across the water, in a cleft in the fells, we see one of the most spectacular waterfalls in the Lake District. This is Scale Force which can be reached on foot from **Buttermere** village. The road skirts Hause Point, a wild headland that juts impertinently into Crummock Water, and suddenly there is a complete change of scenery. Here is gentle

BUTTERMERE

Buttermere is a Cumbrian idyll, judged by many who visit to be the **perfect Lakeland village**. You'll find no shortage of cafés and there are two good hotels. With its clean whitewashed walls and neat slate roof, The **Fish Inn** (☎ 017687 70253) blends perfectly into this happy pastoral scene. But there is a darker side to Buttermere history. In 1802 the landlord's daughter, a celebrated local beauty, was tricked into marrying one **John Hatfield**, who claimed to be a man of means with aristocratic connections. A nationwide hue and cry ensued when it almost immediately emerged that Hatfield was by no means all he purported to be, but rather a bigamist and forger. He met his end at Carlisle the following year, not for his abuse of Mary, but a long catalogue of other crimes. The story did have a **happy ending** however as Mary subsequently married a local farmer.

woodland and sheep pasture as Buttermere is approached.

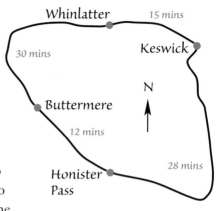

Buttermere's lovely village church is worth a visit. Here you will find a memorial to **Alfred Wainwright**, whose classic walking guides did so much to bring the Lake District to wider public popularity. The memorial tablet is situated by a window, from which there is a clear view to Haystacks, Wainwright's own favourite fell, and where his ashes were scattered. The circuit of the lake is a most rewarding low-level walk; alternatively stroll along the southwest side and rejoin the bus route at Gatesgarth Farm.

Beyond Gatesgarth, the road climbs steeply to the top of **Honister Pass** (1,167ft) – the highest spot on this journey. The slate mine has become a popular tourist attract, and gives some insight into the difficult conditions in which the miners toiled. But the star attraction at Honister is the **panorama**, taking in many of the major Lakeland summits. The eastern side of Honister is even steeper than the climb up from Buttermere, culminating in a heady 1 in 4 gradient on the road that drops down into Seatoller. 'Stay in low gear,' implore the road signs. Our driver obliges.

We have now reached **Borrowdale**, singled out by Wainwright as 'the finest dale in England.' I just sit back and enjoy the view. At Grange Bridge, there is the chance to change on to the open-top bus that skirts the east bank of Derwent Water. I take the easy option, keeping my front seat on the Honister Rambler, as we cruise the west shore of the lake back to Keswick. ■

ABOUT THE AUTHOR | **MICHAEL HOLMES** and his wife have been visiting the Lake District for over forty years, and they eagerly anticipate the next visit.

A NOSTALGIC RIDE THROUGH THE LAKE DISTRICT

Betty Dove

40 Keswick 🚌

Service no. 555 | Journey time 60mins

OS Landranger 90, 97. Runs hourly every day (extra journeys Mon–Fri in school summer hols). Operator: Stagecoach. Connects with Journey 39 in Keswick and with 41 in Ambleside.

Windermere ◄

I have driven from Keswick down to Windermere hundreds of times, and thought I knew every bend in the road. The A591 is a busy trunk road, a route that cuts through the very heart of the **Lake District**. Cars jostle for space on the crowded road and rarely had I a chance to gaze at the scenery. Then I discovered the 555 bus, and before long found a completely new perspective on a route I thought I knew well.

The full 555 journey is something of a marathon among British local bus routes, for many journeys continue south beyond Windermere to Lancaster. The full run from **Keswick to Lancaster** takes 2 hours 40 minutes. For Keswick folk, living in a town which was peremptorily robbed of its rail link to the outside world in 1972, the 555 bus is a lifeline – one that gives easy access to trains at both Windermere and Lancaster.

Now I take the 555 mainly for fun. I gaze at the fells and more often than not am reminded of the happy days when I toiled up steep footpaths on to the open hills, sometimes even in pouring rain. Yes, hiking on the hills can be fun even in the rain, just as the 555 can be a rewarding bus ride in even the most unpromising weather.

The market town of **Keswick**, a place of some 5,000 souls, is hardly picture-perfect. It is a functional sort of place, a popular centre for tourists visiting the Lakes and blessed with a super range of bus routes that radiate out from the town's bus station. Canny visitors know that they can often see far more of the region on the excellent local bus services than is possible on tours organised by various tour companies in Keswick.

Keswick

23 mins

Grasmere

N

23 mins

Ambleside

15 mins

Windermere

My 555 is a double-decker, standard Stagecoach fare, and none the worse for that. Some of the buses on this route are intriguingly decorated to recall significant **Lakeland figures** who have helped shape the image of the Lake District. I have spotted vehicles dedicated to Beatrix Potter, William Wordsworth and Alfred Wainwright.

Hardly are we out of Keswick when the first highlight of the route appears on the side of the fell above the road. Castlerigg Stone Circle was erected on this commanding site by our ancient ancestors for some reason now unknown. Standing on land

COFFEE AND MORE

As the bus rolls down from the summit at **Dunmail**, you will see the **Travellers Rest** (☎ 015394 35604) on the left. This handsome white 16th-century **coaching inn** makes a great coffee stop. Choose a good day and you can enjoy the pub garden before hopping on the next bus south. But be warned! It's a seductive spot. The views are gorgeous, and you'll probably end up wanting to linger. For those who are thus waylaid, the Travellers Rest offers **decent rooms** from about £60. Meals daily from noon through to 21.00.

now owned by the National Trust and maintained by **English Heritage**, Castlerigg Stone Circle is the most visited of the 50 stone circles in Cumbria. It is now generally agreed that it was built about 3000BC at the beginning of the Neolithic period. It is thus one of the earliest stone circles in Britain. It stands on the top of a high moor in an open bowl of hills above **Keswick**. The setting is spectacular at any time but particularly at dawn or dusk. There are **38 stones** in a circle approximately 35 yards in diameter, with a small rectangle of stones within the circle. There is also a small mound, which suggests it might have been a burial place. Happily there is no admission charge to the Castlerigg complex, and it is made all the better by the fact that this atmospheric spot has no facilities.

Our bus cruises confidently south, the **Helvellyn** range towering above us on the left. We pass Thirlspot and Wythburn, well-remembered starting points for routes to Helvellyn's rocky summit. On the right is Thirlmere, visible from the top of the bus over the conifers first planted when Thirlmere became a key source of Manchester's water supply and the surrounding land closed to the public.

We are now about ten miles south of Keswick and cresting **Dunmail Raise**, surely the gentlest of Lakeland cols. It was the site of a battle in the 10th century between King Dunmail, the

Castlerigg Stone Circle (photo © Mille 19 / DT)

last King of Cumbria, and the united forces of Malcolm, the King of Scotland, and Edmund, a Saxon king. Dunmail was defeated and slain, and his sons were mutilated. His men built a stone cairn over the spot where he fell.

Now that the 555 has proved its loyalty to the main road, there comes a happy surprise as we detour through pretty Grasmere, a village so intimately associated with **Wordsworth** that it always pulls the crowds. But it is a place for walkers too as the summits of the relatively lowly Grasmere Fells make manageable goals even for fell walkers well past their first youth.

Back on the main road, Dove Cottage, Wordsworth's home from 1799 to 1808, is just out of sight on the left. The route skirts a lovely duo of lakes, Grasmere and Rydal Water, to reach **Ambleside**, a small town so choked with traffic that I am grateful to be sitting on the top deck of the bus rather than behind the wheel.

We are hardly out of Ambleside when we catch a first glimpse of Windermere. A **steamer** is chugging south from the pier at Waterhead, but too far distant for me to see if it is the *Tern*. This 19th-century boat is a Lakeland institution. It was mentioned in Arthur Ransome's books and is still in service today (for details on cruise services contact ☎ 015394 43360; www.windermere-lakecruises.co.uk).

The bus continues south, stopping off here and there, often with fine views over the lake. A good stop is the National Park Centre at **Brockhole** (☎ 015394 46601). Access to the house, which hosts excellent exhibitions, and the gardens is free. From Brockhole, it is just a few minutes by bus to the town of **Windermere**. We pull up by the railway station, where many change to the waiting train. No rest for our driver, though, as the 555 bus is soon on its way again, now bound for Lancaster. ■

ABOUT THE AUTHOR | **BETTY DOVE** is a retired secretary who has always lived in the south of England, but for over 50 years she spent part of her holiday walking the Lakeland fells.

THE KIRKSTONE RAMBLER

Paul Heels

41 **Bowness** 🚌

Service no. 517 | Journey time 55mins

OS Landranger 97, 90. Runs thrice daily on Sat, Sun and public hols Easter to late Oct and every day in school summer hols. Operator: Stagecoach. Connects with Journey 40 in Windermere and with 42 in Patterdale.

Glenridding ◄

Tourist literature often plugs the Lake District as the most beautiful corner of England. Few will be inclined to dispute this claim as they ride the **Kirkstone Rambler** bus route through the heart of one of England's first generation of national parks. The service is supported by Cumbria County Council and appeals to visitors who want to leave their cars behind and let the bus take the strain. The timetable creatively provides opportunities to climb many of the classic Lakeland peaks around the northern end of the route. For those with a head for heights, Helvellyn via Striding Edge beckons. Those with less energy might opt to cruise Ullswater by boat.

My journey starts at **Bowness Pier** on the morning bus which allows seven hours for exploring Patterdale and Ullswater. The bus runs up the main street just as Bowness shops are starting to open. On the left is the attractive parish church of St Martin's. After just a few minutes, our driver pulls up outside Windermere railway station where a group of fell walkers from Manchester join the bus. Then it's due north up the Troutbeck Valley on the A592 – the road that the Kirkstone Rambler follows for the rest of the run to Glenridding.

A STEEP CLIMB

The gentle valley carved by the Trout is tame but beautiful, yet grander things lie ahead. Soon we start to climb, and our driver deftly shifts down through the gears as the vehicle growls up **Kirkstone Pass**. There are glimpses of shimmering **Windermere** away to the left, and a steep minor road – aptly named 'The Struggle' – joins us from the left. To the east the terrain is severe and forbidding as I gaze over to the fells that mark the Kentmere Horseshoe. In just 20 minutes from Windermere, the Kirkstone Rambler whisks travellers from a placid Lakeland vale to some of the most dramatic hill scenery that England has to offer.

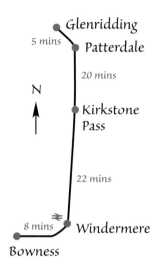

Kirkstone Pass Inn, a traditional coaching inn, makes a fine stop (see box). Just past the inn, we reach the summit of the pass, a breezy 1,489 feet above sea level. This is a magnificent moment,

---

AN INN WITH ALTITUDE

No kudos to the writer for the snappy title, for actually it is **Kirkstone Pass Inn** which styles itself 'an inn with altitude' (☎ 01539 433888; www.kirkstonepassinn.com). And surely true, for this is the **highest inhabited building** in Cumbria. Meals are generally available both lunchtime and evenings, but opening times vary by season – so check in advance. Good en-suite rooms (from £70) are ideal for those seeking a comfortable **mountain retreat**. Keen fell walkers can scramble up the rocky slopes of Red Screes (2,545ft) or take a more gentle climb up to oddly-named High Street (2,718ft).

---

as suddenly Patterdale lies far below us. Steep mountain slopes in the foreground, lakes and verdant green in the dale beyond.

The Kirkstone Rambler is a bus that rarely gets into high gear. It takes skill to drive these mountain roads and our driver today is clearly very adept at coping with all that comes his way. We edge down the steep road, stopping briefly to allow a tourist coach labouring up the pass to go by, followed by a line of frustrated car drivers.

At last the valley floor flattens out, **Brothers Water** on the left and on the right are the slate roofs of the hamlet of Hartsop nestling below the fells. The characteristic stone walls make patchwork of the valley floor. Yet more walls climb up hillsides populated by the ubiquitous and infinitely agile Lakeland sheep. We pass through **Patterdale** village to **Glenridding**, end of the route for the Kirkstone Rambler, but for many aboard the start of a demanding climb into the surrounding hills.

Glenridding is an old mining village with excellent facilities. Try the **Inn on the Lake** (☎ 0800 8401245) for real ale and traditional bar food. This hotel has lovely gardens running down to the lake. **Fellbites Café** (☎ 017684 82781), centrally located, offers a good range of sandwiches, light meals and temptingly delicious cakes.

You don't need to be an accomplished mountaineer to enjoy the hills. Ullswater Steamers (The Pier House; ☎ 017684 82229; see www.ullswater-steamers.co.uk for times and fares) cruise the length of Ullswater from Glenridding to **Pooley Bridge**, a small village with pubs and cafés. Return by boat, or for a different view of the lake, catch the 108 Stagecoach bus running from Penrith to Glenridding via Pooley Bridge. Walkers can take the boat from Glenridding across to Howtown and follow an easy lakeside path at the foot of Place Fell back to Glenridding via Patterdale (7 miles). Boat services on Ullswater operate year round. ■

ABOUT THE
AUTHOR

PAUL HEELS, a retired business studies teacher living in Cumbria, has had a lifelong passion for bus travel.

ESCAPE FROM PENRITH

Ruth Kershaw

42

Penrith 🚐

Service no. 108 | Journey time 50mins

OS Landranger 90. Four to five journeys daily (Sun service runs only from Apr till early Sep). Operator: Stagecoach. Connects with Journey 41 in Glenridding.

Patterdale ◄

Journey 41 approached Patterdale and Ullswater from the south using the seasonal **Kirkstone Rambler** bus service. Now we venture again to the same valley, but this time skirting Ullswater, judged by many to be the most beautiful of the Cumbrian lakes, to reach Patterdale from the north. And happily this service runs year round. As appealing in deep midwinter as it is on a sunny spring day, this is a route for all seasons.

Starting point is **Penrith railway station**, good for direct train connections via the main West Coast route from London, Manchester and Scotland. Travellers from afar are thus already on board when a few minutes later the double-decker stops briefly at Penrith's rather spartan bus station. No-one wants to miss the view from what is locally dubbed the **Patterdale Bus**, so the rush is for the top deck.

THE HILLS BECKON

Most of those aboard are bound for a day in the hills. One or two passengers are really just there for the ride, travelling out and back on the same bus. There is a relaxed atmosphere, as the bus navigates

Penrith ⇌

23 mins

Pooley
Bridge

N ↑

14 mins

Aira Force

7 mins

Glenridding

5 mins

Patterdale

Penrith's streets with their hall-mark red sandstone buildings. Dates prominently inscribed over door lintels attest to the fact that Penrith is no upstart new town. Many buildings date from the 17th century. And settlement in the area dates back far longer. As the bus to Patterdale heads south out of town there is a good view of an ancient **Neolithic henge**. The top deck brings its own rewards on this bus journey.

By the time the bus crosses the M6, we have a sense of really being in the country, and the scenery becomes ever better as we follow a B road southwest towards the hills. Soft Cumbrian farmland area around Tirril gives way to hillier terrain by the time we reach **Pooley Bridge** – a good-sized community that clusters around the northern end of Ullswater.

Much of the remainder of the route, some eight miles in all, clings to the west bank of **Ullswater**, a serpentine ribbon of a lake that has three reaches with two dog-legs. By now passengers who just a half-hour earlier were strangers are chatting amiably with

SOMNAMBULISTS BEWARE!

Aira Force is the scene of a tragedy, recorded by **Wordsworth** in his poem *The Somnambulist*. The legend is of Emma, betrothed to Sir Eglamore, becoming so disturbed by his absence in the Crusades that she took to walking in her sleep by the banks of the torrent. It was there that **Sir Eglamore** found her on his return. He touched her and she suddenly awoke, so surprised by the appearance of her lover that she fell over a precipice into a deep ravine. The knight tried in vain to rescue her. And Sir Eglamore? Well, he is said to have then led a lonely life as a recluse in a cave near the great waterfall.

each other, pointing out landmarks and sharing their plans for the hours ahead.

At the first dog-leg the scenery becomes more wooded and picturesque with a great vista east to Howtown framed by **Hallin Fell**. At just 1,271ft, Hallin Fell is no great mountain, but for one or two of those aboard the bus it has a special meaning. 'That was the first Lakeland fell I ever climbed,' says one lady who reveals that she was only four years old when she made her first ascent of mighty Hallin. Her revelation prompts a man two rows behind to interject: 'And that's where I want my ashes scattered.'

REACHING AIRA FORCE

Now **Helvellyn** is heaving into view, little wisps of cloud lacing the summit that towers high above the west side of Ullswater. We skirt Dobbin Wood and stop near **Aira Force**, where a number of passengers alight. This is a place for all the family. Children can paddle in the stony beck, gentle walks in Gowbarrow Park afford stunning views and the force itself, falling 70ft, is a textbook piece of Romantic scenery (see box on page 193).

Beyond Aira Force comes **Glencoyne Bay**, the shores of which inspired Wordsworth to pen *The Daffodils*. It is still a fine

An Ullswater pier
(photo © Paulmerrett / DT)

spot on an April day when the daffs are in bloom. Now the lake makes its second dog-leg into the final reach. The scenery becomes markedly more rugged and, on a wild day, even forbidding. Over to the left Place Fell drops steeply into the water whilst on the right the cliffed slopes of **St Sunday Crag** look like a landscape of the Gothic imagination. The booted brigade shuffles gear in preparation to leave the bus at Glenridding or **Patterdale** to climb Helvellyn. At 3,118ft, the mountain is judged by many to be the finest of the Lakeland fells.

Journey's end for the Patterdale Bus is the village from which the bus takes its name. I am always struck by the different mood on the return journey. At the end of a long day exploring the area, folk are tired and few are tempted on to the top deck. Travellers chat on the lower deck, and many are already planning their next adventure with the Patterdale Bus.

And a final tip. Don't leave **Ullswater** without taking a short cruise. The Ullswater services (www.ullswater-steamers.co.uk) run year round. You can board the boat at Glenridding, from where it is a 60 to 70-min journey to Pooley Bridge, where you can rejoin the Patterdale Bus to return to Penrith. ■

ABOUT THE AUTHOR | **RUTH KERSHAW** is leader of the Carlisle-based walking group 'Over the Hills' and possessor of a well-used bus pass. She lives in Brampton in Cumbria.

ALONG HADRIAN'S WALL IN AD122

Margaret Brough

 Carlisle

Service no. AD122 | Journey time 2hrs 10mins

OS Landranger 85, 86, 87. Seasonal thrice daily service Apr–Oct only.
Operator: Alba Travel.
Connects with Journey 44 in Carlisle, Haltwhistle and Hexham.

Hexham

There are lots of ways out of **Carlisle**, for the Cumbrian city is blessed with trains and buses aplenty. Take your pick! If you are eastward bound, there is a delightful railway line over the hills to Newcastle upon Tyne, paralleled by a bus route that features as the next journey in this book.

But if you are heading east and, like me, have a sense of history, then you'll want to take the AD122. What an extraordinary number for a bus! AD122. That was the year when Emperor Hadrian visited Britain and fully appreciated the challenge of controlling wayward **Caledonia**. And today it is the number of the seasonal bus route that links key spots along the great defensive wall built at Emperor Hadrian's command.

A DOSE OF HISTORY

I like the AD122 for its friendly informality and for the way that the route deftly combines great scenery with a good dose of history. Often there is a **commentary on key sights** along the way. It is rare that I have travelled the route without there being a nice mix of foreigners and locals on board. And for me this route has a very personal appeal, for it links two English counties that I hold very dear. I have lived in both.

The first leg out of **Carlisle** is through pleasant farming country, with lots of sheep and cattle, to the market town of **Brampton** with its distinctive Moot Hall. The next landmark is Lanercost Priory, founded in 1169 by Augustinian Canons. Like so many buildings along this route, this old priory incorporates stones that were pilfered from nearby Hadrian's Wall. Little did the Romans appreciate that they were providing a ready source of high-quality building material for subsequent generations.

Gatehouse at Vindolanda fort on Hadrian's Wall (photo © Jaime Pharr / DT)

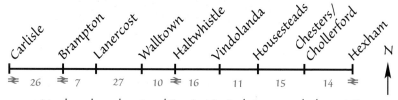

Carlisle — Brampton — Lanercost — Walltown — Haltwhistle — Vindolanda — Housesteads — Chesters/Chollerford — Hexham   N

26   7   27   10   16   11   15   14

Numbers above show travel time in minutes between marked way stations

There were 16 major forts along **Hadrian's Wall**, and the AD122 route is a roll-call of those which boast the richest remains. First up is Birdoswald, often just called Banna by locals. Vindolanda and Chesters are two that boast the most spectacular insights into the architecture and military culture of Hadrian's Wall – the AD122 passes them both later in the route. The entire ensemble of Hadrian's Wall was added in 1987 to the **UNESCO World Heritage List**, an accolade that has done much to ensure a steady flow of overseas visitors to this rather remote part of northern England.

East of **Greenhead**, the terrain becomes more pronounced, with a great ridge of dolerite (called the Whin Sill) threading its way across the landscape. The Romans used the sill as a natural defensive barrier that gave emphasis to the Wall. This is wonderful airy country, with great views north across Wark Forest to the Cheviots and Scotland.

The bus deviates away south of the Wall on three occasions, firstly to serve Haltwhistle, second to stop at the magnificent **Vindolanda fort** (which is located a mile south of the Wall) and then, at the end of the journey from Carlisle, the bus leaves the Wall at Chollerford to run south to Hexham. Both Hexham and Haltwhistle give the opportunity to connect on to the Newcastle to Carlisle rail route or on to Journey 44 in this book.

Chollerford, a classic little Northumbrian community that clusters around an old stone bridge over the North Tyne, is a great spot to linger and combines well with a stop at Chesters Roman Fort. While there is a café at the fort, I would commend an alternative. It is an easy 10-minute walk along the Hadrian's Wall footpath

WALL STOPS

The traveller riding the AD122 will get a good sense of the Wall and its complex fortifications: turrets, mile castles, ditches and forts. But it is worth alighting to explore a little more. The **Roman Army Museum** (☎ 016977 47485; www.vindolanda.com; entrance fee) at Walltown, just east of Greenhead, is a good start. It is situated beside one of the best-preserved sections of the Wall, and offers a captivating insight into the life of the garrisons along the Wall. Don't miss the **film** called *The Eagle's Eye* that is regularly shown at the museum.

Three **forts** make obvious stops. They are (listed from west to east in the order in which the AD122 from Carlisle serves them): **Vindolanda** (☎ 01434 344277), **Housesteads** (☎ 01434 344363) and **Chesters** (☎ 01434 681379).

The Army Museum and all three forts mentioned here are generally open daily from 10.00 until late afternoon, but opening hours are curtailed in winter. It is worth checking in advance, and remember that the AD**122 bus services** do not operate at all after late October. There are cafés at Walltown, Vindolanda, Housesteads and Chesters.

from Chesters to Chollerford, where the **Riverside Tearooms** (☎ 01434 681325; open daily except for a spell over Christmas and the New Year) always welcomes bus-pass explorers with a smile and a great range of homemade cakes. The onward hop from Chollerford to Hexham is easy, with up to 15 buses daily serving the route.

Hexham, the end of our journey, gives insights into history of another kind, less Roman and more medieval in character. But the link with the Romans remains, for some of the stonework used in Hexham's beautiful abbey was plundered from a Roman fort at Corstopitum (on the north bank of the Tyne east of the town). Hexham is a fitting end to one of the most history-laden bus journeys that England has to offer. ■

ABOUT THE AUTHOR | **MARGARET BROUGH** has lived in a village near Hexham for ten years, moving from the Lake District. She retired from teaching in the south, but takes much pleasure from an interest in the village school.

COAST TO COAST

Carol Purves

Carlisle 🚌

Service no. 685 | Journey time 2hrs 10mins to 2hrs 25mins

OS Landranger 85, 86, 87, 88. Runs hourly Mon–Sat, 4 journeys on Sun.
Operators: Arriva & Stagecoach. Connects with Journey 45 in Newcastle and
Journey 43 in Carlisle, Haltwhistle and Hexham.

Newcastle upon Tyne ←

I love this journey for it has the makings of a very relaxing day out, more often than not taking me from my Cumbrian home to meet my Newcastle cousin. These excursions are a chance for tea and cream cake at the Tyneside city's posh Fenwick department store. The journey is a vehicular coast to coast, linking the River Eden which decants into the Irish Sea with the great industrial **River Tyne** which flows into the North Sea. The route generally keeps well south of Hadrian's Wall, but from time to time along the way the Carlisle to Newcastle bus does afford glimpses of the Wall. A parallel seasonal bus route, which more closely follows Hadrian's Wall, features as Journey 43 in this volume.

We leave behind **Carlisle**, the Cumbrian city famous for its castle, citadel and cathedral, as we journey east through lush farmland. The sun highlights the northern Pennine hills on our right, and away to the southwest is a fine vista of the heights of the Lake District. The entire route from Carlisle to Newcastle is in beautiful open landscape with **spectacular views**.

As bus journeys go, this is one of the friendliest. Passengers chat happily to each other, often about inconsequential matters, but occasionally veering on to more controversial topics – and that's

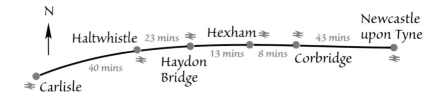

N

Haltwhistle — 23 mins — Hexham — 43 mins — Newcastle upon Tyne

40 mins — Haydon Bridge — 13 mins — 8 mins — Corbridge

Carlisle

when the 685 bus becomes a debating society on wheels. And the bus always attracts a nice cast of local characters. Betty is carrying newly laid eggs to a friend in the next village, Gavin is travelling to his part-time job in Newcastle, while lonely Moira rides the route each day. As the journey east along the A69 progresses I notice how the accents shift from Cumbrian to Geordie.

INTO NORTHUMBERLAND

Before long we are in **Brampton**, little more than a village, but a place that once boasted 63 pubs. Then on across the border into Northumberland. Although the route is a regular hourly service, tucked away in the timetable are some little variations. Three buses a day make an interesting deviation north to the village of **Gilsland** right on **Hadrian's Wall**. No Roman soldiers on patrol today, but plenty of walkers hiking the 84-mile footpath that follows the Wall. It is a walk I've done myself, but today I revel in the comfort of the bus.

We follow the main road, the railway to Newcastle immediately on our left and a fast-flowing burn beyond, and soon we are approaching **Haltwhistle**. This market town makes an extraordinary claim, namely that it is located at the very centre of Britain. I have my doubts, for surely other spots make similar boasts. But the lady in the town's tourist office assertively backs up Haltwhistle's geographical claim to fame with a postcard that shows Haltwhistle perfectly positioned on a straight line linking Portland Bill in Dorset with the Orkney Isles.

I punctuate my regular journeys to Newcastle with stops here and there at villages or towns along the way. **Haydon Bridge**, really a halfway house between Carlisle and Hexham, caught my attention on one journey. It is a place that in 2009 regained its status as a quiet and peaceful village when a bypass was opened. 'Thirty years too late,' says a man in the public library, referring to the bypass. 'But better late than never.'

The **village library** alone justifies the stop in Haydon Bridge. The library, run by volunteers, bristles with community spirit. Books are lent and sold, there are paintings by local artists on sale, and the building (known as 'The Bridge') also serves as tourist information centre and internet café.

THE TYNE VALLEY

The journey continues past fallow fields, ploughed fields and sown fields, all seasons rolling into one. However the area is noted mostly for cattle and sheep. As the bus doors open at each stop we can hear the lowing of cows and the bleating of sheep. This is a happy symphony, a welcome contrast to the deathly silence in 2001 when the area was devastated by foot-and-mouth disease. I still shudder when I recall those awful days.

By far the largest spot along the route to Newcastle is **Hexham**, a market town of some 11,000 inhabitants, and the place where the two Tyne streams, North and South, combine to create the much larger River Tyne. Hexham bustles, for it's the obvious shopping centre for those living in a great swathe of Northumbrian hill country.

The next stop is **Corbridge**, where our bus pulls up outside the Angel Inn. This thriving town, just 18 miles from Newcastle, grew up round the site of Roman Corstopitum. The town was burnt to ground several times by the cross-border raiders known as **Reivers**. These agile horsemen created mayhem for three centuries, but particularly in Tudor times, as they swept down from the hills. So bad were these raids that at one time Tyne Valley communities like Corbridge called for Hadrian's Wall to be reinforced as a defensive barrier against raiders from the north. But today Corbridge is a peaceful spot, no longer harried by wild horsemen, and happily the village's Saxon stone church has survived.

East of Corbridge, the demeanour of the **Tyne Valley** slowly changes as we approach Newcastle upon Tyne. But Northumbrian history still makes an appearance. The place shown as Heddon on the bus timetable is more properly **Heddon-on-the-Wall**. Hadrian's Wall of course. The *vallum* is on either side of the village, where a preserved section of the Wall can be seen. The village of Throckley is also situated on the Wall with splendid views of the distant Pennines. Before long, the city has eclipsed the country and we are travelling along crowded roads through urban **Tyneside**. We pass Newcastle's Royal Victoria Infirmary, the General Hospital and the Freeman Hospital and then there is a glimpse of St James, the football stadium where Newcastle United weave a little sporting magic. Eldon Square is the end of the line. Time for tea and cake. ■

ABOUT THE AUTHOR | **CAROL PURVES** is a freelance writer. She lives in Carlisle and loves exploring her home region – whether by bus, on foot, or even occasionally in a car.

COMMUNITY BUS SERVICES

Brits may be prone to complain about their bus services, but the truth is that we benefit from a dense network that would be the envy of many of our European neighbours. Britain is unusual in having an exceptionally **good network of inter-urban routes**. Using Journeys 44 and 45 in this book, one might travel from Carlisle to Berwick-on-Tweed with just one change of bus – a journey of 150 miles.

But no bus network can perfectly serve everyone, and that's where **community bus services** come in. We praised the merits of locally owned and operated bus services in rural Northumberland (see page 180), yet there are some folk for whom regular scheduled bus services are not a credible option. Nicola Crane is transport manager for **Upper Coquetdale Community Transport** (UCCT). Nicola is a volunteer, as indeed are all who work with UCCT (☎ 01669 621855). The group's 17-seat white minibus is a regular sight on the lanes around **Rothbury**. 'We work with local ramblers who need transport up to Alwinton and beyond,' she says. Every Friday, UCCT runs a **shoppers' special**, collecting elderly residents of Upper Coquetdale at their front doors and taking them to local shops in Rothbury. 'For some of those on board, the ride to Rothbury might well be the social highlight of their week. These are folk who don't get out a lot,' says Nicola, who explains how UCCT passengers shop together and visit cafés in Rothbury.

UCCT caters very much for locals, and the terms of their operating licence do not permit Nicola and her team to operate regular scheduled services for the general public. But at the other end of England, the **Cuckmere Community Bus** does just that. For 35 years, the bus has been ferrying residents of the Cuckmere Valley in East Sussex to nearby towns for shopping, hospital appointments or just for fun. But now they also run a weekend bus service for visitors to the area – which is part of the newly designated **South Downs National Park**. Hourly bus services meet trains at local railway stations. Some on board are bound for the spectacular chalk-cliff scenery at **Seven Sisters Country Park**, while others look for nothing more demanding than cream tea in Alfriston. We are grateful to John Bishop of Hailsham (East Sussex), a volunteer driver with the Cuckmere Community Bus, for drawing our attention to this bus service. NG

North Sea Coastal Splendour

David Beilby

 Newcastle upon Tyne

Service no. 501 | Journey time 3hrs 15mins

OS Landranger 88, 81, 75. Every 2hrs,
limited Sun service. Operator: Arriva.
Connects with Journey 44 in Newcastle and 46 in Berwick.

Berwick-upon-Tweed ←

Journey 45 offers a splendid panorama of coastal Northumberland – made possible by the Arriva 501 bus service. Travellers in a rush to get to Scotland can trim an hour off the journey with the 505 from Newcastle to Berwick, but the 501, albeit slower, is much the more adventurous route. It takes in castles galore: Alnwick, well-preserved and with a flourishing garden, lonely ruined Dunstanburgh and Bamburgh, rebuilt in Victorian times.

The first part of the run from Newcastle is **urban England**, then leafy suburbs, until the bus is eventually clear of the Tyneside conurbation. Here is a bus with attitude, speeding north along the A1, but leaving the main highway here and there to serve communities like **Morpeth** and Felton that are bypassed by the dual carriageway.

This is undemanding country, with views that stretch for ever, and the first half of the journey north is a chance to relax. There are good things to come. At **Alnwick** the fun begins, as the 501 takes to the coast. It loops down by **Alnmouth** station, a reminder of how the speed of modern trains contrasts with the leisurely pace of Britain's local bus services. The fastest direct trains will whisk you from London to lonely Alnmouth in just three-and-a-half hours.

Most buses on this route then head directly for Longhoughton, passing the RAF base at Boulmer, home to a fleet of air-sea search and rescue helicopters which you may well see and hear on your travels along the Northumbrian coast.

Northumberland's coastal path is a superb walk and **Longhoughton** is one place you can easily join it from the bus. The path threads along the coast a mile east of the village but it is well worth the effort. At the north end of Longhoughton you can also alight to walk through woodlands to **Howick Hall**, a tranquil place with large gardens and an historical association with Earl Grey. He was the man who used bergamot to improve the flavour of tea made using local water with a high lime content, so inventing the trademark blend that made Earl Grey a household name.

Berwick-upon-Tweed

Holy Island

44 mins

N

Bamburgh
10 mins

Seahouses
32 mins

11 mins
Craster
23 mins

Alnwick

Alnmouth

37 mins

Morpeth

30 mins

Newcastle upon Tyne

I CAN SEE THE SEA!

You finally get a close encounter with the sea at **Craster** (see box on page 207), as the 501 makes a tour of the village, passing the harbour twice. Quarrying was once a major industry, and whinstone for London's kerbs was shipped from Craster harbour, but there is little sign of that now and it is a pleasant place to enjoy the oystercatchers and eider ducks. Crab pots, flower beds and a lifeboat house make it hard to resist the temptation to linger.

After back-tracking to the main road, the bus heads north to Embleton. From the village centre, where there are several pubs and a shop, you can take a short walk down to **Embleton Bay** and discover another thing that Northumberland has in quantity:

CRASTER

Craster harbour is still used by local fishermen. It is a delightful stop-off point, not just for the harbour and village facilities, but also for coastal walks. A favourite is the amble north through meadows for a mile to what was once the largest castle in Northumberland. **Dunstanburgh Castle** is long-ruined and perched on a rocky promontory. The romance of the location was not lost on Turner, who did several paintings of it.

Craster is famous for its kippers. As you pass on the bus, you may well see smoke rising from the roof vents of **Robson's smoke house**, where they have been produced for over 150 years using traditional methods. For a pint and a snack try the **Jolly Fisherman** where you will find crab and kippers aplenty on the menu (☎ 01665 576461).

superb beaches. It is indeed a blessing that the North Sea is so cold as otherwise this coast would have been developed and spoilt.

Further north the bus makes another detour to the coast to visit **High Newton-by-the-Sea**. If you get off here and it's the right time of year look out for swallows nesting in the bus shelter. It is a short walk south along a quiet lane to Low Newton-by-the-Sea, a slip of a place with the 18th-century Ship Inn and cottages set round a village green. Adjacent is Newton Pool which is a nature reserve with hides for birdwatching.

In contrast, **High Newton beach** has nothing at all which makes it one of the best spots to sit and enjoy this coast as it is so utterly peaceful. The walk to the beach is super with plenty of flowers along the verges of the country lane, the long grass in the adjacent fields shimmering in the wind and – if you are lucky – larks singing high above. To my mind this is what Northumberland is all about and just being there lifts the spirits.

It is five miles to **Beadnell**, where the bus dives down a narrow lane to go through the village centre. Look out for St Ebba's Parish Church, named after the sister of Oswald, the 7th-century Northumbrian king. Near the church is the Craster Arms Hotel.

This building started life as a pele tower, a place of refuge in small settlements where folk feared the raids of the **Border Rievers** and other marauding incomers from Scotland.

A short hop from Beadnell takes you across a golf course to Seahouses which has the feel of a real seaside resort.

CASTLE IN THE AIR

The bus heads through **North Sunderland**, an oddly-named place far distant from Sunderland, prior to a dash along the dunes to Bamburgh. On the other side of the dunes is a particularly fine beach and beyond there are fine views out to the Farne Islands. But **Bamburgh** boasts something special, a castle that is truly one of the highlights of this route. The basalt outcrop at Bamburgh acts as a natural fortress. The castle which you see today is a Victorian creation, restored and reconstructed by the first Lord Armstrong. From the castle there are splendid views all round.

In the village is the **Grace Darling Museum** (☎ 01668 214910; open 10.00–16.00/17.00 depending on season), run by the RNLI Heritage Trust. It tells the story of lifeboats with particular emphasis on the rescue by Grace Darling who is buried at Saint Aidan's Church across the road. Well worth a visit, the church is central to the history of Christianity in this corner of England.

Route 501 has one last close encounter with the sea as the bus skirts Budle Bay. However, unless you catch high tide you are more likely to see waders feeding on the sands than any serious water. Then the bus turns inland to Belford, an old market town which is an important interchange point for local buses.

The rest of the journey to **Berwick** is back on the A1. However, you are rewarded by the sight of Holy Island on the right. At Beal, there is on certain days a connection by bus to the island (see box below). Berwick-upon-Tweed is journey's end. Much of this historic town is perched on a fragment of land on the north side of the Tweed. It is an oddity of geography, and of course a rare spot north of the River Tweed that can be reached with an English bus pass. ∎

| ABOUT THE AUTHOR | **DAVID BEILBY** has long experience as an engineer working in the rail industry. He has enjoyed many relaxing visits to the Northumberland coast. |

BY BUS TO HOLY ISLAND

Perhaps the **quirkiest bus route** in Northumberland, though certainly not the most frequent, is Service 477 from Berwick-upon-Tweed via Beal to **Holy Island**. There are connections at Beal with buses to and from Newcastle upon Tyne. Holy Island relies on a **tidal causeway** for a link to the mainland.

During the brief **summer season**, the bus to Holy Island operates daily except Sundays. For the rest of the year, it is generally Saturdays only with sometimes Wednesday journeys thrown in too. Because the causeway is flooded at high water, the **timetable** for this bus service is necessarily complicated, varying as required to catch low tide. On days when buses do run, there are two journeys out to Holy Island, allowing anything from three to eight hours on the island. Details at www.lindisfarne.org.uk where you will find the current bus schedules under 'general information'.

The bus to Holy Island is not the only bus route in Britain with a timetable governed by the tides. Another example is on the **Hebridean island of Barra**, where services to the island airport are governed by the pattern of arriving and departing flights. As the planes land on the beach, the flight timetable is dictated by the tides. And the buses which serve the airport follow suit. NG

SCOTLAND

The extraordinary range of bus services in Scotland is potentially a prime asset for both locals and visitors alike. Yet in many more rural areas of Scotland, most notably in the **Highland Council area**, poorly co-ordinated timetables and woeful information provision makes it a challenge for those not intimately familiar with the geography of the area to plan complicated journeys across the region. The problem is not pervasive in Scotland. Some Councils, such as Argyll and Bute, do a very good job in providing bus information. And Highland Council do say that they'll have better bus information available on their website for the 2012 season.

Traveline Scotland (www.travelinescotland.com) does a good job in trying to bring some sensible order to Scottish travel planning, but even they evidently don't appreciate that good up-to-date route maps, ideally showing service numbers, bus frequency and operator details, are the basis for planning long itineraries through deeply rural areas. But if you already know which routes you wish to travel, then you'll find a good timetable library on the Traveline Scotland website.

Okay, that's the downside. Yet start **exploring Scotland by bus** and whatever frustrations you might have encountered in planning will quickly evaporate. The experience is awesome, and as long as you go prepared for Scottish weather and the occasional long wait between buses, you really are in for a treat. Many of the most memorable journeys we have ever made by bus were in Scotland. A journey on the slow bus from Inverness to Edinburgh (the M91 operated by Park's of Hamilton) on a May evening was idyllic, the dipping sun catching the **Cairngorms** and Spey Valley at their best. This is a longish journey, a shade under five hours, but the scenery from Inverness to just north of Perth, when darkness finally closed in, was unremittingly beautiful. Then we dozed for an hour or two and awoke as the bus cruised into the Scottish capital in plenty of time for us still to enjoy a wee nightcap at The Dome on George Street, conveniently close to Edinburgh bus station.

RECORD BREAKERS

Scotland boasts the longest routes in the United Kingdom on which **concessionary bus passes** are valid (note that in Scotland these passes are generally referred to as the **National Entitlement Card**). And, just for the record, the longest of them all is the morning departure from Glasgow on Scottish Citylink's 915 service which runs 233 miles to Uig on the Isle of Skye. That's a journey of 7hrs 45mins, and the timetable happily provides for a 50-minute lunch stop in Fort William and then a ten-minute mid afternoon stop for tea in Kyle of Lochalsh. This is Scottish travel at its most civilised.

In a perfect world, with *Bus-Pass Britain* extending to several volumes, we'd have loved to include more Scottish routes. The 95, running south from St Andrews around the Fife coast, is a very fine excursion. Pressure of space squeezed it out, and Lothian Buses 26 through **the heart of Edinburgh** suffered the same fate. It links the beach at Portobello with Edinburgh Zoo, taking in graceful Princes Street along the way. Or, for something really adventurous, why not try the spinal route through the Outer Hebrides? You can travel from Port Nis (Port of Ness) on the Isle of Lewis to the island of Barra by bus and ferry in about 12 hours.

We offer here a choice of five routes for *Bus-Pass Britain*, among them the two longest journeys in this book (nos. 48 and 50). Throw in a lovely **Tweed Valley exploration**, a brave push west to Rannoch's wild moor, and a short but delightful route across the **Cowal peninsula**, and you have the perfect introduction to exploring Scotland by bus. ∎

Richard West

Berwick-upon-Tweed

Service no. 67 | Journey time 1hr 45mins

OS Landranger 75,74,73. Runs every 2hrs Mon–Sat,
5 journeys Sun. Operator: Perryman's Buses.
Connects with Journey 45 in Berwick-upon-Tweed.

Galashiels

I have a long-standing interest in railways, a mode of transport that is nowadays virtually unknown in the **Scottish Borders** (though possibly set to return in three or four years with the reopening of the Waverley Line from Edinburgh to Galashiels). The Tweed Valley rail route from Berwick to Galashiels closed in 1964, and the main line from Carlisle to Edinburgh succumbed five years later.

So us Border folk have learnt to use buses, and the information boards at **Berwick-upon-Tweed** railway station have adapted to the new order by even including some bus departures in their listings. They show, for example, the number 60 services to Galashiels via Duns. It is a tame route, operated by First, and nowhere near as interesting as the 67 which follows the **Tweed Valley** upstream all the way to Galashiels. The latter is not deemed worthy of a mention on the information boards. And that's a pity, for it has the edge over the First route via Duns. The 67 is well run by a respected local operator called Perryman's, a family business worth supporting. Companies like this add colour and variety to the increasingly uniform British bus transport scene. And, like other routes commended in this book (eg: Journeys 19 and 21), the service is essentially a rail-replacement bus link, in this case closely following the route of the erstwhile railway to Galashiels. All that besides, the 67 stops right outside my house.

Perryman's drivers are a friendly bunch, and the 67 is a convivial excursion through splendid Borders scenery. There's always a lively conversation on board – much better, surely, than the tinny rattle of leaking headphones.

Leaving Berwick we have fine views of the magnificent **Royal Border Bridge** and, looking in the opposite direction, the mouth of the Tweed and the North Sea. Berwick is hard to place: this notionally English town has a mainly Scottish hinterland. Its football and rugby teams play in Scottish leagues.

The disused railway along the Tweed Valley haunts this route, and you'll catch many shadows of the old line. Looking out towards the silvery, and here very languid, Tweed, you will see isolated sections of embankment and soon, as our bus passes the hamlet of **Velvet Hall**, the first set of broken bridge abutments. The 1963 Scottish Region timetable shows that while only two daily trains travelled this section of the route towards the end of its life (such was British Railways' keenness to discourage use and make the case for closure), the slowest was still 25 minutes quicker than the current bus service. This rail route, like so many others across Britain, was swept away by the unlamented Doctor Beeching in the name of progress.

We leave the main road to serve **Norham**, a sizeable village that still boasts a handful of real shops. The old railway station

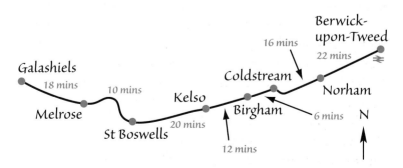

has a little **museum** (☎ 01289 382217 to make an appointment) that recalls life in the days when trains still stopped in Norham. The town's most striking monument is Norham Castle. Besieged 13 times, including once for a year by Robert the Bruce, the castle fell to James IV in 1513 just before he himself was defeated at **Flodden Field**. The present structure, largely rebuilt in the 16th century, is in the care of English Heritage. All in all, Norham is a good point to stop off for a pub lunch or a picnic.

CROSSING THE TWEED

Continuing up the valley, and still on the English side of the border, the bus crosses the River Till – a watercourse with a bad local reputation for drownings – and soon reaches Cornhill. Here, at last, our bus plucks up the courage to cross the frontier. And it's done in style, using Smeaton's elegant seven-arched bridge over the Tweed. Robert Burns crossed the bridge in 1787, the first time in his life that he left Scottish soil. A plaque on the bridge recalls the moment.

Across the Tweed, we arrive in **Coldstream**. 'The First True Border Toon' is home of the regiment of the same name. It has a pleasantly old-fashioned small shopping centre. Just northwest of the town is the **Hirsel Estate**, ancestral home of the Home family who readers of a certain age will recall for Sir Alec Douglas-Home. A remarkably lifelike statue of the former Conservative Prime Minister adorns the entrance to the estate. The Hirsel also offers an excellent tea shop, delightful walks and a herd of instantly loveable Highland cattle. Beyond Coldstream, there are excellent views of the River Tweed on the left. The village of **Birgham** makes a pleasant lunch stop (see box on page 215).

Kelso, the midpoint of the route, has the best-preserved historic townscape in the Borders, a cobbled square, and a fine range of tea rooms. Pick of the bunch is Caroline's Coffee Shop on Horsemarket (☎ 01573 226996; open 08.00–17.00 Mon–Sat, also on Sun during summer), which offers light lunches, and all things Scottish from home baking (including Millionaire's Shortbread and Rocky Roads) to black pudding rolls. Kelso has a **fine riverside location** (of which, it must be said, more could be made), and a ruined abbey. This recalls past monastic wealth and the time when nearby Roxburgh was the seat of King David's power in Scotland. Roxburgh Castle is now but a huge grassy hump crowned by a few stone fragments, while the adjacent meadow lands, once occupied by a thriving community, surely still have many archaeological secrets to reveal.

The jewel in Kelso's crown is undoubtedly **Floors Castle**, home of the Duke of Roxburghe's family since 1721. The fine riverside pile boasts magnificent gardens and, this being Scotland, the Terrace Café offers lunches and Scottish home baking by the duke's own chef (check opening times for the house and café on www.roxburghe.net). The estate can be reached on foot from the town or ask the bus driver to drop you off at the lodge.

We pass the distant, somehow slightly sinister, tower at Smailholm and, after another crossing of the Tweed, the bus reaches **St Boswells**. The penultimate town served is Melrose, with the largest and best-preserved Borders abbey and a decidedly touristy ambience. This is the place for ices, Scottish souvenirs – some tasteful, others best passed over – and some serious ladies' outfitters. Not as self-consciously 'tartan' as Pitlochry, **Melrose** still attracts summer coach tours and on a fine Sunday in August can seem rather overwhelmed. But its townscape has been tastefully developed, its buildings are in good shape and the town certainly exudes prosperity. **Melrose Abbey** itself is well interpreted by Historic Scotland and for those not inclined to vertigo, the climb up the breezy tower offers fine views. A short walk to the footbridge over the Tweed can be rounded off with a pub lunch or, a little further on, the village of Gattonside has the excellent Chapters Bistro (☎ 01896 823217).

Arrival in **Galashiels** is something of an anticlimax. Our journey ends in the town's decidedly down-at-heel bus station, adjacent to the High Street with too many empty shops. But this is set to change when, after a gap of almost half a century, the first trains arrive in Galashiels again. A new transport interchange is being planned. This will transform the town, bringing an injection of Edinburgh money and making Galashiels less than an hour from the Scottish capital. Whether it will change the pattern of bus routes is not yet known but, if you want to enjoy route 67 at its best, head to the border country sooner rather than later. ∎

ABOUT THE AUTHOR | **RICHARD WEST** is a retired civil servant and keen reader of *hidden europe* magazine. He likes seeking out under-publicised journeys by train, bus and ship. He often travels route 67.

The ruins of Melrose Abbey
(photo © Creativehearts / DT)

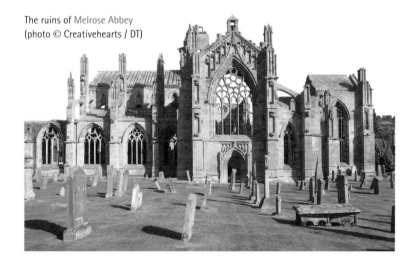

COWAL CONNECTIONS

Douglas Blades

Dunoon

Service no. 478 (part journeys nos. 471, 477, 479) |
Journey time 1hr 5mins to 1hr 50mins

OS Landranger 63, 56, 55, 62. Two to four journeys Mon–Sat (no Sun service).
Operators: West Coast Motors / Tighnabruaich Service Station.
Ferry from Portavadie to Tarbert connects with Journey 48.

Portavadie

Journey 48 in this book will escort us the long way round from Glasgow to the Mull of Kintyre, skirting Loch Lomond and following the A83 over 'Rest and be Thankful'. But there is a credible alterative, using ferries across the Clyde and lower Loch Fyne, and taking the bus across the Cowal peninsula to link those two ferry trips.

Visitors to **Glasgow** are often surprised just how easy it is to escape the city. It takes little more than an hour, using a train and then a boat, to reach Dunoon. And it is the ferry terminal in **Dunoon** that is the starting point for the bus making the 28-mile journey to Portavadie. This is another world from Glasgow and the Clydeside conurbation. Our route includes long stretches on single-track roads with passing places. We skirt lochs, follow deep glens, climb steep hillsides, and you'll not see a lot of people on the way – just the occasional isolated farmstead or cottage. And, although this is wild country, there are some fabulous forests along the way.

'Off to the Bermuda Triangle again,' says our driver as he starts the engine on the bus at Dunoon. It's a local joke that the regulars on board have heard a dozen times before. But fear not!

Deeply rural though Cowal may be, you'll not be lost without trace. The timetable is designed to serve the isolated west Cowal area, providing access to schools and shopping. This does slightly restrict journey opportunities from the Dunoon end of the route. Saturday's timetable is the best chance to cover the whole route and gives time for a walk and a bite to eat in a local café. For guidance on local walks check the **Cowalfest website** (www.cowalfest.org/pwalks.htm), which is looked after by the Cowal Walking Festival Association, a community-led initiative which each October organises a walking and arts festival in Cowal.

LOCHS, HILLS AND GLENS

The bus takes the main road north out of Dunoon, through the main street and over the hill to **Sandbank** with views across Holy Loch to Kilmun and Strone. The US Navy operated nuclear submarines from their **Holy Loch** base for many years and it was a blow to the local economy when they pulled out as part of the peace dividend at the end of the Cold War. Between 1961 and 1992 the view would have been blocked by the presence of a large American submarine depot ship moored in the middle of the loch. A successful and expanding marina has since been established at Holy Loch.

After Sandbank the bus passes former US Navy housing at Sandhaven before turning left on to the B836 which is mostly single track with passing places resulting in frequent stops to allow oncoming traffic to pass. A bit of a novelty if you aren't used to such roads! The first village along this road is **Clachaig**, a collection of a few houses, but over the wall on the left hand side just before the village are substantial moss-covered ruins, seen more easily from the bus than from a car. The extensive ruins are the remains of the **Glen Lean gunpowder mill**. At one time the gunpowder industry employed a substantial number of people in Argyll. The Glen Lean works opened around 1840 and were active until the early years of the twentieth century.

After Clachaig, the road enters open country and starts to climb Glen Lean passing at its summit Loch Tarsan, an artificial loch created in 1951 for a local hydro-electric scheme. We drop down and skirt the head of Loch Striven, then cross another small pass to reach **Auchenbreck** – no more than a hamlet but a strategic road junction. This is where we connect with buses to and from Rothesay, a half-hour journey that includes a short ferry ride across the **Kyles of Bute**. Cowal life is unhurried, so the stop at Auchenbreck is always a social moment. The drivers exchange greetings and messages and also ensure passengers are transferred safely before each bus continues on its journey. The drivers are usually regulars who are on first-name terms with their passengers.

The route now joins the A886 northwards before turning left on to the A8003 for Tighnabruaich. Although classed as an A road, you will be surprised to find that it is mostly single track with passing places. After passing **Ormidale House** – since the late 17th century intimately associated with Clan Campbell – and skirting the edge of Loch Riddon, the route climbs towards the famous Kyles of Bute viewpoint. This really must be the best **scenic drive** in Scotland. Here, the route is lined with rhododendrons and will be bursting with colour if you visit at the right time of year.

As the bus climbs towards the viewpoint, the Kyles (or narrows) come into view. The viewpoint is reached at about 500 feet. There is a bench and a map giving an interpretation of the view as you look down the east Kyles over the small Burnt Islands, down towards the ferry used by travellers to Rothesay.

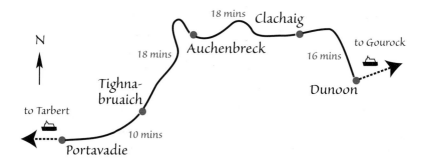

LOCAL CAFÉS

Despite the rural nature of the area and sparse population there are a number of good local cafés. Some are only open on a seasonal basis, so best to check beforehand if travelling off season. Here are two top choices. In Tighnabruaich don't miss the chic **Burnside Bistro** (☎ 01700 811739). This newly renovated restaurant, very ably run for 17 years by Joyce King, offers everything from tasty simple snacks to more formal fare. Joyce also offers rooms (singles £40, doubles £70). At the end of the route, the stylish bar and restaurant at **Portavadie Marina** (☎ 01700 811075) is an essay in modern minimalism with great views out over the new marina.

The view is stunning, a beautiful combination of land, sea and sky. The chances are that you'll see plenty of yachts and if you have chosen your day and time wisely you may catch the famous paddle steamer *Waverley* making her way to or from Tighnabruaich.

The north end of Bute can be seen across the Kyles as the bus route wends its way down towards **Tighnabruaich**, a quiet lochside village popular with the yachting fraternity. Two further villages are passed before reaching the end of the route. These are Kames, which like Tighnabruaich once had its own pier served by Clyde steamers, and Millhouse. The terminus is the isolated ferry terminal at **Portavadie**, an area which is undergoing significant development nowadays. A new marina has been constructed complete with a café. There are some good walks along Loch Fyne from Portavadie. However, this needn't be the end of your journey as an hourly ferry service makes the 25-minute crossing over to Tarbert at the top of the **Kintyre peninsula** where you can join Journey 48 in this book. Service 926 from Tarbert will speed you back to Glasgow in just three hours. ■

ABOUT THE
AUTHOR | **DOUGLAS BLADES** is Public Transport Officer at Argyll and Bute Council and has been involved with the local community in developing the bus routes in this area. This one is a favourite.

ESSENTIAL SCOTLAND

Deirdre Forsyth

Glasgow

Service no. 926 | Journey time 3hrs 40mins to 4hrs 10mins

OS Landranger 64, 63, 56, 55, 62, 68. Three journeys each day in winter, 5 per day in summer. Operators: West Coast Motors / Scottish Citylink. Ferry from Tarbert to Portavadie connects with Journey 47.

Campbeltown

Our previous journey took in a fine fragment of Highland scenery as we crossed the Cowal peninsula. With Journey 48, we take in a great sweep of **West Highland landscape** including Loch Lomond and magnificent Kintyre. For 18 years, the 926 was my local bus route and also a lifeline link to Glasgow and the wider world. Although this is a longer-distance route, Scottish National Entitlement Cards are recognised for free travel.

If you are riding the 926 on a quiet day, make the most of opportunities to swap sides along the route. For the stretch along Loch Lomond, shortly after leaving Glasgow, the right side is the best bet. Then left gives the best views around Loch Fyne, but you'll certainly want to be on the right again south of Tarbert for the glorious run south down the Kintyre coast to Campbeltown.

The 926 cruises authoritatively past local city buses as we head out from **Glasgow**. Speed is the theme on this bus that serves only a very limited number of stops on the first 45 minutes of the journey. But once we get to the shores of **Loch Lomond**, this is just like any local bus and the driver has to be prepared to stop for passengers at any point along the road – even if they are not standing at the bus stop.

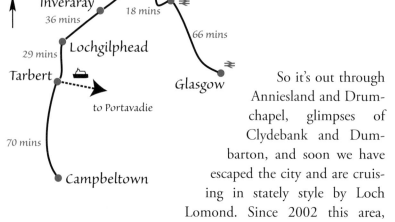

So it's out through Anniesland and Drumchapel, glimpses of Clydebank and Dumbarton, and soon we have escaped the city and are cruising in stately style by Loch Lomond. Since 2002 this area, with the neighbouring Trossachs region, has enjoyed national park status. Ahead lies the clear profile of **Ben Lomond**, said by some to have been the inspiration for the Paramount Pictures logo. This stretch of the route is at its best on a crisp winter's day: skeletal trees, heavy frost and bright sunshine make a magic combination.

Tarbet marks the point when we leave Loch Lomond and cut over a low hill to the head of Loch Long. You'll run across places called Tarbet or Tarbert all over western Scotland. The name comes from a Scottish Gaelic word that refers to a place where it was possible to haul boats between one loch and another. Later on our journey we'll stop at another such spot: Tarbert (this one with an 'r'). The bus just glances **Loch Long**, pausing for a crowd of hikers to alight, and now starts the haul to the top of 'Rest and be Thankful' – a pious name that recalls that this was once a difficult climb. Even nowadays, landslides or heavy snow quite often lead to the closure of this main road.

Over the top, and dropping down to the west, I know that **Loch Fyne** will be my companion for the next 90 minutes. I think spring when the primroses and harebells are out and the air is clear, is the best season to enjoy this part of the route. We stop at **Cairndow**, a wee slip of a place, but well known as the home of Loch Fyne Oysters. From modest beginnings in 1988 on the shores of this remote Scottish loch, the company grew to include over three dozen restaurants. You can still visit the original Oyster Bar on the shores of Loch Fyne (☎ 01499 600482; open daily from 09.00).

INVERARAY AND LOCH FYNE

Inveraray, a conservation village founded by the Duke of Argyll in 1745, is next and here the bus stops for a few minutes. Just enough time to stretch my legs and enjoy the view over Loch Fyne to St Catherines in Cowal. This Inveraray stop on the 926 is always a nice moment. It is as if all aboard have been conspirators in a plot to escape from Glasgow. And now, here in Inveraray, we can take a breath of Highland air, look at each other, and rejoice that 'we've done it.' If you are tempted to stop off in Inverary, the George Hotel (☎ 01499 302111; doubles from £75) is a good bet for rooms. Don't be deterred by the inscription in the hotel, written by Robert Burns, that tells how unhappy the Scottish poet was with the service.

Heading on south, we leave the loch shore just briefly, returning to the water at **Furnace**, a village that once made a decent living from the gunpowder industry. A mile or two south of the village is Crarae Gardens (☎ 0844 4932210; open daily 09.30 till sunset, but note that the visitor centre is open Thu–Mon in Apr–Oct only). The bus driver will stop on request at the gate if you are minded to explore this Himalayan-style woodland garden. Before long we are in **Lochgilphead**, a place with more of a buzz than many Argyll towns for it is the administrative centre of Argyll and Bute Council.

The next village is Ardrishaig with views of Arran to the south. The **Crinan Canal** starts here. It is about 9 miles long and the parallel towpath makes a pleasant walk. The canal was started in 1794 to cut out the 120-mile sail round the Mull of Kintyre from the Firth of Clyde to the Atlantic Ocean. Then on down the banks of Loch Fyne, past the South Knapdale road to Kilberry

EXPLORING KINTYRE

Campbeltown is a little down at heel these days, having lost its regular car-ferry service over to Ireland about 10 years ago. But it is still a good base for travel adventures. In 2011, the local bus company West Coast Motors set up a **summer speedboat link** to Ballycastle on the Causeway Coast of Northern Ireland (details on www.kintyreexpress.com). Landlubbers might prefer the **West Coast Motors buses** to the sands and golf course at Machrihanish (9 buses Mon–Sat, service 200), the southern tip of Kintyre at Southend (5 buses daily Mon–Sat, service 444) or the beautiful 40-minute run up the east side of Kintyre to Carradale. This latter route is numbered 300 or 445 and runs five times daily Mon–Sat only.

and Ormsary, until the fishing village of **Tarbert** – the one with the 'r' – comes into view. From here you can take the ferry over to Portavadie to connect with the previous journey in this book.

South from Tarbert the scenery changes, and now the views are westward towards Gigha, Islay and America. The bus stops near the quays at Kennacraig (for **ferries** to Islay) and Tayinloan (for the short hop by ferry over to Gigha). By now our bus is emptying out. We have dropped off folk here and there, and only those bound for the southern reaches of Kintyre remain. This is Britain's longest peninsula, or, as our bus driver nicely puts it 'Britain's longest cul-de-sac.' Long it may be, but it is anything but boring. I catch a glimpse of seals on the sunny foreshore at Bellochantuy, see Rathlin Island off the far-distant Irish coast and then we are in **Campbeltown**. End of the journey for our driver, but gateway to a good network of local bus services connecting villages in this far-flung corner of Scotland (see box above). ∎

ABOUT THE AUTHOR | **DEIRDRE FORSYTH** worked for Argyll and Bute Council for many years. During that period she lived in Ardrishaig, right on the 926 bus route. Visitors could alight at her front door.

To Rannoch's WILD MOOR

Richard West

 Pitlochry

Service nos. 82 and 85 | Journey time 1hr 40mins to 2hrs45 mins

OS Landranger 52, 43, 42. Two journeys Mon–Fri, 1 journey Sat, no Sun service.
Operator: Broon's Buses and Taxis.

Rannoch Moor

Chat to folk in the **Loch Rannoch area** and you'll rarely hear a bad word spoken of Broon's Buses and Taxis. Until March 2011, a red Royal Mail post bus ran from Pitlochry post office, regularly making a five-hour round trip serving remote villages and farms in the hills beyond Loch Tummel and Loch Rannoch. The service was axed leaving **Broon's Buses and Taxis** as the sole provider of road transport to communities in the area. Broon's, which already operated some buses up the valley, beefed up their schedules and helped plug the gap left by the missing post bus. This journey for *Bus-Pass Britain* has formidably complicated timetables which vary by day of week and also with the pattern of local school terms. So do call Broon's (☎ 01882 632331) before setting out or check current schedules at www.broonsbusesandtaxis.co.uk. Some journeys require a change of bus, often with a longish wait, in Kinloch Rannoch. But let's face it: there are many worse places in which one might be stuck.

Catching the Broon's bus from the centre of **Pitlochry** with its constant traffic of sightseers and tourist buses, its main street lined with coffee shops and hotels and its plethora of souvenir shops and Highland outfitters, it is indeed hard to imagine that in less than two hours you will be at what must surely be Scotland's loneliest and most dramatically located transport interchange.

Pitlochry itself, though undoubtedly overdone, has genuine attractions. The wooded valley setting is very fine and the fish ladder on the **River Tummel** is a remarkable piece of engineering appealing equally to those with a technical turn of mind and those who just want to gaze at the views from its terrace. The Festival Theatre, now into its 60th season, not only offers dramatic productions but arts courses and workshops and has a fine riverside restaurant.

Once on the bus, the Highland landscape is rather marred by an excess of camping and caravan sites, but matters improve once past Queen's View. **Loch Tummel** opens up on the left (from which side of the bus the best views are to be had throughout) as the road twists and turns through the forest above the loch. Forest trails abound for the more energetic and the Loch Tummel Hotel enjoys a magnificent position, but stopping off for refreshments might be tricky with the rather sparse timetable on this route.

Kinloch Rannoch comes as something of a culture shock in the middle of this vastness, with its small and very smart public housing development and its generally practical and workaday feel. The village previously relied on forestry and shooting estates, but both now employ only a fraction of the workforce of earlier times,

Wild Rannoch Moor
(photo © Photos1st / DT)

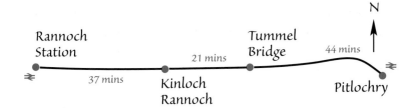

and tourism is the basis of the local economy. But the village is not artificial; the well-stocked shop is full of everyday commodities (as it needs to be in a place so far from a supermarket), and all around are fertile and prosperous looking fields, indicating agriculture continues to make a contribution to the local economy.

WESTWARD BOUND

It is perhaps here that the real adventure begins. West from Kinloch Rannoch you have a sense of heading into **wild country**. The bus is smaller, and passengers are fewer. But if you secure a front seat, the friendly driver will offer a free guided tour of local sights and describe wildlife spotted along the route. Ospreys are seen from time to time and even golden eagles too. The road hugs the northern edge of **Loch Rannoch** and the stopping points in the timetable turn out to be at most small clusters of cottages. A number of small hydro-electric plants are passed, their neatly kept 1930s buildings working monuments to an earlier age of renewable energy. Some local children travel from remote houses hereabouts to **Aberfeldy** every day for school, a marathon commute in good weather and one surely subject to frequent interruption in winter. Broon's Buses and Taxis take care of the school run over to Aberfeldy too.

Once past the head of Loch Rannoch, the landscape becomes almost lunar, with the road twisting between rocky outcrops, dotted with lochans and a distant circle of mountain peaks affording a dramatic horizon. One has a sense of having perhaps stumbled on Conan Doyle's lost world. With low cloud swirling over the moor, it would be no great surprise to find Richard

Hannay standing by the side of the road, his hand raised to hail the omnibus to Rannoch station.

And yet there is life at the end of this long, long road. Here in this ocean of wild moor is an oasis: the white-painted walls of the **Moor of Rannoch Hotel** appear almost to float in the mist. This is the end of the road. A signpost, pointing off rather uninvitingly into the barren desert of wild moor, conveys the intelligence that Glencoe is merely 12 miles distant. A long walk.

But there is a surprise here for Rannoch also has one of Britain's remotest railway stations. Somehow not only the line to Fort William but this tiny train station managed to survive the decimation of our railway network in the 1960s. There are trains north to **Fort William** and the fishing port of **Mallaig**, and south to Glasgow. And, quite against the odds, a direct overnight sleeper to and from London. The Moor of Rannoch Hotel encourages visitors to arrive in this manner. To watch the train disappear into the vastness of the moor, while a stag wanders past the hotel window as you eat dinner, is quite unforgettable. To hear it approach in the morning through the silent emptiness of this landscape at breakfast time is equally memorable. ∎

ABOUT THE AUTHOR | **RICHARD WEST** is a retired civil servant, living in Kelso in southern Scotland. He likes seeking out under-publicised journeys by train, bus and ship.

FOUR FIRTHS IN THE FAR NORTH

Eric Newton

50 Inverness

Service no. X99 | Journey time 3hrs

OS Landranger 26, 21, 17, 11. Five journeys Mon–Sat, 3 journeys on Sun.
Operator: Stagecoach Highlands.

Thurso

When we board the X99 bus on an April morning, we are nearing the end of a two-week journey by bus across Britain. Archie and I had set out from **Land's End**. Archie, it must be said, is smart, intelligent and much-travelled. Few other eight-year-old terriers have seen as much of Britain as Archie. Like another of the Scottish routes in this book, namely Journey 48, the X99 has an ambiguous status. It is more than merely a local bus, but not quite an express coach. But Scottish National Entitlement Cards do allow free travel on the X99, and you can even reserve spaces in advance (go to www.citylink.co.uk for bookings or call ☎ 0871 2663333).

Starting point for our final big hop north is **Inverness**, the city at the top end of Scotland's Great Glen, and the spot where the **River Ness** reaches the Moray Firth. And that sets the tone for this bus journey to the northern reaches of the Scottish mainland, for our route has firths aplenty: Moray, Cromarty, Dornoch and Pentland. Inverness is solid and reassuring, its 19th-century red sandstone castle standing on high ground overlooking the neo-Gothic Episcopalian Cathedral of St Andrew's on the opposite bank. Imposing stuff.

DORNOCH

The improbably small **cathedral town** of Dornoch deserves a stop. The original 13th-century cathedral dedicated to St Gilbert has since been replaced by the present 19th-century building that is more like a large parish church. In the churchyard is a flat stone of fixed length, known as the **Plaiden Ell**, once used for measuring cuts of plaid or tartan cloth. On the way down to the beach is a memorial recalling how in 1727, Janet Horne was convicted of **witchcraft**, rolled in tar, placed inside a barrel and burnt alive. Life in Dornoch seems altogether tamer these days. No witches, no executions. If you are tempted to linger, you'll find many good cafés and pubs. **Luigi's** on Castle Street (☎ 01862 810 893; open daily from 10.00) draws a lively local crowd.

Inverness's road links with the north were transformed in 1982 when the splendid new **bridge at Kessock** opened, making redundant the ferry of the same name. And that impressively graceful bridge is our fast getaway route on the X99. Within a few minutes of leaving Inverness bus station we are speeding across the fertile grazing of the Black Isle. We drop down to Cromarty Firth, crossing the water by a low-slung structure that seems more causeway than bridge. What a far cry from Inverness this is. Now there are **wild moors ahead**, remnants of winter snow on the hills, and we have a sense of leaving civilisation far behind us. Archie is duly attentive to the unfolding landscape, and so am I.

Following the northern shores of the firth, we bypass the small town of Invergordon that is dominated by towering steel megaliths: three oil rigs undergoing repair and maintenance within the safe anchorage of the firth. Continuing along the A9, we reach the historic town of **Tain**, the oldest of all the Scottish royal burghs. The elegant sandstone buildings of the town centre and the Gothic-style market cross are dominated by a tall tower known as the Tollbooth. On past the whisky distillery at **Glenmorangie** located on the southern shores of the Dornoch Firth, and then our bus crosses the newly constructed road bridge that now spans the firth, saving a twenty-mile trip around its head. On a stormy day in 1809, a ferry's passengers and crew, 100 people in all, drowned when the vessel sank while crossing **Dornoch Firth** just by the site of the modern road bridge. Perhaps modern travel has become too easy. Once over the bridge our bus, which has kept up a cracking pace all the way from Inverness, leaves the A9 to serve Dornoch.

The wild Northeast

Back on the A9, Archie is attending to the gulls outside the window and I am swapping notes with a local man who cannot quite believe that I have travelled so far across Britain by bus. 'From Land's End,' he says, a little incredulously. 'So far… so far.' The man points out **Loch Fleet**, a little sea loch which is home to ospreys. The countryside is now becoming quite barren and rocky with few trees visible. And what trees there are have been mightily distorted by the fierce winds that taunt this wild coast. We stop at the fishing village of **Golspie**, with its little harbour and attractive sandstone buildings. Not far beyond Golspie is **Dunrobin Castle**. It is the ancestral home of the Dukes of Sutherland, and the formal

Dunrobin Castle (photo
© Juliane Jacobs / DT)

gardens are said to be based on those at Versailles. From the bus we get no more than a fleeting glimpse of this horticultural oasis in the wilderness.

North to Caithness

Now the road and railway share a narrow stretch of flat land – to our right the sea and to our left the land rising up steeply. **Brora**, once the industrial powerhouse of Sutherland, is the next place of note. For 200 years coal was mined at Brora, which was used in the evaporation of sea water to extract salt that in turn was used to preserve the landed herrings, at one time so abundant in the nearby seas. Today, no coal is mined nor herrings landed.

We continue up the sparsely populated coast to the small fishing villages of Portgower and **Helmsdale** before crossing into Caithness. Here the A9 climbs up to the Ord of Caithness. The scenery is wild with tortuous climbs and descents along the A9 road as it negotiates its way across the **Berriedale Braes**. I can only imagine how the buses fare when travelling this route in winter snowstorms.

This is a land that has been defined by emigration, its residents not always leaving voluntarily. There are signs by the side of the road pointing to **Badbea**, a village that was cleared by ruthless landowners who wanted to introduce sheep farming to this area some 200 years ago. The last residents clung on to their lives and their history, staying until 1911. Today Badbea is a poignant memorial to the Highland

Thurso
to John
O'Groats
35 mins
N
Latheron
35 mins
Helmsdale
Brora
16 mins
9 mins
Golspie
17 mins
Dornoch
18 mins
Tain
50 mins
Inverness

clearances. We drop down to Langwell Water and the small fishing village of **Berriedale**, guarded by two crenulated towers that were used as lighthouses to guide the local fishermen. Berriedale, like Dunbeath and so many other places on this coast, prospered during the herring boom.

We have, by and large, stuck to the coast from Inverness. But at **Latheron**, our bus turns determinedly inland, heading north across eerily empty blanket bog. There are occasional crofts, huge expanses of heather moorland and small lochans. We leave the main road to stop in **Halkirk**, a neat little village with a distillery that closed a hundred years ago. In Halkirk, we cross the River Thurso, and then it is an easy run north along a pleasant B road into tamer country as we approach **Thurso**. Most passengers alight in the town centre, and Archie and I do too. But there are a handful of stalwarts on board for whom this is not quite journey's end. The bus continues round Thurso Bay to the ferry terminal at Scrabster where the elegant blue and white *MV Hamnavoe* is waiting to ferry them over to the Orkney Islands. As for Archie and I, we are off to explore Thurso (see box above). ■

ABOUT THE AUTHOR | **ERIC NEWTON** is a retired civil engineer, once referred to as a 'free-loading wrinkly'. He lives in Lincoln and enjoys travelling, especially using his free bus pass.

LOST AND FOUND

We feared for Archie, Eric Newton's canine companion on the last of the **fifty bus journeys** in this book. Would he remember to alight when his master did? But Archie is a sensible terrier and always took Eric's cue. Not so Chekhov, a lazy Labrador who, when his minder alighted, stayed snoozing on the top deck of a London bus, only to awake when the bus reached the end of its journey.

'The issue is more complicated than you might imagine,' a spokeswoman for Welsh operator **Cardiff Bus** told us. 'Dogs, even cats, opportunely jump on our buses at bus stops, sometimes merely out of curiosity, sometimes looking for a free ride.' Evidently these **freeloading pets** don't always know where to alight, become haplessly lost and end up in the lost property division office at Cardiff bus station. That was Snowy's fate. She hopped on a number 61 in Cardiff while her owner was distracted by a shop window. Thankfully, Cardiff Bus co-opted a dog-loving member of their team to care for Snowy until her frantic owner claimed her.

In London, it is **Sherlock** who presides over the difficult business of reuniting lost property with its rightful owners. Sherlock is a computer who lives in Transport for London's **lost property office** in Baker Street – the very street where Sherlock Holmes was a (fictional) neighbour. Sherlock will process some 200,000 lost items this year, many of them left on London buses. Among the less-probable items that Sherlock processed over the last year were dentures and an empty coffin.

We have always judged Wiltshire to be a very tame county – and all the better for that. But Wiltshire life does have its hazards. Back in 2004, a number 55 bus arrived in Swindon bus station one Sunday afternoon after the one-hour run from Chippenham. On board were a dozen passengers and an eight-foot-long **boa constrictor**. The snake's owner was never traced, and the animal was sent to a new home in Surrey.

Books are of course very frequently left on buses. Last year, Sherlock logged over 30,000 of them. Not to mention lots of manuscripts. Authors are dreadfully forgetful folk and many great writers have left drafts on public transport or at bus and train stations. The first version of *Seven Pillars of Wisdom* suffered just such a fate, when **T E Lawrence** was changing trains in Reading. Lawrence had to start again from scratch. NG

Reference Section: Bus-Pass Basics

Three different **concessionary schemes** for bus travel by older residents operate in Britain – one, respectively, for each of **England**, **Scotland** and **Wales**. Travel may be free to the holder of the relevant pass, but that does not mean that the bus company goes without remuneration for your journey. There is a complex formula by which bus operators are reimbursed for concessionary travel, one that many bus companies forcefully argue leaves them short-changed.

THE RESIDENCE QUESTION

Let's try and clear up some of the misunderstandings associated with these schemes. If you do not live in Great Britain and are merely visiting on holiday, or even making a lengthy stay with non-resident status, then you'll not be eligible for a pass. But if you really are resident and can show evidence of that (for example through regular payment of Council tax), then – provided you meet the age qualifications – you'll be eligible for free travel. This is a **matter of residence**, not a question of nationality.

But if you don't qualify for free travel, don't despair. Travel on local buses in Britain is often **very modestly priced**, and you can follow every route in this book without having to spend the earth. Day tickets and cheap regional passes (valid for a day, a week or longer) allow fare-paying passengers to enjoy the **freedom to roam**.

THE AGE QUESTION

In Scotland, you need to be 60 years old to qualify for free bus travel (which is provided in Scotland as part of a broader package of benefits under the National Entitlement Card). And the 60 threshold applies also in Wales.

For folk in England life is a little tougher. They have to wait till later for their bus passes, and the **qualifying age** is being raised month-by-month, until eventually it stabilises at 65 (for residents of England born on or after 6 April 1955). However legislation proposed by the Westminster government, but still not approved by parliament, would if enacted have the effect of raising the state pension age to 66 by 2020. It has not yet been clarified whether the qualifying age for concessionary bus passes would also then rise to 66. Of course, no-one knows if the concessionary bus-travel scheme will even still exist that long hence.

Residents of England can check when they will qualify for a bus pass by going to www.direct.gov.uk and entering the term 'bus pass' in that website's search field. Here are some **examples of eligibility dates** for readers who might already be anticipating their first concessionary trips:

Year of birth	Qualifying date falls in the range
1950	already eligible for a bus pass
1951	6 Sep 2011 to 6 Sep 2013
1952	6 Sep 2013 to 6 Sep 2015
1953	6 Sep 2015 to 6 Sep 2017
1954	6 Sep 2017 to 6 Sep 2019

TIME RESTRICTIONS IN ENGLAND

In both Scotland and Wales, bus passes may be used at any time of day. Sheer bliss. The English National Concessionary Travel Scheme (ENCTS) offers free bus travel from 09.30 until 23.00 Mon–Fri and at any time at weekends and on public holidays. It is open to individual Councils, who issue the cards to residents of their areas, to relax the time restrictions on all or some of the local bus routes within those areas. And many have, particularly in more rural parts of England. And while **some Councils have relaxed the time restrictions** for *all* ENCTS pass holders, elsewhere you will find that the dispensation applies *only* to holders of passes issued by that particular Council.

CROSS-BORDER JOURNEYS

The general precept that a card issued in England is only valid in England is broadly true. Similarly for Scotland and Wales. But there are intriguing exceptions.

A Scottish bus pass may be used for travel on journeys from Scotland to both Carlisle and Berwick-upon-Tweed (and from those cities back to Scotland again). But Scottish passes are not valid for local travel *within* Berwick and Carlisle. **Holders of Scottish bus passes** keen to flee their fair homeland for free might profitably set their sights on a lovely cross-border service run by Munro's of Jedburgh. Service 131 leaves Jedburgh at 09.10 Mon–Sat, crossing into England at Carter Bar and running to Newcastle upon Tyne. A local dispensation allows holders of Scottish bus passes to use this bus to Newcastle (and the courtesy is reciprocated to pass holders from England wanting to travel to Jedburgh on the afternoon return service from Newcastle upon Tyne).

Similar arrangements apply on the **English–Welsh border**, but note that in many cases the privilege of free cross-border travel is *only* granted to holders of English bus passes issued by an authority that is proximal to the border. A case in point is the arrangement which allows holders of passes issued in Herefordshire to use the X4 bus service from Hereford to Cardiff (though not for journeys entirely within Wales).

It is always **worth checking locally**, for there are many little surprises particularly in border areas. For example, holders of English concessionary passes may travel for child fares on the Beacons Bus seasonal network in Wales.

WHAT DOES 'LOCAL' MEAN?

So now we are getting into the high theology of concessionary bus-pass rules. When is a bus a *local* bus? Rule number one is that it has nothing to do with the outward appearance of the vehicle. Some local bus services in Britain are operated by very upmarket buses, and some even have all the trappings of luxury coaches. The defining issue is whether a route is **registered as a local bus service** with the Traffic Commissioners under the terms of the 1985 Transport Act.

Bus passes can be used on pretty well all regular local bus routes within the country for which your pass is valid (viz: England, Wales or Scotland). A small number of premium-fare services, park-and-ride shuttle buses and airport routes are excluded.

LONG-DISTANCE LOCAL ROUTES

But some so-called 'local' bus routes can be very long. Journeys 12, 13, 45, 48 and 50 in this book are on buses or coaches following routes that most of us would judge to be more than merely local. The relevant national passes are valid on all these routes. The issue is that 'local' is not defined in the relevant legislation by length of route, but by whether or not the service stops to **serve local passengers**, picking them up and dropping them off at frequent stops for a substantial part of the journey. So let's give a cheer for the 915 from Glasgow to Uig (mentioned on page 211) which takes the prize as **Britain's longest local bus route**. This service stops only thrice in the Greater Glasgow area, but for the last seven hours of its journey, from the shores of bonny Loch Lomond all the way to Skye, you can board or alight anywhere where the driver can safely pull in and stop.

Welsh and Scottish perks

The excellent long-distance **TrawsCambria services** in Wales, about to be relaunched in 2012 as TrawsCymru, are almost all local services in terms of bus-pass usage. And that applies to many other long-distance Welsh services, such as the 701 Aberystwyth to Cardiff operated by Coach Travel Wales.

As is so often the case in matters relating to bus passes, arrangements in Wales and Scotland are more traveller-friendly than those in England. The prevalence of very long routes in Scotland and Wales makes undertaking long-distance journeys so much simpler than in England where multiple changes are often needed. Holders of Scottish passes can travel for free throughout the **long–distance networks** in Scotland operated by Scottish Citylink, Scottish Express and Megabus, even though some services are not registered as local bus routes. Pensioners in Scotland may even climb aboard one of the luxurious Citylink Gold services (which connect Glasgow with both Aberdeen and Inverness) to enjoy soft leather seats, Wi-Fi, and a range of drinks and snacks – without having to pay a penny.

National Express

Most express services within England run under the umbrella of National Express Coaches. They also operate routes from England to both Wales and Scotland. Concessionary bus passes are not accepted on any of these services. But anyone over sixty can secure a **handsome**

discount on National Express Coaches. A 50% discount applies on off-peak days, while on peak days that discount is trimmed back to 30%. In 2011, 68 days were designated as peak days (mainly Fridays, summer weekends and bank holidays). This discount for older travellers is not contingent on residency or nationality. Just show evidence of your date of birth and the discount is there for the taking.

Yet National Express also run *local* bus services in a few parts of Britain. Indeed, in the Dundee area and in the **West Midlands** they have a big slice of the local bus market. And on those routes bus passes are of course accepted. Indeed, the **longest urban bus route in Europe** is a Birmingham route operated by National Express West Midlands. It features as Journey 24 in this book. ▪

Planning Longer Journeys
by Janice Booth

As far as I'm concerned, the longer the journey, the better! I'm basing this section of *Bus-Pass Britain* on an eight-day journey from Land's End to Lowestoft with Hilary Bradt in April 2008 (see page 242), and a later trip from Devon to Chester. The Lowestoft journey gave us a serendipitous mixture of sandy beaches, snow, ancient monuments, country walks, remote villages, spectacular views and pleasantly chatty fellow travellers, while the Chester journey was a relaxed and reasonably scenic means of travelling to a conference, with a couple of **attractive stops** *en route*.

THE BUS TRAVELLER'S ARMAMENTARIUM

We started, of course, with **maps**, both general road maps covering the whole journey and detailed Ordnance Survey sheets to specific areas. To my mind they're essential, whether you want to travel straight from A to B with stops along the way or to explore a particular region. But watch out – if you don't keep them under control they may tempt you to places you had no idea you wanted to see.

Then came the **timetables**. For both trips we made good use of the website www.traveline.info, which divides England up into regions, and also provides a gateway to the dedicated **Traveline** sites for Wales and

Scotland. These are superb resources, and the timetable information is very detailed. Yet finding links from one region to another can be awkward: the trick is to pick an 'intermediate' town close to the borders of both and search for buses from there. Traveline is accessible by phone too (☎ 0871 200 2233). The number is helpfully given on bus stops across Britain, so you can phone mid-journey for information or if your bus doesn't come.

Another very handy site is **www.transportdirect.info**. You can use it to plan long journeys across Britain, even specifying your start and end points by postcode. Remember to select the advanced option menu to allow you to identify your preferred transport mode. The only snag is that you cannot specify 'only local bus services'. Buses and long-distance coaches come bundled together as one option.

We also used printed timetables for many of the counties which we traversed on our long journeys. Travellers without internet access can track down printed timetables via local **tourist information centres** (TICs); their contact details are available either in good guidebooks or from telephone directory enquiries.

Although we started by working out our bus times and connections carefully beforehand, as we gained confidence we found we could equally well check those for the following day when we arrived at our overnight stopping place. Even if there was no direct route, we could generally reach our next destination with a couple of changes. Often (in particularly pretty areas) we chose to break our journey anyway and pick up a later bus along the route, so we could explore on foot. It's a question of personality really: some people are fervent pre-planners and others are on-the-spot improvisers. If you can get hold of one, a **bus map** to the area is extremely handy, enabling you to see all the services at a glance. They can be hard to find – sometimes in bus stations and sometimes in TICs – but the local TIC should be able to advise you.

Bear in mind that in areas where bus passes are not valid during the morning peak, the first bus of the day on which passes are valid (generally from 09.00 or 09.30 on weekdays in England) tends to attract more passengers. So buses may be delayed at stops while customers pile on board. We once missed a connection because this first 'free' bus was running late.

Practicalities along the way

As we planned to walk quite a bit between buses, sometimes on footpaths, we kept our **luggage** to a minimum, cramming the essentials into small backpacks which we could carry easily. Country buses don't always have designated space for bags, so something that will squash under your seat is an advantage. If you don't plan to do much off-road walking, a small suitcase with wheels might well be a practical alternative. But don't be tempted to take too much.

For our Lowestoft journey we booked three B&Bs in advance and found other **accommodation** as we travelled. For example the TIC at Avebury (rather surprisingly located in a church) recommended a place outside Marlborough that turned out to be one of our favourites; to reach it from the bus stop we followed a lane off the main road, crossed an old stone bridge, and walked through a hamlet where ducks chattered around a pond. In Hitchin (we'd intended to stay in Stevenage that night but it looked too unappealing) we just got off our bus in the centre, were drawn by the sound of church bells and spotted an attractive inn down a side street. Again it's a question of personality: if you're comfortable about not booking beforehand you've the chance of some pleasant discoveries, but on the other hand you may prefer the security of knowing that a bed is waiting. I'd suggest booking your first night at least, so that you get off to an easy start. We searched and made our bookings online; travellers without internet access can get lists of accommodation from TICs or guidebooks.

A pressing concern, particularly for the older travellers among us, is the availability of **public toilets** *en route*. Our rule was – never pass one by! If you see it, use it. Most towns have them; failing that, stop for refreshment in a pub or café and use theirs. Some bus stations can be pretty unattractive, particularly in cities, but have useful facilities like kiosks selling food and newspapers. Speaking of **food**, we were surprised how many small-town cafés were shut by teatime, when we were gasping for a restorative cuppa. We learnt to carry some fruit or biscuits to fill the gap – and water, of course.

Bags packed and maps and timetables to the ready, you have a wealth of tempting choices and a great deal of countryside to enjoy! However you plan your journey and wherever you go, have a wonderful trip. ■

LAND'S END TO LOWESTOFT

When the national concessionary bus pass for England was announced in 2008, our feet began to itch. Scotland, Wales and Northern Ireland had long had their own schemes, and now England was to follow suit.

With pencil and ruler, we excitedly drew a line across a map between the westernmost and easternmost points on England's mainland. We'd **created our journey**! The pass was to be launched on 1 April 2008 (no fooling...), so we spent the night of 31 March in a B&B at a storm-swept Land's End to be ready for our first free ride. The other half of 'we' was my friend Hilary Bradt.

As we stepped aboard and settled happily into our seats, the storm clouds lifted. The road from **Land's End** to St Ives twists through clusters of pastel-coloured cottages and open, golden moorland. Beyond **St Ives** we paddled in Carbis Bay and walked a sunny two-hour stretch of the South West Coast Path to the stop for our next bus. It took us via Truro to **Bodmin**, where we ended up in jail – because historic Bodmin jail contains an excellent restaurant – and a comfortable B&B that we'd pre-booked.

This was pretty much the pattern for the rest of our **week-long journey** to Lowestoft: two or three buses each day, a bit of walking (sometimes following footpaths across country from one bus route to another), and visits to whatever caught our interest. Often this was a little village church, centuries old and lovingly cared for by its congregation.

In Glastonbury we climbed the famous tor; in Avebury we marvelled at the massive prehistoric stones, great grey guardians of the ancient landscape. On a day of sudden unseasonable snowfall we went to Whipsnade, where ringed lemurs were huddled together against the un-expected cold, and later stopped off by a betting shop to watch the Grand National.

We strolled among the ruins of the abbey of **Bury St Edmunds** as dusk was falling – magical! – and from there visited some beautiful Suffolk villages: particularly Woolpit, its church alive with wing-loads of benevolent carved angels.

On the **final day** – we needed to reach **Lowestoft** that night – we ran out of bus connections so wrote a sign on A4 paper 'Direction Lowestoft please!' and resorted to hitch-hiking; I (with white hair) standing in front to stir the sympathy of drivers. Three enjoyable lifts later we arrived – like a bus – at our terminus, having had a wonderful week. And oh yes, we would certainly do it again! JB

Meet the Team behind Bus-Pass Britain

We explained at the very start of the book (see Welcome Aboard on page 1) how the *Bus-Pass Britain* project has been a co-operative effort by many **bus travellers**. Its origins lay in a serendipitous meeting between **Hilary Bradt** and representatives of U3A (the University of the Third Age). U3A did a splendid job in publicising the idea of a project celebrating the nation's favourite bus journeys. You can find out more about **U3A** at www.u3a.org.uk.

Hilary Bradt's energy and enthusiasm for local buses was our greatest asset. Hilary made the initial selection of routes, and it fell to us as the editors of *Bus-Pass Britain* to find folk to fill in a few gaps. UK-based readers of *hidden europe*, a travel magazine specialising in truly offbeat aspects of Europe, helped us out.

At the end of each route in this book, you will see a short note about the writer. Most of our writers are keen amateurs who showed great generosity of spirit in meeting tight deadlines. Some, but by no means all, live on or near the bus routes about which they have written.

And us? Well, we have long been keen on slow travel. Indeed, a while ago we published the *Manifesto for Slow Travel* (www.slowtraveleurope. eu). We edit *hidden europe* magazine (www.hiddeneurope.co.uk) and run a Berlin-based editorial bureau that works with publishers, tourist authorities and the transport sector to create a vision of travel that is slower, saner and less driven by commercial avarice.

We have for many years used books from **Bradt Travel Guides** to support our own explorations, and it has thus been a special pleasure to take a leading role in managing the *Bus-Pass Britain* project. To Hilary, and all at Bradt, a big thank-you. And most particularly to **Rachel Fielding**, the in-house manager at Bradt who kept us on the proverbial straight and narrow. And to her colleague **Adrian Phillips**, Publishing Director at Bradt Travel Guides.

A thank-you also to **Janice Booth** who contributed 'bus stop' B and some thoughts on planning longer journeys (pages 239–42). The initials JB at the end of a boxed text indicate that Janice penned those words, just as NG reveals that Nicky Gardner was the author. All unattributed text in this book is the joint work of the two editors.

Nicky Gardner and Susanne Kries

Index of Place Names

Use this index to identify places that feature in this book.

FEEDBACK REQUEST

The editors of *Bus-Pass Britain* would **love to hear from you**. Are there things we could have described better? And we would in particular like to **hear of new journeys** which you judge might warrant inclusion in a new edition or follow-up volume. Don't forget to tell us a little about yourself and include your contact details (ideally an e-mail address).

You can **reach us** by post as follows: The Editors, Bus-Pass Britain, Bradt Travel Guides, IDC House, The Vale, Chalfont St Peter, Bucks SL9 9RZ. If you prefer to email us, please use info@bradtguides.com.

Check www.bradtguides.com/guidebook-update-buspass-britain for updates to this volume. This page is maintained by the publisher.